P9-BAV-666

Group Therapies for Children and Youth

Principles and Practices of Group Treatment

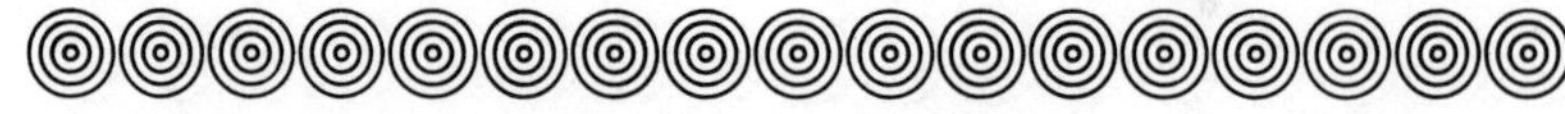

Charles E. Schaefer
Lynnette Johnson
Jeffrey N. Wherry

Group Therapies for Children and Youth

Jossey-Bass Publishers
San Francisco • Washington • London • 1982

GROUP THERAPIES FOR CHILDREN AND YOUTH
Principles and Practices of Group Treatment
by Charles E. Schaefer, Lynnette Johnson, and Jeffrey N. Wherry

 Jossey-Bass Inc., Publishers
433 California Street
San Francisco, California 94104
&
Jossey-Bass Limited
28 Banner Street
London EC1Y 8QE

Library of Congress Cataloging in Publication Data
Main entry under title:

Group therapies for children and youth.

(Guidebooks for therapeutic practice)
Includes bibliographies and index.
1. Child psychotherapy. 2. Adolescent psychotherapy.
3. Group psychotherapy. I. Schaefer, Charles E.
II. Johnson, Lynnette. III. Wherry, Jeffrey N.
IV. Series.
RJ505.G7G76 1982 618.92′89152 82-48061
ISBN 0-87589-545-X

Manufactured in the United States of America

The paper in this book meets the guidelines for permanence and durability of the Committee on Production Guidelines for Book Longevity of the Council on Library Resources.

JACKET DESIGN BY WILLI BAUM

FIRST EDITION

Code 8222

The Jossey-Bass
Social and Behavioral Science Series

GUIDEBOOKS FOR THERAPEUTIC PRACTICE
Charles E. Schaefer and Howard L. Millman
Consulting Editors

Therapies for Children: A Handbook of Effective Treatments for Problem Behaviors
Charles E. Schaefer and Howard L. Millman
1977

Therapies for Psychosomatic Disorders in Children
Charles E. Schaefer, Howard L. Millman, and Gary F. Levine
1979

Therapies for School Behavior Problems
Howard L. Millman, Charles E. Schaefer,
and Jeffrey J. Cohen
1980

Therapies for Adolescents: Current Treatments for Problem Behaviors
Michael D. Stein and J. Kent Davis
1982

Group Therapies for Children and Youth: Principles and Practices of Group Treatment
Charles E. Schaefer, Lynnette Johnson,
and Jeffrey N. Wherry
1982

Therapies for Adults: Depressive, Anxiety, and Personality Disorders
Howard L. Millman, Jack F. Huber,
and Dean R. Diggins
1982

Preface

The importance of the group approach to child therapy cannot be overemphasized. Groups can involve children of different ages actively and experientially in ways that are familiar and nonthreatening, dovetailing psychologically with their socialization needs. A primary developmental task of a child is to become a social being, a process significantly influenced by peer interaction.

Unfortunately, many child therapists have received little or no training in child group therapy. Lacking the necessary instructions and supervision, they are likely to achieve unsatisfactory results when they experiment with psychotherapy groups.

The goal of this book is to provide a practical and comprehensive handbook of group therapies for children from age four through adolescence. Eclectic in scope, the volume encompasses all the major theoretical approaches—including psychoanalytic, behavior modification, and transactional analysis groups—and should be of interest to clinicians of all disciplines: psychiatrists, psychologists, social workers, school guidance counselors, probation officers, childcare workers, and special education teachers.

To make the information as practical and complete as possible, we provide detailed abstracts of the most relevant articles from the group therapy literature, with technical material clarified and simplified whenever possible. Our goal was to make the approaches usable by the wide range of professionals who work with children. The abstracts focus on practical, specific "how to" information. Readers should study the original articles to fully understand the theoretical and research base for approaches described and to avoid any tendency to apply the techniques mechanically. The exact reference for the article is listed at the end of each digest.

The digests in Part One describe the major theoretical approaches to child group therapy, together with a developmental perspective on children's groups. Part Two contains digests of specific group treatments for particular disorders—such as juvenile delinquency, impulsivity, social inhibition, psychosis, and school behavior problems—and digests describing prevention groups for children "at risk" for psychological disturbances, such as children of divorce.

August 1982

Charles E. Schaefer
Dobbs Ferry, New York

Lynnette Johnson
Toledo, Ohio

Jeffrey N. Wherry
Galveston, Texas

Contents

The Authors

Charles E. Schaefer is associate director of psychological services and research at The Children's Village, a residential treatment center in Dobbs Ferry, New York. He received his Ph.D. degree in clinical psychology from Fordham University (1967) and completed a clinical psychology internship at the Institute of Living in Hartford, Connecticut. Schaefer is the author or co-author of ten books on the topics of child therapy, effective parenting, and creativity development, including *How to Help Children with Common Problems* (1981), *Childhood Encopresis and Enuresis* (1979), *How to Influence Children: A Handbook of Practical Parenting Skills* (1978), *Therapeutic Use of Child's Play* (1976), *Developing Creativity in Children* (1973), *Becoming Somebody: Creative Activities for Preschool and Primary*

Grade Children (1973), and *Young Voices: An Anthology of Poetry by Children* (1971). He is also the author of numerous psychological tests and articles in professional journals and co-editor of the Jossey-Bass series Guidebooks for Therapeutic Practice.

Schaefer's current professional interests center on the identification and development of effective child management techniques and child therapy interventions. He is a fellow in the American Orthopsychiatric Association and a member of the American Psychological Association, the American Educational Research Association, and Psychologists in Private Practice.

Lynnette Johnson is completing her Ph.D. in clinical psychology at the University of Toledo. She has worked in a variety of clinical settings, including an adolescent unit at a state hospital, a community mental health center, a residential treatment center for boys, a school program for behaviorally disturbed children, a children's outpatient clinic at a medical school, and a criminal justice training center. Her professional affiliations include the American Psychological Association and the Ohio Psychological Association, and her current research interests include gender identity and adolescent identity development, parent education groups, and violence and aggression in juvenile delinquents.

Jeffrey N. Wherry is a postdoctoral fellow in pediatric psychology at the University of Texas Medical Branch in Galveston. He received his Ph.D. degree in school psychology from the University of Southern Mississippi (1982) and completed a clinical psychology internship at The Children's Village. He has published numerous articles related to the personality of the gifted child. His current professional interests include family therapy, the use of videotape equipment in children's activity groups, and the use of video computer games as reinforcers in residential care. He is a member of the American Psychological Association and the National Association of School Psychologists.

Group Therapies for Children and Youth

Principles and Practices of Group Treatment

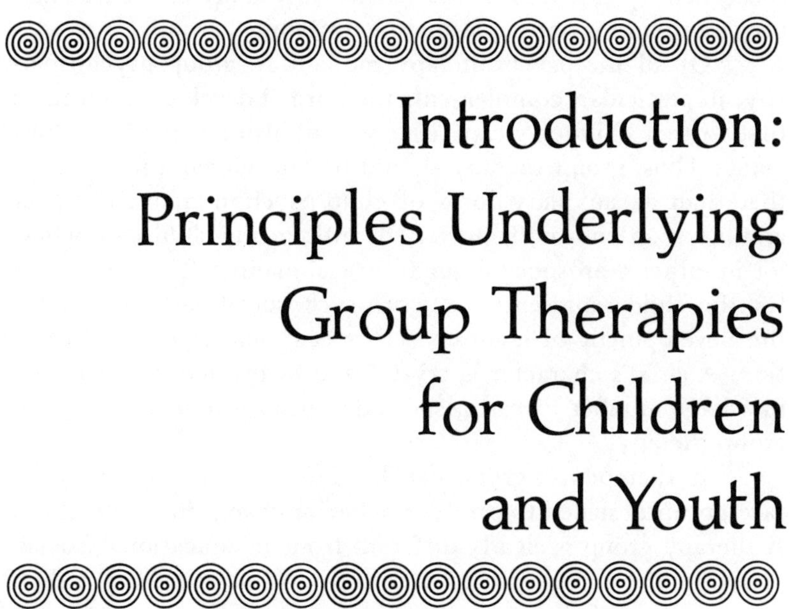

Introduction: Principles Underlying Group Therapies for Children and Youth

All humans possess *social hunger*—an instinctive, affective need for human association—which can be gratified only through communion with other individuals, preferably with peers. Of all available treatments, group therapy is best able to offer opportunities for satisfying social hunger, while at the same time it creates an environment for correcting other emotional problems. Consequently, there is growing recognition that group therapy may be the treatment of choice for a majority of children and adolescents who need psychological help.

Group psychotherapy is particularly effective with youth because it is used during stages of growth and development when social interaction experiences are important. As the early childhood period of nurturance and dependency abates, it is succeeded by experiences that foster autonomy in children and prepare them for participation in extrafamilial groups.

Of all the psychotherapy modalities, group psychotherapy, in particular, complements the normal developmental tasks that further children's capacities for social interaction and intimacy. Thus, group therapy should be considered a primary rather than an auxiliary form of child psychotherapy. The peer group has an enormous power for influencing children's behavior in either a prosocial or an antisocial manner. The peer group for the child represents a major psychosocial pathway toward the development of identity, self-esteem, and character formation. A child's character is crystallized in the social arena, and, in a large number of cases, social deviations can be corrected in group therapy.

A therapeutic group can be defined as a small, face-to-face group designed to produce behavior change in its members. A therapy group is clearly different from an educational, social, or self-improvement group. According to Loeser (1957), a therapy group can function only if the following five properties are present:

1. *Dynamic Interaction.* There must be relationship and interaction among group members. To the extent that the verbal interactions occur predominantly between the leader and individual members, the group process is diminished. When almost all interaction is directed toward the leader, the result is a classroom, an audience, or a troop, but not a true group.

2. *Common Goal.* An aggregate of people can function as a group only with a stated common goal. The absence of a common goal is destructive to group functioning; a loosely defined goal is threatening; a clearly established goal is facilitating.

3. *Size and Function.* There is a direct relationship in all true groups between size and function. Groups that are too large or too small are not able to function efficiently.

4. *Volition and Consent.* Except under very unusual circumstances, a group functions well only with the free consent of its members. Groups composed predominantly of captive, involuntary members do not truly function as a group, except possibly in the sense that all members are in rebellion against authorities. Hostility and aggression by group members reflect their absence of volition and consent.

5. *Capacity for Self-Direction.* All efficient groups function on a democratic basis. Under an authoritarian leader, the individuals become followers or adherents, or subjects, but not group members. In this regard Dreikurs (1955, p. 65) has stated, "The therapeutic group cannot exist save in a democratic atmosphere, and in turn it creates a democratic atmosphere."

Historical Background

Until the beginning of this century, child therapists were concerned with the behavior of individuals and not with the behavior of groups. Group psychology was left largely to sociologists. In 1911, however, J. L. Moreno began working with children as a group. Using a method that he called psychodrama, he encouraged the children to act out their fantasies, usually on a primitive, fairy-tale level. In 1934 Slavson began to work with latency-age children in groups. His approach, activity group therapy (Slavson, 1943), keeps the therapist in the background in a passive, rather shadowy role; such a permissive atmosphere encourages group interaction in the children. Subsequently, Redl (1944) advocated that the therapist be more active in children's groups and make interpretations to change maladaptive behaviors. About this time, the writings of Konopka (1949) did much to establish group work as a full-fledged clinical modality.

Until recently, psychoanalytic, Adlerian, and client-centered principles have dominated the practice of group therapy with children. Within the past twenty years, however, group treatment strategies based on the successful application of social learning theory to individual cases have started to emerge. Treatment goals in behavior modification groups are limited to changing specific behavior patterns.

In recent years, there has been a decline in the number of published articles on child therapy groups, although these groups are widely used in clinics, schools, and inpatient settings. One reason for the scarcity of published reports may be a hesitancy to reveal work that is poorly evaluated and often conducted in a "groping-in-the-dark" manner. According to Frank and Zilbach (1968), child group therapists tend to have poor education and training in this modality, and turn to it as a way of giving treatment to a large number of children.

Outcome Research on Child Group Therapy

The available evidence regarding group therapy outcome is inconclusive. According to Abramowitz (1976), about one third of the studies have yielded positive results, one third have generated mixed results, and one third have produced null findings; among the positive and mixed outcome studies, behavior modification groups have been overrepresented. Parloff and Dies (1977) observe that groups have not proved successful with juvenile delinquents. Of the seven studies they reviewed, only two showed evidence of positive effects on postinstitutional adjustment. Apparently, then, little can be concluded regarding the efficacy of group therapy with children and adolescents.

There is a need to evaluate various group therapies for specified classes of problems. Without a clearer evaluation of client, therapist, and treatment variables, there is little likelihood that outcome research in this area will progress beyond its present impasse.

Group Dynamics

A group is composed of a number of people in interaction with one another, and it is this interaction process that distinguishes the group from an aggregate of individuals and from individual psychotherapy. The term *group dynamics* refers to these interactive forces that operate in a group and influence the behavior of the group's members. This group process itself is often more helpful than the therapist's efforts in getting people to change. Various articles describe the therapeutic factors inherent in a group. A brief review of this literature follows.

Curative Factors in the Group Process. Based on extensive research, Yalom (1975) has identified the following as curative factors that lead to successful group therapy: imparting of information, instillation of hope (that is, belief in one's ability to control his own behavior); altruism (others offering support, reassurance, suggestions), universality (learning that others have the same feelings), corrective recapitulation of the primary family group, development of socializing techniques (interpersonal input and output), imitative behavior, interpersonal learning, group cohesiveness, and catharsis.

Corsini and Rosenberg (1955), in a literature review, identify nine classes of curative factors, which overlap significantly with Yalom's:

Emotional

1. *Acceptance of, Empathy with, and Involvement with Others.* Acceptance requires the development of group identification, a communal feeling, an end to isolation, and the development of increased feelings of belonging. It is in the group that one has an opportunity to find one's place.

2. *Altruism or Social Interest.* Altruism is developed in an atmosphere and a setting that encourage the group members to help one another.

3. *Transference.* Group members develop strong emotional feelings toward the leader or separate members of the group. These feelings may be either positive or negative, and they become a strong therapeutic agent.

Cognitive

4. *Spectator Therapy.* The group provides an opportunity for one member to observe others, to imitate behavior, and to learn from the transactions in the group.

5. *Universalization.* Group members come to realize that their concerns can be shared. These concerns may be related to incompetence in life tasks or feelings of inadequacy. Universalization is a factor that helps to bring about group cohesiveness.

6. *Intellectualization.* Learning goes on through the pro-

cess of feedback and insight, so that group members have an opportunity to explore feelings, purposes, values, and perceptions.

Actional

7. *Reality Testing and Interpersonal Learning.* The opportunity to learn from the real things that happen in the group and to test one's behavior in a safe and nonthreatening atmosphere is therapeutic.

8. *Ventilation.* Group members can express negative or positive feelings instead of holding them within.

9. *Interaction.* The relationships that occur in the group permit the counselor and group members to see how an individual's goals and purposes are revealed in interpersonal transactions in the group.

Similarly, Levy (1977) has identified eleven processes inherent in self-help groups. They include four behavioral processes—(1) social reinforcement of ego-syntonic behavior and elimination of problems; (2) training, indoctrination, and support for self-control behaviors; (3) modeling of methods of changing and coping with stress; (4) an agenda and rationale to change the social environment—and seven cognitive processes; (5) rationale for problems and distress and the group's way of dealing with it, demystification, and increasing expectancy for change; (6) provision of normative and instrumental information; (7) generation of alternative perceptions of members' problems and ways to change them; (8) enhancement of discriminative abilities toward stimulus and event contingencies; (9) support for change in attitudes toward self, behavior, and society; (10) reduction or elimination of a sense of isolation or uniqueness regarding problems through social comparisons and consensual validation; (11) development of a substitute cultural and social system in which members can develop new definitions of identity and new norms on which to base self-esteem.

Hill (1975) combines the change mechanisms found previously by Yalom and by Corsini and Rosenberg into a single list, ranked by degree of consensus among the theorists. The mechanisms having clear consensus are ventilation, acceptance, spectator therapy, and intellectualization. Of secondary importance are universalization, reality testing, altruism, and socialization. It seems likely, then, that the more the group leader is aware of and makes an effort to strengthen these therapeutic factors, the more effective the group experience will be for the members. In a similar manner, the therapist must be alert to and head off antitherapeutic or destructive forces inherent in a group situation, such as group condemnation or rejection of a member.

Cohesion. Cohesiveness—the forces acting on the members to stay in a group—results psychologically in a fusion of individualities in a common whole, so that a sense of "we" develops out of the common life and purpose of the group. Numerous studies have found that the greater the cohesiveness of a group, the greater its ability to induce change in its members, not only at the level of public conformity but also at the level of private belief. So the more cohesive the group, the more the members are apt to accept the attitudes that it prescribes.

The cultivation of cohesiveness in group members is, then, a central task of the therapist (Yalom, 1975). It is well known that a deviant group member tends to drop out early, benefits the least, and is most likely to suffer harm.

What forces act to produce group cohesiveness? One study found that the caring and self-expressiveness of group leaders are positively related to cohesiveness (Hurst and others, 1978). The sharing of one's private thoughts and feelings implies that the group is a safe, trusting environment. According to Frank (1957), cohesiveness occurs in therapy groups if (1) the group provides direct fulfillment of members' needs and also promises future satisfaction; (2) members find that they can be mutually helpful to one another; (3) the group provides rewards for successful performance; and (4) mutual attraction of members develops. Interpersonal attraction of members is derived from such factors as common goals, shared norms and values, and stability of membership.

Stages of Group Development. A group developmental theory helps us pay close attention to the core tasks that group members must cope with in therapy groups. Groups seem to pass through different stages of development during their existence. Each stage is said to be characterized by distinguishable behaviors exhibited by the members. Various models have been proposed to describe the behavior patterns occurring in groups over time.

Schutz (1958) has described three essential phases of group development. During the first phase, that of "inclusion," the members are concerned primarily with acceptance and non-acceptance. Do the others like me? Does the leader give me equal time? Will I be able to keep up with this group? These are the typical, often unverbalized, questions with which group members are preoccupied in the inclusion phase. Once members feel safe in the group, they start to be concerned about the degree of autonomy the group leader will permit. They find satisfaction in challenging each other, especially the strong group members but, above all, the therapist. The members want to show that they are different from the others. The struggle for individuation in a group is called the "power phase." The prime concerns at this stage are: Who among us are the strong ones? Now I am going to challenge the therapist and some members. I am glad I am different from the others. The third and final group stage in Schutz's scheme, the "intimacy phase," is characterized by cooperation and comradery among members and is achieved only if a lot of challenge has been expressed in the power or strength phase.

Garland, Jones, and Kolodny (1965) propose five stages or growth-problem levels through which members and groups as a whole pass in the course of their development: (1) preaffiliation, (2) power and control, (3) intimacy, (4) differentiation, and (5) separation.

In the preaffiliation stage, the members are becoming familiar with one another and the group situation and have not yet formed close ties. They are typically ambivalent about the group and manifest an approach-avoidance conflict. That is, they are attracted by the group experience but anxious about becoming involved. They manifest that anxiety by coming late to meetings or impulsively leaving a meeting. In short, at this stage members *scout* issues and relationships at the same time that they are *skirting* them.

In Stage Two, the power and control stage, there is a testing of the therapist and other members and an attempt to form cliques and alliances. This stage is reached only after the members have decided that the group is potentially safe and rewarding and worth a preliminary emotional investment. To pass the group through this phase, the therapist must allow the members to resist her authority somewhat (so that they come to know that they have a degree of control over their own affairs and operations) and assure each member a reasonable degree of safety from physical and psychic attack.

The third stage of development, the intimacy stage, is characterized by intensification of personal involvement in the group, more willingness to bring into the open feelings regarding the therapist and the group, and striving for satisfaction of dependency needs. Sibling-like rivalry tends to appear, as well as overt comparisons of the group to family life. There is a desire to know and be known, to share emotions arising out of common experience, and to become immersed in group life.

In Stage 4, differentiation, members begin to accept one another as distinct individuals and to see the therapist as a unique person. In the final stage, separation, the members begin to move apart and find new resources for meeting social needs. The process of termination in this stage may involve some regression and recapitulation of former group experences.

Both models described above emphasize the central themes of power and intimacy. Power refers to the members' feelings of control over their lives in the group, while intimacy pertains to how emotionally close the members will come to one another. Different groups will progress through these developmental tasks at different rates of speed. Some groups will never really develop beyond the first step.

Roles. Therapy groups, like all human groups, encourage the development of roles: the monopolizer, the isolate, the help-rejecting complainer, the self-righteous moralizer, the therapist's assistant, helpful Hannah, and the professional patient. The "professional patient" comes across as an expert in all areas of human conflict and functions as a pseudotherapist. The monopolizer seeks to control the group by excessive verbalization. The misfortune hunter has had so many bad-luck experiences, tragedies, and accidents that he comes across as a depressive martyr. The isolate is the emotionally separated member of the group—the member who is hiding, mysterious, or fearful.

These roles can be either fluid or fixed. Fixed roles can evolve into a condition called role lock (Bogdanoff and Elbaum, 1978), which impedes therapeutic progress. According to Bogdanoff and Elbaum, the therapeutic management of fixed roles involves encouraging the individual locked in a role to change. Both the individual and the group must assume some responsibility for producing change. The therapist might confront the individual and the group by saying, "George, you are doing most of the talking. How come the rest of you allow this to go on?" So the dual focus of the therapist is to point out that it is both the individual's problem and the group's problem.

Selection. The careful selection of group members is important for the success of group treatment. First of all, it is best to avoid too great a variation in age, developmental level, or degree of disturbance. In regard to diagnosis, the most common reason for referral is faulty interpersonal relations: "Cannot get along with people," "Needs to improve social interactions," "Cannot relate to groups." So children with "social inhibition," "social aggressiveness," and "social prejudice" have problems that are best suited to group rather than individual therapy. All these problems come up immediately in the group and can be dealt with efficiently. Other common problems referred to group therapy include disruptive behavior in school, poor self-concept, and academic underachievement.

A group's mix or balance means that the group process is facilitated by a balance of active/passive and verbal/nonverbal participants. If too many withdrawn children are in a group, the group may have little energy to invest in group activities. If there are too many aggressive children, frequent fights and disturbances may make it impossible for the group to function well. Consequently, a group composed of differing personalities, ages, ethnic backgrounds, and socioeconomic levels seems preferable.

Another consideration is that any child whose functioning is widely deviant from the group's norm will slow the group's progress. So most therapists would not include in a group of reasonably well functioning children a psychotic child, a psychopath, a drug addict, or a severe narcissistic personality. Group methods for such cases require special considerations.

It should also be noted that children in crisis require immediate help that is best provided by individual therapy. Unless the group is organized around a shared common crisis—for example, children of divorce—group cohesion does not take place rapidly enough to give new members the necessary support and guidance that individual therapy can provide.

Size. In the final analysis, group size is a matter of the therapist's ability to follow and respond to a number of individual concerns. The complexity of interaction increases with the size of the group. Yalom (1975) cites seven as an ideal number for adult groups, with five to ten as an acceptable range, and this number also seems appropriate for adolescent groups. In general, group therapists tend to begin a group with eight to ten members, expecting that after some attrition seven to eight will remain in the group. In groups of less than five, the therapist must become much more active, and members may experience a high level of anxiety. Many therapists find that they do not get significant interaction among members of children's groups with fewer than seven in a group. With groups of only four or five children, the children tend to interact mainly with the therapist, so that the therapeutic value of the group itself is nil or minimal.

Duration. The ninety-minute hour has become the standard in group therapy with adolescents and adults. Some adolescent group therapists, however, prefer sixty-minute sessions, which can run an additional ten to fifteen minutes when needed. How many sessions should a group last? Usually adolescents do not begin to trust the group and begin talking about important issues until about the ninth session. Consequently, adolescent groups can last six months or a year. With children, however, most group therapies tend to be brief—about ten to fifteen sessions. Moreover, because the attention span of children is more limited than that of adolescents, children's groups are rarely scheduled for more than sixty minutes per session.

Limits. The responsibility for establishing and enforcing

group rules is shared by the therapist and members. They must spell out standards of conduct to minimize negative behaviors, while maximizing the learning and modeling of positive behavior. Rules should encompass details of unacceptable behavior in the group, confidentiality, and attendance. The more disturbed and fragmented the members, the greater the need for a *highly structured approach.*

Leadership Style. What is the best leadership style for group therapies? Galigor (1977) found that group members who regard their leader as "open, accepting, responsive, and confident" were less likely to drop out than those who saw their therapist as "neutral, professional, and distant." Lieberman, Yalom, and Miles (1973) found that the outcome of groups led by therapists of many different persuasions was correlated not with the leader's theory but with his behavior in the group. The most favorable outcome and the fewest dropouts occurred when the leader provided considerable cognitive structuring but where he used authority neither too much nor too little and stimulated the group in a judicious manner.

Preferably, the leader should not be too dominant or too passive. A leader who is too dominant turns members off because he intrudes too much, doing everything possible to ensure that something is happening at all times. A leader who is too passive loses control of the group. Research indicates that a nondirective leadership style results in increased aggressive behaviors in children (Bole, 1971). Also, insecure children may become anxious because a passive leader does not provide sufficient structure.

Adolescent Groups

Group psychotherapy is particularly suitable for adolescents because it can influence personality growth. During adolescence the individual needs to develop a stable feeling of identity, become independent, form important relations with other persons of the same age, become sexually mature, and clarify goals and values.

According to Godenne (1965), an adolescent therapy

group is an entity very different from an adult therapy group. An adolescent is rarely self-motivated to attend the group meetings; instead, he is pressured to attend by parents, teachers, or the court and feels threatened when there is a sudden focus on his problems. The adolescent, therefore, has to find something enjoyable in the group, something personally needed, and some support to reduce anxiety.

Probably the most difficult challenge confronting the group therapist is handling the various resistances shown by adolescents. Rosenthal (1971) found that the most frequently occurring resistance in adolescent groups is the *craving for excitement,* whereby group members keep the group on a level of aggressive-sexualized excitement. This resistance allows the group to avoid experiencing the negative feelings of anxiety, depression, fear, and hopelessness in coping with life's problems. Other common resistances of adolescents include a frequent banding together of group members against the therapist, a characteristic group restlessness, and a tendency toward limited and diffused conversation (Hauserman, Zweback, and Plotkin, 1972). Furthermore, when group membership is required rather than optional, the above characteristics become especially pronounced. Adolescents usually seem uninterested in the group treatment and are extremely reluctant to discuss their difficulties with anyone else.

To cope with the above tactics, the therapist must be active, ego supportive, and in control of the group situation at all times. According to a recent survey (Corder, Haizlip, and Walker, 1980), the therapist in adolescent groups typically is verbally active, personally open, directive, and confronting (to counter adolescent denial mechanisms) and models adult problem solving and functioning.

Three main strategies for leading adolescent groups are offered by Hurst and Gladieux (1980). The first strategy, validation and affirmation, involves affirming and validating the worthiness and inner strength of the group and of each member. The therapist must emphasize the positive happenings in the group, such as instances of caring, positive feeling, and personal strengths of the members. Second, the leader should share his thoughts about the group. In general, interpretation is not effective with adolescents. Rather, the therapist should offer various explanations of why a particular behavior took place and let the adolescent choose those that are relevant for her. Or the therapist may simply state the dilemma, or the bind, that a certain difficulty poses and ask group members to help resolve the dilemma. Third, the leader must become skilled at handling special management problems of adolescent groups, such as intoxicated members, sexual attraction or hostility between members, and overtalkative or overquiet members. As a general rule, it is best to acknowledge the troublesome behavior, point out its consequences for the group and the individual, and attempt to make camouflaged feelings overt.

Other authors have suggested the following guidelines for leading adolescent groups:

1. It is generally best to work with adolescent groups of limited age ranges, such as puberty (twelve and thirteen), early adolescence (ages thirteen and fourteen), and middle through late adolescence (ages fourteen to seventeen). In some circumstances, girls of sixteen or seventeen would overwhelm boys of fourteen in the same group but the older girls might not be so different from girls of 14 in an all-girl group.

2. With adolescents, few limits are set, but they are clearly stated and consistently respected. No action that might result in bodily injury is permitted, although verbalization is usually not restricted. Socialization with group members outside the group is discouraged.

3. Generally the rule is for the therapist to communicate to the group what the parents said but not, except in emergencies, to give information about group happenings to the parents. Such confidentiality ensures that the group does not become an instrumentality of the parents.

4. A mixture of boys and girls in the group is in keeping with adolescents' need to focus on identity issues, and interaction with opposite-sex peers is a vital source of feedback for establishing a sexual identity.

5. In beginning an adolescent group, the leader must ac-

complish several tasks at the first meeting: (1) lower the members' anxiety by establishing a tone of openness, comfort, and safety; (2) define the group's limits and boundaries by clarifying the agreements and structure within which the group will function; and (3) engage members' interest and evoke their sense of responsibility for determining the group's direction.

6. Male and female cotherapists seem advisable for adolescent groups composed of both boys and girls.

References

Abramowitz, C. V. "The Effectiveness of Group Psychotherapy with Children." *Archives of General Psychiatry,* 1976, *33,* 320-326.

Bogdanoff, M., and Elbaum, P. L. "Role Lock: Dealing with Monopolizers, Mistrusters, Isolates, Helpful Hannahs, and Other Assorted Characters in Group Psychotherapy." *International Journal of Group Psychotherapy,* 1978, *28,* 247-262.

Bole, T. J. "Systematic Observation of Behavior Change with Older Children in Group Therapy." *Psychological Reports,* 1971, *28,* 26.

Corder, B. F., Haizlip, T. M., and Walker, P. A. "Critical Areas of Therapists' Functioning in Adolescent Group Psychotherapy: A Comparison with Self-Perceptions of Functioning in Adult Groups by Experienced and Inexperienced Therapists." *Adolescence,* 1980, *15,* 435-442.

Corsini, R., and Rosenberg, B. "Mechanisms of Group Psychotherapy." *Journal of Abnormal and Social Psychiatry,* 1955, *51,* 406-411.

Dreikurs, R. "Group Psychotherapy and the Third Revolution in Psychiatry." *International Journal of Social Psychiatry,* 1955, *1,* 1-151.

Frank, J. D. "Some Determinants, Manifestations, and Effects of Cohesiveness in Therapy Groups." *International Journal of Group Psychotherapy,* 1957, *7,* 53-63.

Frank, M. G., and Zilbach, J. "Current Trends in Group Therapy with Children." *International Journal of Group Psychotherapy,* 1968, *18,* 447-460.

Galigor, J. "Perceptions of the Group Therapist and the Dropout from Group." In A. R. Wolberg and M. L. Aronson (Eds.), *Group Therapy 1977: An Overview.* New York: Stratton Intercontinental Medical Book Corp., 1977.

Garland, J. A., Jones, H. E., and Kolodny, R. "A Model for Stages of Development in Social Work Groups." In S. Bernstein (Ed.), *Explorations in Group Work.* Boston: Boston University School of Social Work, 1965.

Godenne, G. D. "Outpatient Adolescent Group Psychotherapy." *American Journal of Psychotherapy,* 1965, *19,* 40-53.

Hauserman, N., Zweback, S., and Plotkin, A. "Use of Concrete Reinforcement to Facilitate Verbal Initiations in Adolescent Group Therapy." *Journal of Consulting and Clinical Psychology,* 1972, *38,* 90-96.

Hill, W. F. "Further Consideration of Therapeutic Mechanisms in Group Therapy." *Small Group Behavior,* 1975, *6,* 421-429.

Hurst, A. G., and Gladieux, J. D. "Guidelines for Leading an Adolescent Therapy Group." In A. R. Wolberg and M. L. Aronson (Eds.), *Group and Family Therapy.* New York: Brunner/Mazel, 1980.

Hurst, A. G., and others. "Leadership Style Determinants of Cohesiveness in Adolescent Groups." *International Journal of Group Psychotherapy,* 1978, *28,* 263-277.

Konopka, G. *Therapeutic Group Work with Children.* Minneapolis: University of Minnesota Press, 1949.

Levy, L. H. "Self-Help Groups: Types and Psychological Processes." *Journal of Applied Behavioral Analysis,* 1977, *12,* 310-322.

Lieberman, M. A., Yalom, I. D., and Miles, M. E. *Encounter Groups: First Facts.* New York: Basic Books, 1973.

Loeser, L. H. "Some Aspects of Group Dynamics." *International Journal of Group Psychotherapy,* 1957, *7,* 5-16.

Parloff, M. B., and Dies, R. R. "Group Psychotherapy Outcome Research 1966-1975." *International Journal of Group Psychotherapy,* 1977, *27,* 281-319.

Redl, F. "Diagnostic Group Work." *American Journal of Orthopsychiatry,* 1944, *4,* 53-67.

Rosenthal, L. "Some Dynamics of Resistance and Therapeutic

Management in Adolescent Group Therapy." *Psychoanalytic Review,* 1971, *58,* 353-366.

Schutz, W. C. *FIRO.* New York: Holt, Rinehart and Winston, 1958.

Slavson, S. R. *An Introduction to Group Therapy.* New York: Commonwealth Fund, 1943.

Yalom, I. *The Theory and Practice of Group Psychotherapy.* (2nd ed.) New York: Basic Books, 1975.

Part One

Therapeutic Approaches to Group Treatment

The group approaches discussed here have been divided into two categories. Chapter One presents the major theoretical approaches to group therapy with children, including psychoanalytic, transactional analysis, behavioral, and diagnostic groups. Chapter Two describes the most appropriate group activity to use with children of different ages, from preschool through adolescence. It also contains miscellaneous group approaches—such as psychodrama groups—that do not fit well into either a theoretical or a developmental perspective.

In recent years therapists have become adept at more than one of the group approaches described in the following three chapters. As a result, they may combine two or more group approaches for maximum effectiveness. In particular, therapists are combining structured group activities, such as role playing or games, with a talk or discussion period. Clearly, group therapists should be knowledgeable and skilled in the use of several methods, using the ones most appropriate to the particular members of the group.

1 Major Theoretical Orientations

The major psychological theories utilized in group therapy are psychoanalytic, transactional analysis (TA), and behavioral theories. Each theory offers a different perspective from which to view pathology and treatment. Specifically, the theories may give rise to different views about the role of the therapist and the group composition—although, in practice, many of the therapeutic mechanisms are often similar. The following sections describe the essential aspects of these three theoretical approaches. In addition, diagnostic groups are presented, as they are representative of an innovative approach to diagnosis and group therapy.

Psychoanalytic

Psychoanalytic groups are used primarily with older children and adolescents. In these groups the members typically share their feelings about a variety of topics and are usually allowed to move at their own pace in resolving conflicts. Consequently, the duration of treatment often is lengthy. Some therapists view such a group as a collection of individuals; others perceive it as a single unit. When viewed as a unit, the group most often functions as a symbolic family. The activities of the psychoanalytic group therapist include confronting, interpreting, reflecting, modeling, and occasionally setting limits. Transference and countertransference issues are often intensified in the group atmosphere.

Transference-Countertransference Issues

AUTHOR: Fern J. Azima

PRECIS: Examining transference and countertransference issues in group therapy with adolescents

INTRODUCTION: The author presents a theoretical discussion of transference and countertransference issues using case examples from a therapy group for adolescents. The group was composed of male and female outpatients, ages fifteen to eighteen. The patients were between the low average and superior range of intellectual functioning. A variety of diagnoses and socioeconomic levels was represented. The group met for weekly eighty-minute sessions. Group therapy was the only form of therapy received by the participants.

TRANSFERENCE: Azima defines transference as "the wide array of repetitive or emotionally significant manifestations of patient behavior in relation to the therapist, to other group members, and to the group as a whole" (p. 52). As such, it may be diluted by the presence of others in the group, or the combination of individuals may magnify its intensity. The experienced therapist identifies transference and then assists members in working through it. Transference issues encountered by the author were (1) attitudes toward authority and peers, (2) acting out, (3) silence, and (4) somatization.

Problem attitudes toward authority include active or passive rebellion against the leader. When angry feelings are expressed by adolescents, the therapist utilizes confrontation in addition to or as a substitute for interpretation of the transference. Transference problems related to peers also may revolve around attitudes toward authority. That is, the therapist must monitor and modify the use of confrontation lest it be considered as condemnation by the remaining peers. Under such perceived circumstances, the adolescent group might retaliate against even the best-meaning therapist. Additionally, the therapist can model appropriate responses to criticism from the group. Similarly, acting-out behavior is often related to the transference attitudes toward authority and peers.

Silence often occurs within the group context and is difficult for many adolescents to tolerate. Silence may be utilized to test the therapist or as a response to the fear of self-disclosure.

As the emotional stress within the group increases, numerous physical symptoms (such as headaches, flushing, palpitations, encopresis, vomiting, and hypochondriasis) often increase. These symptoms present a physical reality, which is more easily accepted by the adolescent than elusive emotional problems. Occasionally, the physical symptoms may even be linked with specific transferential objects.

COUNTERTRANSFERENCE: Countertransference includes feelings and reactions arising in the therapist, which if unacknowledged or unmodified may impair and block therapy. The author suggests that countertransference is stronger in group therapy than in individual therapy. The therapist needs a high frustration tolerance in order to withstand the personal questions, sarcasms, put-downs, and direct attacks from adolescents. Countertransference issues encountered by the author included (1) omnipotence, (2) fear of self-disclosure, (3) overidentification with the adolescent, (4) somatizations, and (5) blind spots.

Omnipotent therapists may be initially welcomed by group members because they serve as all-powerful protectors who are fantasized as their problem solvers. However, the adolescents soon realize that they are unable to match the therapist's image of infallibility. Furthermore, group members often become overdependent on an all-powerful therapist.

The therapist of an adolescent group must also be sensitive to requests for self-disclosure. Inquisitive adolescents may make honest requests based on curiosity. Such inquiries deserve honest replies. A therapist who neutralizes honest inquiries by statements like "What do you think?" may seem excessively rigid and lacking in spontaneity. The result may be a reduction in the group's ability to trust the therapist. Conversely, therapists can overidentify with adolescents, communicating their excessive needs for closeness and acceptance.

Somatizations (for example, blushing, perspiring, teeth clenching, nausea, cramps, and chest pressure) often occur and if noticeable may communicate quite vividly the therapist's thoughts and feelings. Thus, awareness of these somatizations, especially observable acts, is essential. Similarly, therapists often have blind spots with which they are unfamiliar. Discovery of these areas and focused attention on them can be crucial to the professional growth of the therapist.

COMMENTARY: Azima has pointed out important issues (in individual or group therapy) that require attention by the therapist. Unfortunately, many of these issues may remain beyond awareness without the assistance of an observer or a consultant/supervisor. This especially holds true in group therapy, where such feelings may be intensified. An approach for dealing with this problem would be the utilization of a cotherapist.

SOURCE: Azima, F.J. "Transference-Countertransference Issues in Group Psychotherapy for Adolescents." *International Journal of Child Psychotherapy*, 1972, *1*, 51-70.

Para-Analytic Groups for Adolescents

AUTHOR: Norman S. Brandes

PRECIS: Providing para-analytic group therapy to adolescents in outpatient treatment

INTRODUCTION: The peer group is a major influence during adolescence, affecting the individual's attitudes, values, and modes of behavior. Although the peer network cannot be exactly duplicated in a therapeutic milieu, the group experience closely approximates it. As an adjunct to individual therapy, or when used in combination with family therapy, group therapy often is the treatment of choice for many adolescents.

TREATMENT: Brandes emphasizes the importance of carefully selecting adolescents to participate in para-analytic group therapy. Adolescents who are either too young or nonverbal may not respond favorably to this verbal, dynamic approach to outpatient treatment. In beginning a para-analytic group, the therapist identifies goals of group therapy as viewed by the adolescents and by the therapist. It may be necessary to reiterate these goals during later sessions or to modify them as treatment progresses. Additionally, the author recommends the use of a contract between individual clients and the therapist.

The para-analytic group as described by Brandes is a long-term, open-ended, continuous, group experience for adolescents with a variety of diagnoses. Although it is closely related to traditional psychoanalytic treatment in its emphasis on unconscious processes, the para-analytic group places additional emphasis on here-and-now life situations. In addition, the therapist in a para-analytic group departs from traditional analytic practice by giving suggestions, directions, reassurance, reeducation, and support. Generally speaking, the group provides a greater range of reality testing than does individual therapy. The therapist is able to view patients dealing with interpersonal relationships within the group, and group members can view the therapist from a different perspective as well.

Brandes recommends that a para-analytic group be led by a male and a female therapist, thereby providing identification models for both sexes. Meetings between cotherapists are scheduled before and after group sessions in order to facilitate honest feedback and the communication of opinions and feelings. Cotherapists must display flexibility in dealing with the adolescent group, since rigidity thwarts responsible interaction. Furthermore, since the cotherapists must present healthy models for identification, they need to be spontaneous, honest, and tolerant.

COMMENTARY: The departures from traditional psychoanalytic procedures, as recommended by Brandes for para-analytic groups, seem warranted for two reasons. First, the group experience changes the dynamics of the transference relationships and requires additional flexibility on the part of the therapist(s). Second, the developmental demands of adolescence require reality-oriented assistance, in addition to symbolic transference relationships. Thus, suggestion, direction, reassurance, reeducation, and support—not used in "orthodox" psychoanalytic therapy—become key aspects of the para-analytic group.

SOURCE: Brandes, N. S. "Adolescent Therapy Through the Eyes of a Group Therapist." *Groups: A Journal of Group Dynamics and Psychotherapy*, 1977, *8*, 2-7.

Group Psychoanalytic Treatment for Disturbed Juvenile Delinquents

AUTHORS: Girard Franklin and Wallace Nottage

PRECIS: Treating seriously disturbed juvenile delinquents in intensive psychoanalytic group therapy in order to effect substantial changes in personality

INTRODUCTION: The rationale for providing psychoanalytic group therapy was threefold. First, this approach was useful in diluting the hostility toward the therapist as an authority figure. Second, the group served to expose the members' problems—for instance, their distrust of other people. Third, the group provided peer support to foster an active, self-responsible approach to solving internal problems. The goals of therapy were as follows: to explore one's personality, to understand oneself, and to rebuild and remodel one's character structure.

TREATMENT: The group was an ongoing, open one whose

members were adjudicated mid-adolescent delinquents with the following characteristics: (1) They had demonstrated a poor response to probation. (2) They could not relate to authority figures. (3) They resisted any focus on themselves or their problems. (4) As a condition for their probation, they were required to attend therapy.

The group met five times each week. The reasons for the frequent meetings were the members' low tolerance of frustration and anxiety, their propensity to impulsive behavior for the discharge of tension, and their intense needs for support in order to combat profound feelings of worthlessness. Thus, the frequent meetings were important in providing the necessary support and encouragement that ultimately facilitated greater self-awareness. Furthermore, the intensive treatment served to emphasize the serious nature of each member's personality problems and legal situation.

Members were encouraged to share their feelings on a variety of topics in group discussions. Individuals were generally allowed to move at their own pace (unless otherwise confronted by their peers), and for many the experience was the first opportunity to recognize their feelings and to be exposed to alternate approaches to handling them. Although the therapist and peers accepted certain impulsive behaviors (such as explosive verbal outbursts), resistances were readily confronted by the group members. Such honest confrontation was possible because of the similarities in backgrounds, the practice of self-disclosure, the admiration for self-disclosure, and the developing friendships. Accurate feedback provided in a supportive atmosphere helped the group members realize that inappropriate behavior was separate from the total self. Furthermore, members discovered that their behavior stemmed from feelings and desires common to other adolescents.

RESULTS: The following results of treatment were noted: (1) Members seldom returned to the court system. (2) Individuals often sought further assistance in the community—so that they could achieve constructive goals. (3) Members often maintained close personal contact with their group therapist. These positive behaviors were attributed to the members' developing capacities to cope with intrapsychic and interpersonal difficulties, as well as their new ability to experience friendship and love for one another and for the therapists.

COMMENTARY: Two conditions of the group were monumental to its success as described in the authors' reports. First, the adolescents presumably were motivated to attend the group sessions, since this was a condition of probation; thus, resistance manifested by sporadic attendance was virtually eliminated. A second condition (related to the first) was the intensive nature of the treatment. As a result, the group members were provided with an ongoing, safe environment where they could deal with their internal problems and their daily, real-life adjustment difficulties. Furthermore, the intensity of the program surely served to communicate the intense, genuine commitment of an adult authority figure (the therapist) and peers to the resolution of each member's problems.

SOURCE: Franklin, G., and Nottage, W. "Psychoanalytic Treatment of Severely Disturbed Juvenile Delinquents in a Therapy Group." *International Journal of Group Psychotherapy,* 1969, *19* (2), 165-175.

An Analytic Play Therapy Group

AUTHOR: Maria Rita Mendes Leal

PRECIS: Interpreting the play themes of preadolescent girls involved in group play therapy to effect greater verbalization and understanding of their emotional problems

INTRODUCTION: Leal categorizes children's groups as (1) groups where activity serves a recreational and instructional purpose, (2) groups where free expression through play and art serves a cathartic purpose, and (3) groups where play is viewed solely as a symbolic language. She then reviews the progress of a girls' activity group that evolved into an analytic play therapy group.

TREATMENT: The group, six preadolescent girls with pronounced behavior and learning problems, met once a week for fifty-two sessions. Meetings were held in a room that was once a kitchen. After several sessions an informal petition dividing the room (a cupboard) was replaced with a permanent wall and door. The rooms were furnished with tables and chairs. One room was supplied with toys and "conventional preschool play material." As the group sessions progressed, the room without toys was declared by the girls to be a room for "older children who preferred talking about things instead of doing what they liked."

During the initial two months, the girls participated in activity group therapy. Activities included painting, playing with clay, playing with dolls, and reenacting mother-father conflicts. At the end of the two-month period, the girls' teacher reported "greater access" to individual children; however, the therapist noted that the girls had not verbalized situational problems. Additionally, the girls' behavior continued to be marked by sudden motor outbursts, fantasy play, and nonverbal expression of primitive impulses. Thus, the therapist determined that a move from the supportive activity group to a more analytic approach was necessary.

The therapist began to interject interpretive statements of play themes while concurrently providing continued support and acceptance. Gradually, the girls moved from nonverbal communication through symbolic play to verbal discussions of situational problems. After a time, the group as a whole preferred the discussions and occupation of the "talking room" (the room without play materials).

RESULTS: According to the therapist, the change from activity-oriented group therapy to the analytic approach resulted in the development of improved communication and greater verbalization of problems. Additionally, the girls' teacher reported the following improvements: increased attention, progress in abstract reasoning, increased attendance, and greater acceptance of responsibilities, authority, and independence.

COMMENTARY: Leal's account of the evolution of the group illustrates the importance of flexibility on the part of the therapist. By being sensitive to the needs and progress of the girls, the therapist was able to effect changes in the group format and ultimately in the behavior of the individual girls. While the success of interpretation may also depend on the intellectual level of the individual group members, the readiness and need to move on were equally important factors.

SOURCE: Leal, M. R. M. "Group-Analytic Play Therapy with Preadolescent Girls." *International Journal of Group Psychotherapy,* 1966, *16* (1), 58-64.

Psychoanalytic Groups for Adolescents

AUTHOR: Melvin Singer

PRECIS: Using the "classic techniques" of psychoanalysis in long-term, open-ended group therapy for adolescents

INTRODUCTION: During adolescence individuals withdraw into a narcissistic realm. Libido, which was object cathected, is now free floating. One of the adolescent's tasks is to search for substitutions for this previously object-cathected libido. Additionally, the adolescent must bridge the gap between the ideal and the real self in order to avoid a reduction in self-esteem. These developments often result in an impulsive, action-oriented, and distraught individual with feelings of emptiness and despair. Thus, the goal of the psychoanalytic group is to provide emotional growth through understanding and insight.

TREATMENT: Members of the group were high school and college students, sixteen to twenty-one years old, from middle- and upper-middle-class families. Participants were excluded if they were excessively sociopathic, impulsive, destructive, narcissistic, withdrawn, or overtly psychotic. Six to eight individuals met twice a week when possible for three to four years.

The role of the therapist was to provide an actual substitute for parent objects. Thus, the therapist became an ego ideal who provided security, guidance, and a suitable model for identification. Also, the therapist occasionally set limits in order to curb the expression of impulses. Through constructive ego-building comments, the therapist aided participants in acquiring freedom for the reintegration of ego and superego structures.

Group members provided needed support and additional models for identification. Gradually, cohesiveness and loyalty developed among group members. The resulting therapeutic alliance reduced the likelihood of flight and sustained members through difficult periods. The real contact with peers allowed for an emphasis on interpersonal conflicts, rather than on intrapsychic ones. Also, the group provided the individual members with (1) a mechanism for reality testing; (2) confrontation experiences, which reduced expansive aspirations and goals; (3) numerous transference relationships; (4) the opportunity for modification of punitive superego structures through acceptance; and (5) suitable sublimatory channels for the development of vocational and avocational skills through identification and the rechanneling of energies.

When the psychoanalytic group was used in conjunction with individual therapy, members were provided with a useful opportunity to explore in greater depth situations and/or responses arising in the group. Singer warns potential group leaders to choose group members carefully, since individuals with poor self-esteem require good models; to expect and allow acting out (for example, missed sessions, silences, and rebellious behavior); and to guard against countertransference reactions that are too restrictive or inhibitory.

COMMENTARY: When the psychoanalytic group is used with adolescents, the support of the members and the therapist is essential. Additionally, the group provides real, rather than merely symbolic, relationships. The reality-oriented confrontations and limit setting, when blended with support and constructive feedback, provide the adolescent with the information and opportunity to gain insight and to grow emotionally.

SOURCE: Singer, M. "Comments and Caveats Regarding Adolescent Groups in a Combined Approach." *International Journal of Group Psychotherapy,* 1974, *24,* 429-438.

Interpretive Group Psychotherapy: An Overview

AUTHOR: Max Sugar

PRECIS: An overview of interpretive groups, with attention focused on group composition, characteristics of the playroom, general considerations, and the three phases of the group

INTRODUCTION: The interpretive group is designed to elicit the child's demonstration of various conflicts, defenses, and fantasies through play and verbalization. The therapist's primary activities are observation and interpretation. Prerequisites for the interpretive group therapist are a knowledge of the latency child's type of thinking, psychosexual level, and typical defenses. Also, experience in individual child therapy is necessary.

GROUP COMPOSITION: Sugar suggests that children manifesting a variety of symptoms should be considered as candidates for interpretive groups. Symptoms treated by Sugar have included ulcers, asthma, "transvestite tendencies," psychosis, anxiety, and phobias. Children may come from intact or broken homes, institutions, or deprived backgrounds. Excluded from group participation are children who are intellectually retarded, autistic, severely antisocial, totally action oriented, or prone to panic reactions when close to other children. The possible candidate should also be able to use play or language in order to express conflicts and fantasies. Children described as most suitable are those who display a behavior disorder in the neurotic range, a psychosomatic disorder, inhibitions, neurotic symptoms, or sexual problems. Other viable candidates for group membership are children involved in individual therapy who have settled many personal conflicts but continue to demonstrate difficulties with their peers or siblings.

Sugar suggests that the optimal size for a group is six members. If the children are overanxious, hostile, or hyperactive, a group composed of four to five members is recommended. Same-sex groups are also recommended. In deciding a suitable age range for participants, one should consider the level of maturity, social adjustment, and achieved school grade. However, general guidelines for preschoolers are that group members be within a year or two of each other. With latency-age children, a three-year age span is suitable.

TREATMENT ROOM: A room eight feet by fourteen feet should be sufficient for interpretive group therapy. The room should be designed and furnished so as to be conducive to the production of questions and fantasies and the expression of certain conflicts through play or language. Toys serve as a means of nonverbal communication and help the children reenact life scenes that are difficult for them to verbalize. The author provides a lengthy list of recommended toys and furnishings. The room should also be furnished with a comfortable chair for the therapist, placed to one side for the purpose of observing without intruding. It is also helpful to soundproof the walls of the playroom so as not to disturb others or excite parents in the waiting room.

GENERAL CONSIDERATIONS: Before a potential participant is introduced to the group, the child and his parents should have the rationale of therapy explained to them. The duration of therapy (a recommended minimum of six months), the length of sessions (forty-five to sixty minutes), and fees should be discussed. Rules regarding confidentiality should be explained to the parents and the child. A trip to the playroom before beginning in the group is also recommended.

Children are advised of the rules of conduct for the group. Chief among these rules is the stipulation that children may play with any toy but are not allowed to destroy property or to hurt other group members. Children are allowed to bring personal toys and even food to the session. These items may serve as means of communication for the child and may provide for useful interpretive statements by the therapist. The therapist should strive to avoid becoming centrally involved in the child's play activities. Instead, she should assume a nonauthoritative, nondirective role.

GROUP PHASES: During the initial phase, the child is a social isolate, concerned only with his personal problems. During the first few sessions, dependency needs, disappointments, and frustrations may peak, resulting in the child's expressed desire to drop out of the group. Similar reactions may occur in response to occasional fighting between members; however, the therapist should insist to parents that the child return to the group in order to deal with the problem in the context of the group. Early meetings may also be characterized as dull, with long silences, feelings of embarrassment, repetitious play, isolation, and the avoidance of one another. However, as the therapist continually insists that members interact with one another and not with her, the group members gradually learn how to get along. The end of the initial phase is signaled by the development of group cohesion, as manifested by involvement with one another in games, activities, and conversations. Additionally, negative cohesion may develop, as demonstrated by the exclusion of the therapist in group activities.

The middle phase of the interpretive group is marked by the following: (1) The group members realize that the therapist will not direct them, teach them, or give them advice. (2) Group members begin to ask personal questions of one another. (3) Individuals begin discussing their troubles. (4) Individuals ask for the opinions of other group members. (5) Members identify with one another. (6) Comparisons of families occur. (6) Dreams and nightmares are discussed. (7) Absences decline. Additionally, multiple transferences begin to develop, and it is during this phase that most of the work in therapy is done. This phase may last from three months to three years.

During the terminal phase, the child is more functional overall, with an accompanying reduction in symptoms. At this point the child is able to give more, to play cooperatively, and to get along better with all group members. In effect, the child no longer needs the group, although the group may profit from contact with the child. This phase should last from three to six months.

COMMENTARY: This article is recommended reading for any therapist involved in group psychotherapy. The author provides practical suggestions and recommendations for beginning and conducting a group. Especially useful are the list of recommended toys and furnishings and the expectations for behavior at various stages in the evolution of the group.

SOURCE: Sugar, M. "Interpretive Group Psychotherapy with Latency Children." *Journal of Child Psychiatry,* 1974, *13* (4), 648-666.

Psychoanalytic Group Therapy for Pubescent Boys with Absent Fathers

AUTHOR: Max Sugar

PRECIS: Providing psychoanalytic interpretations and emotional support within a group context to boys from father-absent families

INTRODUCTION: Sugar reviews research findings that suggest a relationship between paternal deprivation and the following conditions in boys: emotional illness, juvenile delinquency, intense sexual anxiety, poor school performance, enuresis and encopresis, and gang delinquency. He suggests that group therapy led by a male therapist can help troubled boys resolve oedipal conflicts. A description of events in a boys' group, led by the author, is presented.

TREATMENT: The group was an open one whose size never exceeded ten boys. Boys ranged in age (eleven and a half to thirteen years) and in socioeconomic status. Referral problems included neurotic disorders, adjustment reactions, behavioral disorders, schizoid conditions, and passive-aggressive disorders. The boys participated in the group for from two to fifteen months. All boys had fathers who were absent from the family for a variety of reasons.

Operating within a psychoanalytic framework, the male therapist utilized the symbolic, family aspects of the group to explore changing transference relationships with the boys. That is, the boys initially exhibited transference to the therapist as a mother figure. As the group progressed, transference to the therapist as a father figure became more positive and prevalent. Interpretations and emotional support were offered by the therapist.

During early sessions the boys exhibited hostile and rebellious behavior. The therapist viewed this as representative of their search for a father—that is, someone to control and help them. Additionally, the male therapist provided a figure with whom the boys could identify and have fantasies.

With time mothers were brought into individual therapy and ultimately with their sons in therapy. This arrangement symbolically re-created the original intact family, wherein the therapist represented the lost fathers. In this situation the mothers' cathexis on and seduction of their sons gradually reduced, allowing the sons to become aggressive and separate from them. Additionally, the symbolic relationship between the male therapist and the mothers allowed the sons to surrender their roles as "protectors" of their mothers. Simultaneously, the boys were then able to deal with the loss of their fathers and to resolve oedipal conflicts. Thus, boys developed suitable superegos and were able to proceed with the usual developmental demands of adolescence.

COMMENTARY: Although the therapist's role as a male model was important, his symbolic role as the lost father for these paternally deprived youngsters cannot be understated. Another key aspect of the group therapy as described by Sugar was the timely inclusion of mothers in the therapy. This procedure allowed the boys to relinquish their roles as "protectors," thereby allowing for resolution of oedipal conflicts.

SOURCE: Sugar, M. "Group Therapy for Pubescent Boys with Absent Fathers." *Journal of Child Psychiatry,* 1967, *6,* 478-498.

Additional Readings

Becker, B. J., Gusrae, R., and MacNicol, E. "A Clinical Study of a Group Psychotherapy Program for Adolescents." *Psychiatric Quarterly,* 1963, *37,* 685-703.

The authors describe a group therapy approach for adolescents and present five case histories illustrating certain therapeutic processes. The goal of the group was to reach the positive forces in the adolescents' personalities by creating an atmosphere less threatening than that found at school or within their families. The group members were encouraged to discuss their problems and feelings. The following therapeutic processes were utilized: ventilation, group relationships and interactions, emotional release, dreams, humor, and interpretations by group members.

Brandes, N. S. "Multidimensional Treatment of Adolescents and Young Adults." *Groups: A Journal of Group Dynamics and Psychotherapy,* 1977, *8,* 1-6.

The author describes a multidimensional approach to the treatment of adolescents, wherein the youth participates in individual, group, and family therapy. A psychoanalytic framework serves as the foundation for group work; however, the following para-analytic methods are used to make the analysis less threatening: teaching, guidance, direction, reassurance, suggestion, support, periodic coaxing, and confrontation. The author also addresses the need to attend to group composition factors and issues related to transference and countertransference.

Day, M. "Psychoanalytic Group Therapy in Clinic and Private Practice." *American Journal of Psychiatry,* 1981, *138* (1), 64-69.

Day describes psychoanalytic group therapy as an interactive process in which members develop a strong feeling toward the leader and one another. The leader permits the forces of suggestion, intuition, contagion, projection, and acting out to develop group issues. Through confrontation, clarification, and interpretation, members gradually achieve a degree of insight and are able to change their methods of coping outside the group. The author also addresses the following issues as they relate to psychoanalytic groups in clinical and private practice: the type of patient referred for group therapy, factors related to group composition and patient diagnosis, beginning a group, therapeutic processes, and terminating a group.

Fisher, H. S. "Adolescent Group Psychotherapy: Collaborative Opportunity for Patients, Parents, and Therapist." *International Journal of Group Psychotherapy,* 1977, *27* (2), 233-239.

An adolescent group therapy session is described; and a new approach—which allows collaboration opportunities for patients, parents, and therapist—is suggested. Fisher points out that adolescents face the critical tasks of freeing themselves from childhood and parents and learning to be adults. Because of rapid changes in cultural standards and mores, adolescence was particularly confusing in the 1960s and 1970s. As a result, the following triphasic approach to analytic group therapy with adolescents has appeared: (1) An attempt is made to convert resistant, hostile teenagers into a productive, talking group. (2) The therapist introduces verbal exploration of the parents in absentia. (3) Parents are invited to join several sessions, in which parents and children have an opportunity to hear one another and, with the therapist's help, come to understand one another's roles and expectations.

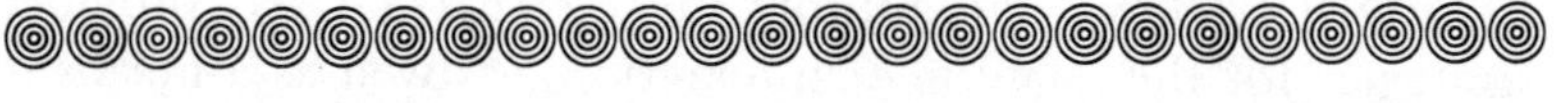

Transactional Analysis

Another theory represented in the group therapy literature is transactional analysis (TA). The duration of a TA group depends on the children's needs or the group therapist's preferences; thus, some groups meet for weeks while others continue for more than a year. The purpose of most TA groups is to provide insight into one's functioning. TA groups typically incorporate more structure than psychoanalytic groups do. The methods utilized in these groups include role playing, Gestalt exercises, and discussion sessions. Issues examined in the activities include one's ego states, transactions, and games utilized by group members.

A Transactional Analysis Group with Emotionally Disturbed Boys

AUTHORS: Tim J. Arnold and Richard L. Simpson

PRECIS: Assessing the effects of a transactional analysis (TA) group on the self-concept and behavior of emotionally disturbed boys

INTRODUCTION: The authors suggest that TA has provided strategies for the analysis of interactions, as well as a means to help individuals discover the "meaning of their existence." As individuals acquire insight into their own behavior, they are better able to exercise self-control and to make changes in their lives. Although the popularity of TA strategies has increased, this interest has not been matched by empirical studies designed to evaluate the effectiveness of TA. Thus, the purpose of this study was to measure changes in behavior and self-concept arising from involvement in a TA group.

TREATMENT: Eight emotionally disturbed boys, ages ten through sixteen, participated in group meetings conducted three times a week over a six-week period. Although all participants demonstrated average intellectual abilities, their academic functioning was below expected grade levels. During the initial meeting, the boys were introduced to the basic principles of TA. To help them understand the basic concepts, the coleaders utilized A. M. Freed's books *TA for Kids* (Jalmar Press, 1971) and *TA for Tots* (Jalmar Press, 1973).

After gaining an understanding of TA principles, the boys participated in activities designed to provide enlightenment regarding ego states, transactions, and games. Role playing was utilized and was followed by group discussions. Group members also cut out and discussed pictures demonstrating TA concepts. Additionally, each boy participated in a special project. Projects included puppet shows, audiovisual recordings, and the development of comic books. Each project was structured and guided by the coleaders to illustrate TA concepts and their applications. Sessions were recorded, so that absent members could review the proceedings.

RESULTS: The authors utilized pre- and posttreatment measures from the Piers-Harris Self Concept Scale, the Peterson-Quay Behavior Checklist, and classroom ratings to assess the effectiveness of the TA group. The results failed to indicate positive changes in the dependent measures used. In fact, increases in inappropriate behavior were noted by teachers' aides. However, the authors reported other beneficial aspects of treatment, including (1) the use of TA terms, principles, and concepts outside the scheduled therapy meetings; (2) insight into "games" and behavior in day-to-day school activities; and (3) the voluntary continuation by all boys in the TA group.

COMMENTARY: Although the objective results are not particularly encouraging, these findings may reflect a difficulty in the experimental methodology and not in the group procedures. That is, the effects of group participation were evaluated after only six weeks; if more time had elapsed, the results might have been positive. In fact, the increase in inappropriate behaviors, as suggested by the ratings of teachers' aides, *may* reflect a change from passive compliance by the boys to active participation in guiding the events of their lives. That is, the boys may have begun to assert themselves, and their behavior may have caused discomfort to some adults. The techniques deserve further exploration.

SOURCE: Arnold, T. J., and Simpson, R. L. "The Effects of a TA Group on Emotionally Disturbed School-Age Boys." *Transactional Analysis Journal,* 1975, *5* (3), 238-241.

Transactional Analysis Groups in Residential Treatment

AUTHOR: Richard Roth

PRECIS: Using a transactional analysis (TA) group as an adjunct therapy for adolescents in residential treatment

INTRODUCTION: TA is a psychological theory and treatment method developed by Eric Berne. The language of TA is intentionally colloquial and utilizes the following constructs:

1. Structural analysis is the study of the ego states of the "Parent," "Adult," and "Child."
2. Transactional analysis proper is the study of the way people "transact" with each other.
3. Game analysis is the study of repeated transactions that result in bad feelings.
4. Script analysis is the study of the way people compulsively follow unconscious life plans.

The TA approach, when used in a group setting, allows children and adolescents to see themselves more clearly. Thus, they are provided with information that allows them to make desired changes and additions to their personality.

Roth describes four treatment issues relevant to the use of TA groups with adolescents. First, the influence of the peer group is important in the family and in therapy. That is, the peer group relationship may take temporary precedence over family ties, resulting in strained relationships within the family. Similarly, the influence of the peer group may interfere in the occurrence of transference with the therapist. Second, adolescence is marked by conflict and ambivalence related to independence. Thus, the adolescent involved in a TA group may complain about the infringements on his privacy, followed later by contradictory requests for more time in therapy. Third, most adolescents come to therapy unwillingly or, at best, reluctantly. Consequently, strong negative feelings toward parents and professionals may delay effective treatment. Fourth, the group described by Roth utilized a childcare worker as a coleader of the TA group. This arrangement requires a careful balance between playing the roles of peer, parent, and therapist.

TREATMENT: The TA group was composed of six to eight boys, ages twelve to sixteen. Boys were randomly assigned to the group upon admission and were heterogeneous with respect to referral problems and intelligence (dull normal to bright average). The group met weekly for approximately one year with the stated goal of learning TA.

A caseworker (a social worker) and a childcare worker were the coleaders of the group. This arrangement was useful because it promoted interdisciplinary communication and cooperation. Also, the interactions with adults allowed adolescents to observe these professionals and caretakers as unique individuals. Consequently, a healthy and constructive reappraisal of parents and parent figures could occur.

Adolescents were told that the TA group was designed to help people learn what "makes them tick." Learning occurred with the aid of visual materials and Gestalt exercises. Thus, the format provided for affective and cognitive learning. For example, in discussing the concept of the "Child" ego state, the coleaders utilized visual aids to present theoretical material and visual imagery exercises to develop an affective understanding of the concept. Coleaders also used the following statements to make the "Child" ego state more real: "Imagine you are a little boy again. What is the nicest thing anyone ever said to you? Who said it? How does it feel?" (p. 782). Thus, the TA group became a setting in which life data were gathered and reviewed. Since changes and revisions were explored in individual therapy, the group members were not anxious during group meetings.

RESULTS: The overall response to the TA group was positive. Voluntary attendance averaged about 80 percent, and many members expressed disappointment when meetings were unavoidably canceled on occasions. Additionally, youngsters not involved in the TA group sought membership in the group, and both natural and foster parents reported favorable reactions. Similarly, the childcare staff accepted and supported the group, as demonstrated by their voluntary, regular attendance at in-service training meetings related to TA. Finally, the members of the group said that they felt better after group sessions.

COMMENTARY: Although Roth does not provide empirical data to demonstrate the effectiveness of the TA group, the subjective data warrant the consideration of this approach under similar circumstances. Particularly important, apparently, is the availability of individual therapy offered in conjunction with the TA group. Individual therapy was used to deal actively with the issues arising from the group session and thus was a necessary component in the "treatment package."

Another characteristic of Roth's TA group was the use of the childcare worker as a coleader. Again, although its effectiveness was not empirically demonstrated, this approach seems extremely helpful in promoting interdisciplinary cooperation and in presenting significant adults to group members in a different and positive light.

SOURCE: Roth, R. "A Transactional Analysis Group in Residential Treatment of Adolescents." *Child Welfare,* 1977, *56,* 776-785.

Additional Readings

Erskine, R. G., and Maisenbacher, J. "The Effects of a Transactional Analysis Class on Socially Maladjusted High School Students." *Transactional Analysis Journal,* 1975, *5* (3), 252-254.

The authors describe a transactional analysis (TA) class in which twelve socially maladjusted and academically deficient students enrolled for a semester. The class met for one hour each day, and participants received course credit on a pass/fail basis. Students were required to learn the basic concepts of structural, transactional, and game analysis. Discounts, time structuring, and basic life positions also were emphasized in the class. Results from the study indicate a significant decrease in discipline referrals, a significant decrease in truancy, and a significant increase in grade averages for participants in the TA class.

Hipple, J. L., and Muto, L. "The TA Group for Adolescents." *Personnel and Guidance Journal,* 1974, *52* (10), 675-681.

The authors describe a program wherein four adolescent boys participated in a six-session group that utilized transactional analysis principles. Homework exercises were assigned to the participants at the end of each session. Hipple and Muto conclude that the structured, time-limited transactional analysis group approach is useful in working with adolescents.

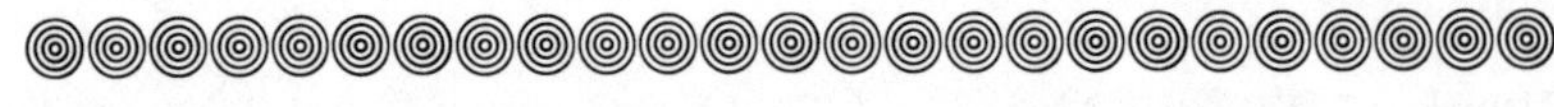

Behavioral

A theory gaining increased acceptance in group work is behavioral or social learning theory. Whether utilized as a singular method for group therapy or as part of a multimodal framework, behavioral group therapies are successful with a wide variety of children in diverse settings. Learning and social psychology principles often used include the following: modeling of appropriate behavior by the therapist and/or peers in the group; reinforcement (for example, with tokens or verbally) of group behavior, including the frequency and quality of verbalizations; and generalization of behavior sought through the use of role playing and "homework" assignments. Behavioral approaches are usually more brief and structured than in either psychoanalytic or TA groups.

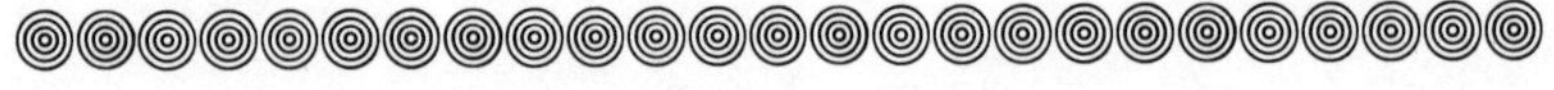

Use of Appropriate Peer Models in Counseling Groups for Children

AUTHORS: James C. Hansen, Thomas M. Niland, and Leonard P. Zani

PRECIS: Providing appropriate peer models in reinforcement counseling groups with sixth-grade students

INTRODUCTION: Many problems exhibited by adolescents develop before they begin secondary school—often as a result of interactions with undesirable peer models or the absence of desirable models. Since interactions with other persons are important, group counseling can serve as an excellent vehicle for learning or relearning appropriate behaviors. The authors suggest that the equivocal findings of some studies of group effectiveness may have resulted because homogeneous groups—groups composed of socially unpopular youngsters whose social interactions are inappropriate—were used. As a possible solution to this problem, they suggest that appropriate peer models be incorporated into counselor reinforcement groups.

TREATMENT: Utilizing a learning theory approach to counseling, the authors established two types of counselor reinforcement groups. One type of group was composed of six students, three boys and three girls, who *all* received low sociometric ratings. A second type of group was also composed of three boys and three girls; however, there was one appropriate peer model (a person who received high sociometric ratings) for each sex. Additionally, a control group reported for an "activity period."

Participation in the groups was voluntary, and the groups met twice a week for four weeks. The purpose of the groups, as presented to the students, was to discuss social behavior in school. During each session the counselor introduced a specific topic, which was related to getting along with others. Also, relevant reading materials were utilized to stimulate discussion. The discussions were semistructured and focused on the reading materials and personal experiences. The counselor verbally reinforced insights, ideas, and suggestions that were relevant to appropriate social behavior.

RESULTS: After eight sessions pre- and posttreatment sociometric ratings were compared. Low sociometric students who had participated in counselor reinforcement groups with appropriate peer models made significant gains in social acceptance. Also, the gains in sociometric ratings were maintained two months later. However, learning did not sufficiently generalize so as to *increase* social acceptance from posttreatment measures to follow-up measures.

COMMENTARY: While the authors provide empirical data supporting the inclusion of peer models in group counseling, the practicality of this procedure may be limited in certain settings. For example, the psychologist or counselor who removes "healthy" peer models from regular classes to participate in group therapy for troubled youngsters may encounter considerable, and perhaps justified, resistance from parents. Although the "healthy" peer models would undoubtedly benefit from the group experience, parents may view their youngsters' academic preparation as preferable to emotional growth gained from the group experience. Additionally, parents of "healthy" peer models might fear that the troubled group members will adversely affect their children.

As an alternative to actual models, the authors suggest that videotapes depicting appropriate models in action might be viewed. At the very least, groups could be more heterogeneously composed with regard to students' presenting problems.

SOURCE: Hansen, J. C., Niland, T. M., and Zani, L. P. "Model Reinforcement in Group Counseling with Elementary School Children." *Personnel and Guidance Journal,* 1969, *47* (8), 741-744.

A Behavioral Perspective on Group Therapy

AUTHOR: William G. Johnson

PRECIS: Using learning theory principles to effect changes in behavior within the group therapy context

INTRODUCTION: The empirical foundations of behavioral groups rest in learning theory principles and social psychological research. The behavior one initially seeks to change in the group is the individual's verbal performance. The appearance, mannerisms, and behaviors of individuals serve as discriminative and reinforcing stimuli. Role-playing and rehearsal activities utilize reinforcement and modeling principles. As the group develops knowledge of group norms, majority opinions provide an impetus for change. The group influence is used to secure a verbal commitment from participants to small, gradual changes in behavior. Since problem behaviors occur at home, work, school, and play, the therapist attempts to move from increases in appropriate verbal performance to changes in behavior outside the group. These changes are initiated by role playing and "homework" assignments.

TREATMENT: In selecting members to participate in behavioral groups, Johnson recommends that groups be heterogeneous with respect to age, sex, problem area, and socioeconomic class. The rationale for this course is to provide a "melting pot" from which rich opportunities for role playing emerge. Regarding group size, the key is to keep the group small enough to encourage individual participation, yet large enough to provide sufficient resources. Johnson suggests that seven to eight members provide a workable group even in the event of absences or withdrawals. Before therapy, each participant's behavior is individually observed and analyzed. Data are collected from interviews, records, self-report questionnaires, and other similar sources. Behaviors targeted for change are mutually agreed on by the client and therapist. Then the therapist offers strategies and contingencies for dealing with the problem. Changes both within and beyond the group context are emphasized.

The therapist takes time before each meeting to plan specific individual and group goals. To begin a session, a summary of the previous meeting is presented. This generally leads to a productive discussion of previous "homework" assignments and experiences outside the group. If problem areas are ignored in the ensuing discussion, the therapist prompts and shapes the discussion toward these more relevant topics. With time, group members gradually begin to assume more responsibility in shaping each other's discussion. If the verbal interactions remain nonproductive, the therapist interrupts and interjects more crucial topics. Role playing is utilized at appropriate moments, and sufficient time is allocated for the discussion of role plays. As the session closes, the meeting's progress is reviewed. Finally, "homework" assignments are made for the next session.

During the initial phase of the group, appropriate ground rules are established. Also, considerable time is devoted to the identification of problem behaviors. Occasionally, the contract between the therapist and individual members may require reiteration. During this phase the therapist immediately acknowledges (reinforces) verbal target behaviors, keeps interventions simple, speaks directly to clients, and limits excessive focus on any one content area during a given session.

During the middle stage, there is frequent use of role playing. Group members are reinforced for offering alternative solutions for themselves, as well as others. Outside the group it is expected that clients will initiate solutions to problems and then return to the group to report on their efforts. The emphasis changes from maintenance of appropriate behaviors within the group to generating and maintaining behavior outside the group.

In the termination phase, the influence of the therapist and group decreases in order to encourage independence in problem solving. As the last sessions approach, there is usually an increase in activity. Members who meet with success outside the group receive verbal reinforcement, while those who offer "empty explanations" for their lack of effort often encounter disappointment from the group. Finally, as the group ends, the therapist seeks feedback and impressions from the group. The author recommends that the length of treatment—from two to six months, depending on the individuals' needs—be specified beforehand.

COMMENTARY: An important focus of the behavioral group as outlined by Johnson is to generate and maintain desired behaviors in the group, followed by similar efforts outside the group context. Maintenance of behavior, or response generalization, is a key therapeutic issue regardless of the theoretical orientation. The use of role playing and "homework" assignments seems to lead to response generalization; however, Johnson does not provide empirical data supporting the group's effectiveness.

SOURCE: Johnson, W. G. "Group Therapy: A Behavioral Perspective." *Behavior Therapy,* 1975, *6,* 30-38.

Application of a Token Economy in Group Therapy

AUTHORS: James M. Stedman, Travis L. Peterson, and James Cardarelle

PRECIS: Using a token economy plus group therapy to improve the behavior of preadolescent boys within a group and at school

INTRODUCTION: The authors established a token system within the framework of an already existing activity group for boys. The purpose of the token system was to eliminate deviant behavior and, simultaneously, to increase appropriate behavior in the group. The authors also sought to improve academic and social behaviors for the boys while at school.

TREATMENT: The group was composed of eight boys (ages ten to twelve years, five months) with diagnostic classifications ranging from withdrawn to aggressive. The group met weekly for approximately one hour. To evaluate the effects of the procedures more closely, the authors selected two boys for closer study prior to the initiation of the token system.

Boy 1 was age eleven and was diagnosed Unsocialized Aggressive Reaction of Childhood. He frequently engaged in fighting, had temper tantrums, and used "bad" language at home and school. He was placed in a special education class for students with minimal brain injuries and received *B*s and *C*s on his schoolwork. Although he was on "stabilizing" medication, his behavior in the group continued to be aggressive and unpredictable.

Boy 2 was twelve years, five months old, with a diagnosis of Anxiety Reaction. His behavior at home and school was described as erratic, with variations from extreme politeness to aggressive outbursts. Similarly, his academic grades varied from *A*s to *F*s. He received medication; however, its effects were negligible. His behavior in the group was immature, and he continuously sought to gain the attention of the therapists and the other boys in the group.

Observations also were made of the whole group, and frequent disruptive behaviors were noted. Negative behaviors were restated positively and were assigned the following token values:

1. *Beginning the Group.* One token was awarded for coming to the group, staying in the waiting room, and so on.
2. *Cooperation in the Group.* One token was available during the beginning, middle, and end of the group session (for a total of three tokens per behavior) for participating and trying group activities, "acting like a friend," helping others to get along, and the like. Also, one token was delivered if a boy stayed in the group for the entire daily session.
3. *Cooperation in Group Discussions.* One token was available during the beginning, middle, and end of the group session for listening to others, talking seriously about a problem, and so on.

4. *Behavior Outside the Group.* Any improvement in a school conduct grade resulted in twenty tokens. Maintaining a conduct grade of either *A, B,* or *C* resulted in five, four, and three tokens, respectively. Students also received ten tokens for maintaining all academic marks received on report cards. Academic improvements resulted in five tokens per *A,* four tokens per *B,* and three tokens per *C.*

Although Boy 1 and Boy 2 received tokens for the positive behaviors mentioned previously, the following inappropriate behaviors were recorded and graphed:

Boy 1: Acts of physical aggression and acts of verbal aggression.

Boy 2: Verbal interruptions and interruptions initiated by some distracting physical action

At the outset the token economy was explained to the parents of the boys. Since daily parties with refreshments were initiated, parents were requested to refrain from providing children with snack money, so that they would be optimally motivated. Handouts explaining the desired behaviors and corresponding token values were given to each boy. Additionally, the following privileges with the necessary token earnings were explained: returning to the next group session—ten tokens, attending the ten-minute party at the end of each session—five tokens, and attending occasional student-determined field trips—the number of required tokens varied. After explaining the procedure, the therapists answered questions from the boys.

The delivery of tokens during the activity group session was decided by the consensus of the therapists. If an infraction occurred, the boy was given immediate feedback. Occasionally, bonus tokens were delivered for "outstanding adaptive behaviors" (such as returning a dropped token to one of the therapists). The number of tokens earned was tallied near the close of each session. Although most group members earned from fourteen to sixteen tokens during a session, additional tokens from their school performances provided more leeway for attaining the privileges.

RESULTS: Empirical data for Boy 1 and Boy 2 indicated a "dramatic" decrease in all deviant behaviors, especially for Boy 2. In addition, socially positive responses increased. Although Boy 1 suffered a relapse on two days, it was noted that he had failed to take his medication on those two days.

The therapists' subjective ratings of the other group members suggested increases in appropriate behavior. Only one boy failed to earn enough tokens to participate in the party throughout the fifteen sessions; and all boys earned enough tokens to return to the group each week. At school, five boys either maintained adequate conduct and academic grades or made improvements. Two boys showed mixed patterns, and one demonstrated little change.

COMMENTARY: This study shows the importance of a similar contingency system applied across different treatment settings for maximal improvements in behavior. While empirical data were offered for two of the boys, the qualitative data for the group as a whole seem equally impressive. Thus, the activity group can serve a therapeutic purpose when used independently or when utilized in conjunction with a token economy.

SOURCE: Stedman, J. M., Peterson, T. L., and Cardarelle, J. "Application of a Token System in a Pre-Adolescent Boys' Group." *Journal of Behavior Therapy and Experimental Psychiatry,* 1971, *2,* 23-29.

Token Reinforcement in an Adolescent Group

AUTHOR: Stanley Zweback

PRECIS: Using token reinforcement to influence the frequency and specific content of hospitalized adolescents' verbalizations in group therapy

INTRODUCTION: Group therapists frequently report resistance by adolescents in group therapy. This resistance is often manifested by infrequent verbalizations, avoidance of discussing one's own problems as well as those of others, and/or banding together against the therapist. While therapists have sought to increase the frequency of verbalizations in a group by using verbal-social reinforcement, this study sought to increase verbalizations by using concrete reinforcers (tokens).

TREATMENT: Individuals participating in the therapy group were eight adolescents, five girls and three boys, who were patients in the adolescent unit of a state hospital. All were described as "verbal" and of at least average intelligence. Although they represented a wide variety of diagnostic categories, none was considered organically impaired.

The group met for twenty-one semiweekly sessions lasting thirty minutes each. Sessions were conducted in the hospital's adolescent unit by a dynamically oriented psychologist. Group therapy was an integral part of the overall treatment program.

During the first meeting, the four data collectors were introduced, and the purpose of the procedure was explained. Baseline data were collected during the first four sessions. Two types of verbal behavior were recorded: Class I and Class II verbalizations. Class I verbalizations focused on one's own problems, whereas Class II verbalizations focused on the problems of another group member. On the fifth day, the baseline period was terminated, and Phase 1 began. One of the observers delivered tokens (metal washers) to group members on a variable-ratio 3 (VR3) schedule for the production of the requested verbal behaviors. Tokens were already utilized within the hospital's token economy and were redeemable for a variety of items and privileges. Tokens were awarded during Phase 1 for Class I verbalizations; during Phase 2 for Class II verbalizations, and during Phase 3 for Class I verbalizations. Each phase was terminated when all group members had increased their number of required verbalizations by 50 percent over baseline.

RESULTS: All group members increased their Class I verbalizations by the end of the fourth session in Phase 1. No systematic 50 percent increase in Class II verbalizations was recorded during Phase 1. During Phase 2 all members increased the frequency of Class II verbalizations to the criterion by the end of the fifth day of that phase. There was no systematic increase in Class I verbalizations during this time. For Phase 3 all members increased Class I verbalizations to the criterion level by the eighth day of that phase. Again, no systematic increase in Class II verbalizations was noted during this phase.

COMMENTARY: This study illustrates a useful technique for increasing the frequency of potentially therapeutic behavior within the group context. However, while the tokens were effective in increasing verbalizations, no data were noted regarding improvements in functioning outside the group. Thus, the ultimate utility of this procedure for the group therapist remains unclear.

SOURCE: Zweback, S. "Use of Concrete Reinforcement to Control Content of Verbal Initiations in Group Therapy with Adolescents." *Psychological Reports,* 1976, *38,* 1051-1057.

Additional Readings

Hauserman, N., Zweback, S., and Plotkin, A. "Use of Concrete Reinforcement to Facilitate Verbal Initiations in Adolescent Group Therapy." *Journal of Consulting and Clinical Psychology,* 1972, *38* (1), 90-96.

Token reinforcement was delivered to six hospitalized adolescents contingent on verbal statements in a therapy group. Results indicated that typically nonverbal adolescents can be shaped into emitting a higher rate of verbal initiations. Also, once the rate of verbal initiations increased, group pressure brought about a decrease in silly, off-topic verbalizations and an increase in appropriate and relevant initiations.

Heckel, R. V., Hursh, L., and Hiers, J. M. "Analysis of Process Data from Token Groups in a Summer Camp." *Journal of Clinical Psychology,* 1977, *33* (1), 241-244.

Forty-two campers attending a summer camp for disturbed children were treated by a combined group therapy-token economy approach in which peer judgments were the basis for tokens awarded for behaviors that occurred during the preceding twenty-four-hour period. Behaviors were studied to determine whether this approach would produce positive verbal behavioral change. Four variables changed significantly: environmental (irrelevant) responses declined; group responses increased; leader-directed responses declined; and decision making—reflected by summarizing, testing feasibility, and consensus—increased.

Small, A. C., and Cooper, G. D. "Convergent Effects of Behavioral and Dynamic Factors in Group Psychotherapy with Adolescents 1, 2, 3." *Groups: A Journal of Group Dynamics and Psychotherapy,* 1978, *9,* 6-10.

Learning principles were used to facilitate verbal interactions in group psychotherapy of adolescents displaying a wide range of pathology and living in a group home setting. Eight target behaviors were selected for reinforcement. The frequency of these behaviors during week one was compared with their frequency during week five. Results indicated that the continued application of learning principles was instrumental in altering target behaviors in three of the four groups. Two groups led by an experienced therapist showed greater enhanced results. The recognition or use of both dynamic and behavioral principles appeared to be advantageous in maximizing therapeutic effects.

Diagnostic

Diagnostic groups provide a relatively effective and efficient means of diagnosis. Although the diagnostic procedure occurs within the group setting, the focus remains on the individual. An important advantage of the diagnostic group is that it provides a sample of behaviors in a variety of settings—not just an examiner's "sterile" office. These behaviors may provide useful information regarding an individual's relationship with adults in the presence of peers, knowledge of social skills, and relationships with peers. The probability of success with certain treatment modalities also can be determined.

The Social Group as Diagnostic Tool

AUTHOR: Sallie R. Churchill

PRECIS: Using a group as the milieu in which diagnostic observations are made

INTRODUCTION: Churchill describes an evaluation of a social group used as part of an interdisciplinary diagnostic effort. Although group work is typically reserved as a treatment method, the author suggests that the group milieu provides essential information regarding peer relationships. This information differs from other diagnostic impressions in that it samples behavior in a variety of situations. The focus of the diagnostic group is the individual and not the group itself.

TREATMENT: The author recommends that short-term groups, consisting of no more than six members, be formed. A series of four meetings provides an adequate number of observations while still minimizing the children's emotional investment in the group. Although carefully balanced groups are not required, severely handicapped and retarded children are not accepted in diagnostic groups. Groups consist of one sex, since groups composed of both sexes may split into two homogeneous groups anyway. Also, the optimal age range is two years.

In preparing the child for the diagnostic group, both the parents and the practitioner should explain its purpose and format. In fact, the total diagnostic procedure, including the group observations, should be explained during the child's first interview with the practitioner. If the child expresses extreme anxiety about the group, efforts are made to clarify the nature of the protected and confidential group experience.

All participants begin the group simultaneously. During the first session, the following activities occur: (1) The children's perceptions of why they are there are explored, as well as concerns and fantasies about the group experience. (2) The basic rules of the group are explained. (3) Crafts, games, and activities are utilized to provide opportunities for group activity and constructive isolation. During the second session, the demands for peer interaction and social skills (for example, participation in group games or sharing equipment) are increased. In the third meeting, the child's behavior and interactions outside the safety of the treatment room are examined. Typically, the children travel together to a store, museum, or ball park. After the third session, initial impressions are shared with the diagnostic team. A final group session, individually planned for each child, is then conducted.

The four meetings permit a subjective evaluation of the child's behavior and adaptive ability. The areas of behavior typically observed by the practitioner are (1) the child's relationships with other children, (2) the child's relationship with an adult in the presence of other children, and (3) the child's knowledge and use of social skills. Each of these response patterns also may be reviewed within the context of the child's initial approach to the group, ability to change over a period of time, stresses that precipitate regression, behavior that provokes unhappy or unpleasant reactions, and reactions to group pressure.

COMMENTARY: Although the diagnostic group requires additional time, the pragmatic information provided by the group experience minimizes the degree of speculation required in formulating a diagnosis. Furthermore, specific and individualized treatment recommendations could be offered and/or even pretested. This approach to diagnosis would be especially valuable when the referral problem includes disturbed peer relationships.

SOURCE: Churchill, S. R. "Social Group Work: A Diagnostic Tool in Child Guidance." *American Journal of Orthopsychiatry,* 1965, *35,* 581-588.

Predicting Accessibility to Treatment from Diagnostic Groups

AUTHORS: Grace Ganter and Norman A. Polansky

PRECIS: Using diagnostic groups to predict accessibility to individual treatment

INTRODUCTION: Ganter and Polansky suggest that in order to maximize the efficiency and effectiveness of individual treatment, additional information beyond the traditional psychosocial evaluation is useful. The authors describe and evaluate the use of diagnostic groups designed to provide additional information on children referred for treatment.

TREATMENT: Diagnostic groups were composed of four to seven children, ages six to twelve years, who were making their initial visits to a clinic. Each group met for three to four one-hour sessions with a social worker. Primary to the group's activities were play and verbalizations encouraged to ventilate the children's uncertainties and confusions about reasons for their coming to the clinic. The purpose of the clinic also was explained to them. Thus, the group provided a bridge to the world of the clinic and an opportunity for the staff to observe the child in action.

The diagnostic utility of these groups was examined empirically. Trained observers rated 135 children on ten dimensions. Of these children, the first 50 to complete four months of treatment were then rated and dichotomized into either High-Accessible or Low-Accessible groups. These groups were determined by rating clients on such qualities as insight, motivation, trust, and verbal accessibility.

RESULTS: Of the ten dimensions or behaviors observed, five significantly discriminated between High-Accessible and Low-Accessible individuals. The two most significant were (1) the child's ability to verbalize the purpose of the clinic and his reason for coming there and (2) the child's ability to plan and follow through on activities involving a number of related steps over an extended period of time. Additional discriminating behaviors included receptivity to others' talk of painful feelings, response to imposed controls, and dependence on the group worker.

COMMENTARY: These findings emphasize the importance of first clarifying the purpose and expectations for treatment within the diagnostic group context. Surprisingly, many children may demonstrate confusion, or at best a limited understanding, of why they have been referred for treatment. Thus, sufficient preparation of the child by parents and the therapist is indicated in order to maximize accessibility to treatment. Furthermore, the relationship with the worker, response to group rules, sensitivity to others, and the ability to follow a sequence of related steps are important prognostic indicators of accessibility.

SOURCE: Ganter, G., and Polansky, N. A. "Predicting a Child's Accessibility to Individual Treatment from Diagnostic Groups." *Social Work,* 1964, *9* (3), 56-63.

Additional Readings

Kernberg, P. F. "Use of Latency-Age Groups in the Training of Child Psychiatrists." *International Journal of Group Psychotherapy,* 1978, *28* (1), 95-108.

A training program in conducting group psychotherapy with children is described. An average of eight first-year child psychiatry Fellows participate in the program annually. The training program consists of six half-hour orientation sessions followed by four lecture and seminar meetings. Students are introduced to actual diagnostic groups in the context of a diagnostic scheme that includes two individual play therapy interviews, one family diagnostic interview, and two group diagnostic interviews. Four case vignettes are presented to illustrate various aspects of the learning experience for the Fellows. Supervisors consider the training exercise valuable even though anxiety producing and often painful in its impact on the trainees. The program provides enrichment of the clinical skills of observation and special psychotherapeutic techniques.

Rabiner, E. L., Wells, C. F., and Zawel, D. "The Assessment of Individual Coping Capacities in a Group Therapy Setting." *American Journal of Orthopsychiatry,* 1975, *45* (3), 399-413.

The authors describe a psychotherapy group used to allow clinicians to observe a variety of demands made on newly admitted inpatients by the therapist and other group members. Groups typically consist of ten to fourteen patients and one to three staff members. The groups usually meet three times a week. The group sessions consist of two portions—one devoted to history taking from new arrivals and one to encouraging and observing patient-to-patient interactions. Thus, diagnostic impressions are formed, therapeutic issues are pursued, and the patient's response to treatment is evaluated over time. During history taking or the diagnostic portion of the sessions, the following information is sought: (1) What factors led to admission? (2) Who initiated the admission? (3) What is the patient's attitude toward others involved in the admission? (4) How does the patient feel about being in the hospital? (5) Does the patient see hospitalization as the appropriate course? Why? (6) How much responsibility does the patient take for behaviors leading to hospitalization? Once this information is gathered, the therapist invites comments from the group, offers his own impressions, and notes the patient's reaction to the whole procedure. The interactional portion of the session is more like traditional group therapy. The authors also present the factor analytic findings for the Group Discussion Rating Form (GDRF), which is used in the group. The factors of the GDRF include the following: observing ego, impulse control, intensity of affect, object relations, and appropriateness of affect. The authors conclude that participation in the diagnostic group and results from the GDRF are useful in exposing symptoms and attitudes otherwise undetected in individual interviews.

Taboroff, L. H., Brown, W. H., Korner, I. N., Reiser, D. E., Talmadge, M., Goates, B. L., and Stein, E. "A Note on Intake Diagnosis in Groups." *International Journal of Group Psychotherapy,* 1956, *6,* 193-196.

Six adolescent boys referred for therapy because of similar behavioral and learning problems were evaluated independently by two separate teams in individual and group interviews. Each team consisted of a psychiatrist and a psychologist. The team assessing the boys individually conducted a psychiatric interview and administered several psychological tests to individuals during a one-hour period. The team assessing the identical boys in a group met with all the boys twice for one hour. The boys were asked to introduce themselves and to explain the reason for their coming to the clinic. Diagnoses in the group setting were formulated from observations of individual behavior and group interactions. When reports from the two teams were compared, similar information and essential agreement were reported. The authors conclude that findings from a group diagnostic team are not only sufficient for an accurate diagnosis but also more efficient than individual interviews and/or testing.

2

Types of Groups

Group therapists who work with children must have a sound knowledge of normal development during childhood and adolescence. This knowledge can help the therapist select appropriate group members and an approach congruent with the cognitive functioning of those members. For example, play therapy may be indicated for children with limited verbal abilities. For latency-age children, activity group therapy (AGT) or activity group guidance (AGG) may be indicated. Finally, as the children enter adolescence and their verbal and reasoning abilities increase, discussion groups may serve as the most effective means for resolution of difficulties common to this period.

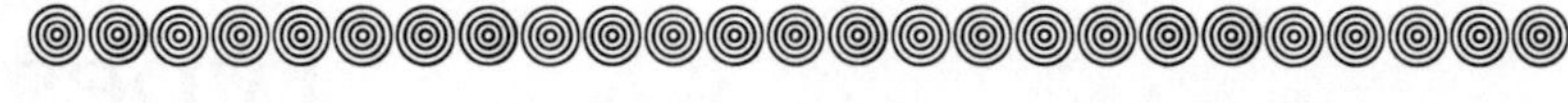

Play Groups

Play group therapy is used primarily with children between the ages of four and six; however, it also has been used with latency-age children. Based in psychoanalytic theory, play therapy typically utilizes the following dynamic constructs: relationship, catharsis, insight, reality testing, and sublimation. Children are provided with a variety of play materials, and the therapist observes the content of play, group interactions, and the children's affect. The degree of control exerted by the therapist varies; however, a blend of spontaneity and structure is usually sought. The therapist may also offer interpretations or implement interventions in a manner appropriate to the child's age level.

Play Group Therapy with Hospitalized, Emotionally Disturbed Children

AUTHORS: Robyn M. Abramson, Leon Hoffman, and Christine A. Johns

PRECIS: Using play group therapy to improve social, cognitive, and intrapersonal skills in early latency-age children hospitalized for psychiatric disorders

INTRODUCTION: The authors assert that the appropriateness of play group therapy with latency-age children is well established. However, relatively little has been written regarding its use with hospitalized, emotionally disturbed children. The purpose of the article was to describe its use as part of a multidimensional approach to the treatment of severely disturbed, impulsive children on a short-term inpatient unit.

TREATMENT: The typical group was composed of three to five children, depending on the number of children on the unit at any given time. Group balance was not considered a crucial factor. The room used for the play therapy was furnished with two large circular tables and the following play materials: a sandbox, a water table, a wooden bench, a record player, puppets, puzzles, clay, board games, and writing materials.

The play therapy group met twice weekly for forty-five-minute sessions. Treatment typically lasted two to three months. At least two adults were present at each meeting—a leader and a coleader. The leader was seated so as to maintain a constant view of all the children. The coleader was free to move about, providing individual attention as needed. Although the adults did not initiate play, they engaged in play if approached by a child.

The leader and coleader (or cotherapists) utilized interpretation and intervention in a way that was compatible with each child's cognitive and emotional development. However, the therapists were careful in their use of interpretation. For example, they did not interpret sublimative activities. In making comments to a child, cotherapists mentioned the content of the child's play, group interactions, a child's affect, and/or occurrences in the child's life. Since the child's life (past and present) affected his behavior, the cotherapists were required to have a thorough knowledge of each child's history and current progress on the unit.

The consistent atmosphere of the group was also a crucial factor. The cotherapists were required to provide stable leadership and a blend of permissiveness and structure. Absolute permissiveness was inappropriate with these severely disturbed children. Instead, the therapists set protective and supportive limits in order to provide external support for the children's fragile egos. If aggressive behavior occurred, the cotherapists employed any of the following methods: (1) They encouraged other group members to identify the problem. (2) They discussed the situation and interpreted it to the group. (3) They verbally set limits to stop the disruptive behavior. (4) They instituted voluntary time-outs with the disruptive child. (5) They resorted to physical removal of the aggressive child. Throughout the group process, the therapists sought to transform the child's actions into feelings, and feelings into words. With an increased capacity for verbal expression and some developing insight, the children were helped to develop self-control.

COMMENTARY: A unique aspect of the play group was its relatively short duration (two to three months). Since groups often continue for many months or even years, this article provides encouragement for the use of play therapy groups with severely disturbed populations requiring intensive, short-term, inpatient care. However, the authors did not collect empirical data, and the relative effectiveness of the play group was difficult to evaluate, since it was only part of the total therapeutic milieu to which children were exposed.

SOURCE: Abramson, R. M., Hoffman, L., and Johns, C. A. "Play Group Psychotherapy for Early Latency-Age Children on an Inpatient Psychiatric Unit." *International Journal of Group Psychotherapy,* 1979, *29* (3), 383-392.

Guidelines for Play Group Therapy

AUTHOR: Clesbie R. Daniels

PRECIS: Incorporating unobtrusive observations with limited interpretations in play group therapy with children

INTRODUCTION: Play group therapy as described by Daniels is based on the assumption that children's play is most spontaneous when they are unobserved by adults. Thus, the purpose of play group therapy is to create an atmosphere closely approximating the child's natural, adult-absent world of play. Under these circumstances, the play group can provide additional diagnostic information, as well as serving a therapeutic function.

TREATMENT: Daniels recommends that a play group be comprised of a maximum of eight children. Ages may vary within the group from five years to twelve years, and both boys and girls are mixed in the same group. The rationale for the heterogeneous composition is that children must live harmoniously in the "real world" with children who are neither their age nor their sex.

Each child receives a complete psychological, psychiatric, and social history evaluation. This information is used to determine the most appropriate mode of therapy for the child. If group therapy is indicated, a decision is required concerning whether a discussion or play group would be preferable. Although a wide variety of diagnostic categories may be represented in a play group, the author suggests that a balance between children who are active and passive, realistic and imaginative, and dependent and independent be achieved. Additionally, some potential play group members may require individual preparation or therapy before participating in the group experience.

The author recommends that a large room be utilized in play group therapy. The following furnishings are suggested: a sink for water play, chairs, tables, toy cabinets, dolls and doll equipment, stuffed animals, puppets, carpentry equipment and materials, a sandbox, cars and trucks, clay, a library of children's books, and materials for building any "missing items." Guns, arrows, and other shooting devices are excluded because of their tendency to create unhealthy excitement and to stimulate destructive fantasies and games. If a child should repeatedly request a toy gun, one of the therapists might encourage the child to make one of wood, thereby channeling the hostile and/or aggressive energy into positive achievement.

Two adult therapists are recommended, although not absolutely necessary. The cotherapists observe the child's play, listen quietly, and enter into the play only when asked. They may also occasionally offer interpretations of the play. However, they do not initiate discussion; if asked a solution to a problem, they defer the question if possible, attempting to guide the children in discovering the answer themselves.

The children in the play group are free to do whatever they like; however, two rules require obedience. First, children are not to ask each other why they are in the group. Second, no child is allowed to hurt another child.

Children play and frequently talk with each other. Conversations may focus on television shows, dreams, friends, family, or school. However, the therapist does not encourage conversation between group members. Through their play and accompanying discussions, children express varying amounts of emotion. Subgroups form and dissolve, and the overall group cohesiveness varies from session to session. Thus, the play group provides insight into many aspects of the child's thoughts, emotions, and general behavior.

COMMENTARY: Although this article provides useful guidelines for composing and conducting a play therapy group, neither empirical data nor case report data are provided to substantiate the effectiveness of these guidelines. In addition, the criteria used in determining what type of child should receive group therapy as opposed to individual therapy are not specified. Finally, while interpretations of play are offered to the children by the cotherapists, guidelines regarding the nature and timing of the interpretations are not specified.

SOURCE: Daniels, C. R. "Play Group Therapy with Children." *Acta Psychotherapeutica,* 1964, *12,* 45-52.

Nondirective Play Group Therapy

AUTHORS: Louise Fleming and William U. Snyder

PRECIS: Encouraging children to express their feelings through nondirective free play in a group setting

INTRODUCTION: The authors applied nondirective principles in a play group and measured their effects by administering three tests before and after therapy. The tests administered were the Rogers Personality Test, the "Guess Who" Test, and a sociometric test. These three objective tests were administered to forty-six children, seven of whom were selected for therapy.

TREATMENT: Children participating in play group therapy were residents in a "progressively operated" children's home with a service capacity for 100 children. Most of the children came from broken homes, and all were between the ages of three and seventeen. Two groups were formed for play therapy —one comprised of three girls and one of four boys. All participants in therapy were within a two-year age range.

The groups met twice weekly over a period of six weeks. Group sessions lasted approximately a half hour and were conducted in the playroom of a university psychology clinic. The playroom was equipped with the following materials: clay, paints, crayons, dolls, play furniture, guns, a sandbox, nails, and a "pounding log."

A female therapist led both the boys' group and the girls' group. Principles utilized in individual nondirective play therapy were applied to the group setting. Thus, the primary activity for the children was free play. The therapist's goal was to create a permissive atmosphere and to encourage the children's expression of their feelings. The therapist restated and reflected the children's feelings.

RESULTS: The authors provide objective and subjective data regarding improvements for individuals and the group in general. The following statements are based on the data: (1) Four subtests from the Rogers Personality Test showed "marked" improvements. (2) Improvements for the girls' group were greater than those for the boys' group. (3) Girls showed a greater change in personal than in social adjustment.

COMMENTARY: Although the authors provide data indicating the effectiveness of the nondirective play therapy group, the specific techniques utilized are not clearly defined. Additionally, the authors appropriately note that the differences in treatment success between the boys' and girls' group were perhaps due to the sex of the therapist. This possibility indicates the importance of providing male and female cotherapists wherever appropriate. With opposite-sex cotherapists, both boys and girls can be provided objects for transference and modeling.

SOURCE: Fleming, L., and Snyder, W. U. "Social and Personal Changes Following Nondirective Group Play Therapy." *American Journal of Orthopsychiatry,* 1947, *17,* 101-116.

A Theoretical Framework for Play Group Therapy

AUTHOR: Haim G. Ginott

PRECIS: Examining the role of relationship, catharsis, insight, reality testing, and sublimation in play group therapy

INTRODUCTION: The purpose of any therapy is to effect

changes in one's personality functioning. Ginott suggests that such changes are made through relationship, catharsis, insight, reality testing, and sublimation. He examines the operation of these elements in play group therapy.

RELATIONSHIP: The presence of other children can be particularly helpful in play group therapy, since it promotes a relaxed atmosphere and reduces tension and thereby helps to establish a desirable relationship between the child and therapist. In addition, the group provides for multiple relationships, which would not be available in individual play therapy; other children provide numerous models and ego ideals, and the therapist may serve as a parent surrogate for children. Although the focus of treatment remains on the individual, the group makes it possible for each child to be a giver and a receiver of help.

CATHARSIS: Ginott asserts that play is the child's natural language of self-expression—the medium through which statements about self and significant others are made. Although play is the primary vehicle for catharsis in play group therapy, verbal expression presents another alternative for the child. In addition to catharsis through self-expression (either verbal or symbolic play), the group provides for "vicarious" and "induced" catharsis. That is, some children are able to participate as spectators, and others can gradually move from passive to active roles in the group.

INSIGHT: The author suggests that the stimulation of ideas and feelings by the group may lead to insights for individual members. Once the problem is brought to awareness, the child can face it and reflect on it.

REALITY TESTING: The group provides an actual social setting where new insights are tested. The presence of other children serves to anchor the therapy situation in reality. For example, if a child exhibits infantile feelings, the group may expose and modify them for the child. Thus, the child learns what behaviors are acceptable and rewarding. Additionally, reality is experienced as satisfying, helpful, and safe.

SUBLIMATION: Play group therapy provides actual sublimative activities within the therapeutic situation. That is, toys, materials, and the rules accompanying their use may channel certain impulses or interests. For example, aggressive impulses may find their discharge through involvement by the child in competitive games, or "oral interests" may be sublimated through play involving "cooking."

COMMENTARY: Although these therapeutic elements are involved in play group therapy, the therapist must exercise good judgment in forming a group for therapy. That is, while there is the potential for therapeutic effects resulting from relationships between group members, there is also the potential for ostracism of participants by the group. Similarly, if a group contains too many inappropriate models, it may exert a negative influence on the child. These caveats indicate that the therapist must use discretion in picking group members and must observe group activities closely and sometimes be involved in the activities.

SOURCE: Ginott, H. G. "Play Group Therapy: A Theoretical Framework." *International Journal of Group Psychotherapy,* 1958, *8,* 410-418.

Play Group Therapy

AUTHOR: S. R. Slavson

PRECIS: Theory and practical advantages of play therapy within a group context

INTRODUCTION: An advantage of the group in play therapy is the catalytic effect that each child has on the other. This facilitates the acting out of fantasies and ideas through behavior.

Also, the group reduces the tendency toward repetition of activities by individual children. Finally, children assign themselves roles that express their emotional problems.

TREATMENT: The author recommends that the therapist be active and fully in control of the group's activities, since children have limited controls. With the therapist in control, acting out can be limited, restrained, and directed. The therapist also interprets the latent meaning of behavior to the children. Slavson suggests that, as with all psychotherapy, the fundamental elements of the play group are relationship, catharsis, reality testing, insight, and sublimation.

Interpretation is important because a relationship akin to transference is established when the child feels understood by the therapist. Furthermore, the relationships among the children in the group are important because they provide acceptance and support, which may facilitate the expression of hostility toward the therapist. Catharsis is achieved through play in the presence of a permissive, understanding adult. That is, the child is able to express repressed feelings, conflicts, and emotions fixed through traumatic experiences in early childhood. Regarding reality testing, the tangible objects and relationships with others are more real to the child than ideas and words are. Through the child's successes and failures, the play activities become a measure of the self in relation to reality. Slavson also suggests that insight, which is of "paramount importance" in older persons, may manifest itself in different forms in children. That is, often the insight acquired is a more perceptive type and less verbalized or ideationally organized. The play group may also provide situations, materials, and relationships whereby primitive drives can be sublimated or transformed into controlled, socially approved patterns of behavior. Finally, Slavson illustrates these dynamics by presenting a transcript from a play therapy group session.

COMMENTARY: Many of the elements discussed in this article are not unique to the group setting. However, the principle of the catalytic effect of group members on each other is of primary significance. Such a setting gives the individuals an opportunity for interactions within a natural setting that closely approximates the environment where the emotional problems manifest themselves.

SOURCE: Slavson, S. R. "Play Group Therapy for Young Children." *Nervous Child,* 1948, *7,* 318-327.

Additional Readings

Ammon, G. "The Role of Prevention in Children's Play: Psychoanalytic Kindergartens Within Dynamic Psychiatry." *Dynamische Psychiatrie,* 1978, *11,* 174-190.

Psychoanalytic kindergartens—their goals and preventive tasks—are discussed as an integrative part of Ammon's dynamic psychiatry. The preventive aspect of these kindergartens is based on early recognition of deficient ego structure, which can be observed and therefore influenced by kindergarten staff and parents. Children's play activities are excellent indicators of identity development and also represent possibilities for giving corrective support, structuring ego boundaries, and dissolving rigid defense operations. Various play modes (role playing, family imitation, structured group plays, rival conflicts) and characteristics (isolated, group, creative, fantasizing) can indicate pathological symptoms and are discussed in detail. The work of these kindergartens serves not only as prevention and treatment but also as a search for new and better ways for families and groups to live together.

Anderson, R. F., and Cook, W. "Play Activities in Groups." In J. A. Duncan and J. Gumaer (Eds.), *Developmental Groups for Children.* Springfield, Ill.: Thomas, 1980.

The authors outline several systematic approaches to using play in groups: (1) nondirective approaches, in which children engage in free play and the counselor reflects feelings;

(2) play process, consisting of structured activities designed to help children focus on areas of special concern; (3) activity group counseling—that is, free play followed by structured discussions of topics emerging from the play activity. In addition to a review of these major approaches, the following play techniques are presented: the use of puppets, drama and role playing, guided fantasy, games, and art media.

Ginott, H. G. "Group Therapy with Children." In G. Gazda (Ed.), *Basic Approaches to Group Psychotherapy and Group Counseling.* Springfield, Ill.: Thomas, 1968.

Ginott discusses group play therapy as the treatment of choice for many children between the ages of three and nine. However, he stresses the importance of carefully selecting and assigning children, so that the group will exert a remedial impact on its members. Some of the major group considerations are as follows: (1) Group members should not differ in age by more than twelve months (however, the child's "social age" may take precedence over his chronological age). (2) Same-sex groups are indicated for school-age children; opposite-sex groups are suitable for preschool children. (3) A balance of quiet and aggressive children is suggested. The aim of group therapy is described as an enduring personality change in the form of a strengthened ego, a modified superego, and an enhanced self-image. These changes are effected through (1) the relationship between the therapist and each individual child; (2) the use of play and talk to facilitate free-associative, vicarious, and induced catharsis; (3) the acquisition of insight or self-knowledge through experience in many group relationships; (4) reality testing enhanced by a friendly yet neutral adult, helpful yet demanding peers, and stimulating yet challenging materials and tools; and (5) activities that allow children to sublimate primitive urges. Finally, guidelines related to physical settings and limit setting are presented.

Activity Groups

Activity group therapy (AGT), an approach for children between the ages of eight and twelve, is typically used in "clinical" settings. In AGT the therapist generally is permissive, in order to capitalize on the therapeutic mechanism of identification. That is, the individuals, the therapist, and the group as a unit serve as objects of identification. In a sense, the group becomes the child's symbolic and/or ideal family. A second therapeutic mechanism used in AGT is reinforcement. The following reinforcers are available in any activity group: interactions and activities with the therapist, verbal praise delivered by the therapist and/or peers, and the inherent fun of playing with others. A third therapeutic mechanism is insight. Children engage in activities and may follow these activities with group discussions. Insight is possible with latency-age children because of their increasing capacity to use reason. A fourth mechanism used by the therapist is the presentation of alternate behaviors. The typical format for AGT is participation in some activity (varying from games to videotaping one-act plays) followed by a discussion period. Since the peer group is also growing in importance to the latency-age child, the group is often able to exert a corrective influence on its members.

A Game of Insults Played in a Group of Adolescent Boys

AUTHOR: George Dyck

PRECIS: Examining the function of a game of insults in an adolescent boys' analytically-oriented activity group

INTRODUCTION: Psychoanalytic theory holds that play and games provide for the discharge of aggressive drives. The author describes a game of insults, "The Dozens," in which adolescent boys move toward renouncing physical violence by discharging their aggressive impulses on a verbal level.

TREATMENT: The children involved in treatment were eight boys, ages fifteen and sixteen. Five were Caucasian, two Hispanic, and one mixed Hispanic and Black. The boys were committed to a boys' industrial school for a variety of minor offenses, usually involving theft. All were from families of low socioeconomic status, and the mother was usually the dominant figure in the family.

Group therapy was offered to the boys on a voluntary basis. The group met weekly, and the boys were expected to stay in the group for a minimum of nine months. The group was a para-analytic group in which the therapist sought to address the behavior and ego functioning of the group members. Unconscious material was allowed to surface and was utilized to provide insight into behavior.

During the course of group therapy, it became clear that the boys' verbal exchanges were actually games with explicit rules. The most frequent game, "Talking the Dozens," involved the expression of aggressive and sexual drives in relatively undisguised forms.

"Talking the Dozens" most often took two forms. The first form was less derogatory and usually involved remarks about a boy's habits, appearance, features, or background. In the more aggressive form, a boy usually would insult another boy's mother, linking her first name with obscenities or a sexual reference. The "game" was played in the presence of onlookers, who cheered the participants and appeared to derive vicarious pleasure from the episode.

On one level "The Dozens" represented a step toward the renouncing of physical violence. The boys were able to discharge aggressive impulses on a verbal level, although the game still involved primitive projection and denial. In addition, "The Dozens" provided a vehicle for the enhancement of verbal skills as well as favor from peers. On another level "The Dozens" represented the discharge of forbidden wishes, although the game left such wishes disguised enough to allow the child to bear the anxiety. That is, a boy whose mother was insulted could identify with the aggressor, thereby achieving a simultaneous discharge of hostile and incestuous wishes. In summary, "The Dozens" provided a method adapted to the psychological needs and limitations of the boys' environments for the playing out of sexual and aggressive feelings.

COMMENTARY: The author describes a phenomenon that requires astute cultural sensitivity. Given any similar cultural occurrence, the group therapist who is aware of both the manifest and the latent meaning of the "ritual" can interpret these cultural games/rituals and help the youths gain insight into their behavior.

SOURCE: Dyck, G. " 'Talking the Dozens': A Game of Insults Played in a Group of Adolescent Boys." *Bulletin of the Menninger Clinic,* 1969, *33,* 108-116.

Therapeutic Mechanisms in Activity Discussion Groups

AUTHOR: Merritt H. Egan

PRECIS: Explaining the therapeutic mechanisms (or dynamisms) of identification, reinforcement, and insight, which are operational in activity discussion group therapy (ADGT)

INTRODUCTION: In Egan's view, group therapy that combines activities and discussions is especially appropriate for latency-age children. He suggests that ADGT should utilize the therapeutic dynamisms of identification, reinforcement, and insight rather than one single theoretical principle or technique. The goals for the ADGT therapist are (1) to understand the tasks, defenses, and developments of latency; (2) to be aware of the problems specific to the group members; and (3) to determine which techniques will help bring about emotional health. The particular techniques utilized should be in accordance with the individual's maturity, intelligence, degree of deprivation, psychopathology, and stage in therapy. Furthermore, the techniques and treatment plan should be constantly monitored and adjusted in order to ensure constant growth and progress in therapy.

IDENTIFICATION: The dynamism of identification (copying or modeling behavior) is exerted through the therapist, group members, and both the therapist and group as a symbolic family. To make identification possible, the therapist must develop a warm, trusting, accepting, and confident relationship with the group. That is, early in therapy the therapist must allow the children complete freedom, short of injury or destruction of property, so that they can act out their fantasies but realize that extreme behavior will not be permitted. As the group progresses, the group members begin to compete with the therapist, challenging his power over the group. Group members may even unite against this parent surrogate, through direct verbal attacks or through sublimated games against the therapist. However, as the therapist points out the inconsistencies of their words and actions, the children gradually become aware of their problems. With this awareness comes a gradual change in their view of the therapist. If resistance by a particular child is high, the therapist may identify with the child (reverse identification). This facilitates positive transference and countertransference and allows the penetration of resistance.

Children also identify with other group members, since the group or "club" approximates the neighborhood gang. That is, in ADGT defeated, withdrawn, compulsive, and aggressive children are usually all present, and a particular child is not able to escape beyond the confines of the group. This approximation to the neighborhood gang facilitates identification, as well as the generalization of therapeutic gains beyond the group setting. Also, the presence of other children leads to appropriate gender identification (in groups of same-sex children) and healthy identity development (through separation from parents). Since the other members exert an influence on the individual, it is important to provide suitable models through the careful selection of group members.

The final mechanism for identification is the symbolic family provided by the therapist and group members in combination. The food, table, and discussions around refreshments approximate the healthy family's dinner hour. This arrangement and the accompanying discussions help to develop verbal skills as well as problem-solving skills.

REINFORCEMENT: The best way to decrease an undesirable behavior is to discontinue the reward received for its occurrence (extinction), and the best way to increase a desirable behavior is through positive reinforcement. The reinforcers or rewards used in ADGT are either extrinsic (for example, a "donkey ride" on the back of the therapist), social (verbal praise), or intrinsic (the fun of playing with others). To modify behavior in ADGT, one takes the following steps: (1) Decide the target behavior. (2) Determine how to measure the behavior and obtain a baseline. (3) Select a desirable reward. (4) Develop the plan with the child. (5) Shape the desired behavior by rewarding successive approximations. (6) Reinforce intermittently to consolidate gains. (7) Use fewer extrinsic reinforcers available in the group only, thereby relying more on extrinsic reinforcers available in the natural environment. After a behavior is modified within the group, behaviors at home and school are examined and then modified. The ultimate goal, however, is to lead children to the point where they can deliver self-rewards. Consequently, individuals who are maturing emotionally are allowed to try various ways of relating and getting a payoff. Although mistakes are inevitably made, the children's failures stay in the room with the group.

INSIGHT: To achieve insight the child must be able to use reason. This ability is facilitated in ADGT through participation in conversations and in discussion groups. Inherent in the process of reasoning is the intrinsic reward gained from the satisfaction of thinking through a problem and arriving with alternative solutions. Reason is also important because it helps the child progress along the morality continuum.

The therapist's role in developing insight is to encourage discussion of real-life situations, to reality-test with the group, and to offer alternatives (as do the other group members) to behavior. If the group process becomes routine and the progress is minimal, the therapist might invite parents and/or teachers to the group to increase insight for the child. In addition to insight resulting from verbal discussions, insight may develop from actions, feelings, and experiences of members; feedback provided by peers; and games used to help children learn lessons that are applicable to life.

COMMENTARY: Several important principles elucidated by Egan's discussion of ADGT are applicable to almost any group therapy approach. First, the selection of members to achieve a suitable balance with regard to presenting problems is imperative. Second, the group therapist must be flexible enough to use a variety of techniques and to apply several principles (for example, identification, reinforcement, and insight). Third, therapists must become more accountable for the progress made in therapy. Therefore, they must monitor the individual's progress more closely and make adjustments in strategies where indicated. Fourth, and finally, the group technique provides a setting that approximates real life and thus enhances the generalization of the therapeutic effects. This emphasis is extremely important if children and youth are to truly benefit from therapy.

SOURCE: Egan, M. H. "Dynamisms in Activity Discussion Group Therapy (ADGT)." *International Journal of Group Psychotherapy,* 1975, *25,* 199-218.

Variations in Activity Group Therapy

AUTHOR: Alvin I. Gerstein

PRECIS: Varying the approach in activity group therapy according to the diagnostic category involved

INTRODUCTION: The author argues for varying the activities and roles of the therapist in activity group therapy according to the types of children in the group. He suggests that one group be composed exclusively of children from a "neurotic" category and that another group be composed exclusively of children from an "ego-impaired" category. The neurotic group includes children who are neurotic or developing in a neurotic direction or who manifest behavior disorders. The ego-impaired group includes "hyperkinetic" children, children prone to rapid regression of thought processes, and children inclined to "affective displays."

TREATMENT: Children participating in the activity groups were diagnosed and placed into one of the aforementioned groups. The diagnosis was based on psychological testing, a developmental history, and an individual interview. All participants in the activity group were boys between the ages of eleven and thirteen. No more than two severely aggressive boys were placed in any one group. Each group was composed of six members and two therapists. The group met weekly for sixty-minute sessions. In addition to their involvement in the activity group, each boy participated in individual therapy.

In the neurotic group, there was a minimum of physical materials and no access to the workshop. Materials provided were a length of rope, a soccer ball, crayons and paper, a piano, tables and chairs, and a tape recorder. As the boys engaged in activities, the therapists labeled and described both the behaviors and the affective states of the boys. The therapists also encouraged the discussion of fantasies and concerns and occasionally were required to set limits.

The sessions for the ego-impaired group were divided into two daily phases. One phase consisted of either some physical activity or participation in a woodshop activity. Before either activity began, the group discussed and established rules for the activity or game to follow. A prerequisite for participation in each day's activities was the completion of previous tasks. For activities requiring materials and/or tools, the therapists intentionally provided a less than adequate supply, so that the boys would be encouraged to share and cooperate. If a boy became distressed or behaved inappropriately, he was temporarily removed from the stimulating situation. The therapists helped the boys understand social responsibility and causal relationships; they also stood as auxiliary egos for boys with difficulty in self-control or poor planning skills.

RESULTS: For the neurotic group, the initial effect of group participation was an increase in activity level. Their fantasy play was marked by its aggressive content, and discussions were typically of sexual or "cannibalistic" content. Thus, because they were constantly confronted with anxiety, there was a breaking down of inhibitions, accompanied by an increase in behavioral outbursts and destructiveness. In the ego-impaired group, the youngsters were able to settle down into the routine of the activity and discussion after only a few sessions. In fact, they sought the structure of the woodshop and the rules of the game. Their discussions with one another were not marked by the degree of sexual and cannibalistic content found in the neurotic group.

COMMENTARY: Gerstein noted that the results of group involvement by the two diagnostic groups were contrary to expectations. That is, he had posited that the boys in the neurotic group would quickly adjust and devote time to discussing their concerns. However, as the anecdotal results suggest, the boys in this group showed increases in inappropriate behavior, attributed to the breaking down of inhibitions. Conversely, the boys in the ego-impaired group enjoyed improved behavior in school, as suggested by reports of better work habits, declines in disruptive behavior, and increased academic achievement. Although Gerstein's results are fraught with experimental shortcomings (no empirical data, vaguely specified diagnostic categories, and varying treatments for the differing groups), the findings suggest the limited use of activity groups with children who manifest certain neurotic and/or socially aggressive behaviors. At the very least, greater structure would be necessary for children who are neurotic and/or aggressive.

SOURCE: Gerstein, A. I. "Variations in Treatment Technique in Group Activity Therapy." *Psychotherapy: Theory, Research and Practice,* 1974, *11* (4), 343-350.

Female Therapists in Activity Group Therapy for Boys

AUTHORS: Beryce W. MacLennan and Barbara Rosen

PRECIS: Evaluating the effect of a female therapist in activity groups for latency-age boys

INTRODUCTION: The authors review the model of activity groups as outlined by Slavson. In such activity groups, children typically are able to act out difficulties in relationship to one another and to one adult therapist. Traditionally, this adult therapist has been of the same sex as the children participating in the activity group. The therapist's role is to provide a relationship whereby children can obtain love, interest, help, and encouragement. Specifically, the therapist helps bring about success experiences for group members, encourages certain values and behaviors among group members, and assists members in changing perceptions of themselves. However, when the therapist is of the opposite sex (for example, a female therapist leading a boys' activity group), the roles become more complex. In such an arrangement, the female therapist may serve as a mother substitute, as an adult authority figure, and as a nonrelated love object (for boys entering puberty). Thus, the authors sought to evaluate the specific effects of a female therapist leading three boys' activity groups in two outpatient clinics.

TREATMENT: Group 1 was composed of eight boys, ages nine to ten years, described as anxious and phobic; hostile and withdrawn; passive, dependent, and depressed; infantile and demanding; and/or aggressively defiant. The group met for approximately forty sessions during one school year. The therapeutic atmosphere was described as positive, with active involvement by the boys. Issues receiving attention in the group included feeling liked, developing confidence, handling anger and fear, dealing with sibling rivalry, and acting assertively versus aggressively with peers. This group responded similarly to groups led by male therapists, except that the boys kept the therapist in a culturally feminine role (as was done in all three groups). For example, the boys would not allow the therapist to participate in such "masculine" activities as baseball.

Group 2 was composed of seven boys, ages ten to eleven. The group met for approximately forty sessions during a twelve-month period. Two boys were carried over from Group 1, and the group also included boys described as constricted, withdrawn, immature, and/or sexually confused. From its beginning the group behaved more aggressively than Group 1. Consequently, the therapist was required to intervene more often. Issues receiving attention included handling anger, jealousy, and disappointment. The therapist sought to offer assertive methods for dealing with these problems instead of the aggressive approaches more commonly employed by the boys. Additionally, as the group progressed and as some boys entered puberty, there was a rise in anxiety with an accompanying resurgence of aggressive acting out. Simultaneously, the pubescent boys began to relate to the female therapist as a love object, rather than as an authority figure. In order to resolve this development, an additional male therapist served as a focus of identification and provided protection for the boys against their own impulses. As a result, the overaggressiveness gradually diminished, and the group atmosphere became more positive.

Group 3 was composed of six boys, ages eight years, nine months to ten years, described as passive, infantile, and dependent; constricted and phobic; demanding and immature; aggressive; and/or neurotic. The group met for approximately fifty sessions during a thirteen-month period. As in Group 2, this group began with much aggressive behavior, especially among those boys entering or nearing puberty. Rather than introducing an additional male therapist, the female therapist dealt with the boys' competition for her as a love object by discussions related to the natural changes associated with puberty. As a result of these discussions, the anxiety and acting out diminished.

COMMENTARY: The authors report generally favorable results associated with the use of a female therapist in a boys' activity group. Although the therapist's sex temporarily complicated group behavior in Groups 2 and 3, the therapists were able to deal with these problems by either introducing an additional male therapist or by utilizing group discussions of natural pubertal changes. Thus, the authors provide evidence challenging the traditional notion that success in activity groups is contingent on the therapist's sex. Although sex-related issues may arise in such groups, this article suggests that these problems are not insurmountable. In light of the higher incidence of emotional problems and therapeutic referrals among boys, these findings offer encouragement to mental health facilities staffed by female therapists.

SOURCE: MacLennan, B. W., and Rosen, B. "Female Therapists in Activity Group Therapy with Boys in Latency." *International Journal of Group Psychotherapy,* 1963, *13* (1), 34-42.

Activity Group Therapy for Preschool Children

AUTHOR: Agnes M. Plenk

PRECIS: Utilizing a variety of intervention strategies in an activity therapy group for emotionally disturbed preschoolers

INTRODUCTION: The author describes an activity group used as part of the total therapeutic approach by a comprehensive treatment center for preschool children. Activity groups were used because in such groups various techniques can readily be combined to help children investigate their social environment; learn what to expect from others; and explore options for change in a safe environment with active, concerned adults.

TREATMENT: Children referred to the center were evaluated and diagnosed before intervention strategies were formulated.

Long-term goals were expressed in psychodynamic terms; however, short-term goals were formulated based on observable, measurable behaviors. Problems represented by the children included: delayed speech, poor self-care skills, short attention span, intellectual deficits, immature interpersonal relationships, oppositional tendencies, impulsivity, inadequate toilet training, autistic behaviors, acting-out disorders, and neurotic disorders. Children were heterogeneously grouped (eight to nine children in a group) with regard to sex and presenting problems.

Although the children were encouraged to express both positive and negative feelings, the following limits to behavior were established: (1) No hurting one's self or others. (2) No willful destruction of property. (3) No leaving the premises prematurely. Other rules were added to meet individual needs on an occasional basis.

Children were observed in play, in managing daily activities, and in accepting new experiences. On the basis of their observations, the therapists intervened with the following methods: behavior management, on-the-spot interpretation, modeling, and verbalization of alternate behaviors. The general aim was to create or enhance coping strategies.

COMMENTARY: This article suggests the use of activity groups for children with a variety of problems. Also, the description of the group illustrates an eclectic approach to formulating goals and to implementing varied intervention strategies within the activity group context. That is, Plenk's activity groups combined elements of both psychodynamic and behavioral approaches to goal setting and treatment methods.

SOURCE: Plenk, A. M. "Activity Group Therapy for Emotionally Disturbed Pre-School Children." *Behavioral Disorders,* 1978, *3,* 210-218.

Effects of Countertransference in Activity Group Therapy

AUTHOR: Leslie Rosenthal

PRECIS: Avoiding errors in countertransference that may interfere with the therapeutic process in activity group therapy

INTRODUCTION: Activity group therapy provides actual life situations to children in order that they might act out their hostile and destructive impulses. The child's self-esteem is enhanced as a result of the therapist's acceptance and the increased status accorded by fellow group members. The activity group also provides an "ideal family" in which relearning can occur. Thus, the role of the therapist requires neutrality, unconditional acceptance, and passivity. Initially, members of the group may test and challenge the therapist, seeking to cast this new adult figure in a more familiar, rejecting role.

Rosenthal defines countertransference as the therapist's needs, feelings, and irrational likes and dislikes that obstruct the goals of therapy. When these unresolved conflicts emerge, the neutral, accepting role becomes difficult to maintain.

ERRORS INVOLVING TRANSFERENCE: The following needs and feelings represent undesirable, unresolved conflicts that may impede progress in the activity group: resentment toward the child who refuses to share; anxiety arising from struggle and conflict; hostility as rivalries develop among group members; insecurity in relation to the group, often resulting in special treatment to a "preferred sibling"; weakness, resulting in drives to function in an authoritative and controlling manner; loneliness and helplessness, resulting from a combination of overidentification with the children and exclusion from the group's activities; needs to be loved, which interfere with the ability of the children to express their hostilities against the adult world; and identification with the weaker, "attacked" child, which often results in protective interventions. When these unresolved conflicts are reactivated in the context of the activity group, the resulting countertransference may negate the passive, accepting, and neutral role of the therapist.

COMMENTARY: Rosenthal reminds the reader of the potentially obstructive qualities of countertransference. The activity group accentuates the possibly harmful effects because special attention, either positive or negative, interferes with a crucial aspect of activity group therapy—acceptance. Even positive attention to one member may be detrimental, since it affords status to one group member in relation to another member. Thus, to monitor, minimize, or eliminate negative countertransference, psychotherapy for trainees in activity group therapy is recommended (thereby providing insight into unresolved conflicts and needs).

SOURCE: Rosenthal, L. "Counter-Transference in Activity Group Therapy." *International Journal of Group Psychotherapy,* 1953, *3,* 431-440.

Kinetic Group Psychotherapy

AUTHOR: Robert S. Schachter

PRECIS: Combining playground games and group therapy to encourage the expression of feelings

INTRODUCTION: Kinetic psychotherapy (KPT) is a version of group therapy used with children who have difficulty in expressing feelings. The premises of KPT are (1) that feelings should be expressed and can be mobilized if the body is mobilized and if individuals are placed in situations that trigger feelings and (2) that there is a link between the body and the mind. The goals of KPT are catharsis, insight, increased self-esteem, better reality testing, development of mechanisms for sublimating, better coping and organizational skills, acceptance of responsibility for one's actions, reduction of anxiety through play, expression of feelings, and attention to resolving difficult life situations rather than passively accepting them.

TREATMENT: The vehicles for interactions are children's games, which have been slightly modified to permit more social interaction. The games—"bombardment," "freeze tag," and the like—are nonthreatening to children and evoke emotional responses—anger, joy, disappointment—comparable to those aroused in real-life situations. Schachter suggests a thirty-minute game period followed by a forty-five-minute discussion period, during which the emotions arising from the game are discussed and related to real-life interactions outside the game experience.

With time, children are able to get "in touch" with their feelings and to deal with them in constructive, socially appropriate ways. The therapist's functions are to prevent destructive behavior (such as intimidation) by other children in the group, encourage group discussions, and provide nonjudgmental and noninterpretive feedback.

According to Schachter, KPT groups help children verbalize rather than act on their feelings. As more verbalization occurs, inappropriate behavior changes spontaneously. Thus, children who verbalize are viewed more positively by the group.

RESULTS: The results of an uncontrolled retrospective study indicated that, of seventy-four children, fifty-nine (or 79.7 percent) were functioning more effectively at the end of KPT.

COMMENTARY: KPT is promising for several reasons. First, the therapist has the option of suggesting immediate coping alternatives or providing feedback in the context of the group discussion. Second, this approach could be utilized in a number of settings (such as schools, clinics, and hospitals) and with children exhibiting a wide variety of symptoms. Third, it would be a useful strategy for preventing problems if incorporated into the regular activities of schools, parks, or community center programs.

SOURCE: Schachter, R. S. "Kinetic Psychotherapy in the Treatment of Children." *American Journal of Psychotherapy,* 1974, *28* (3), 430-437.

Developing a Sense of Industry Through Activity Group Therapy

AUTHOR: Holly Van Scoy

PRECIS: Using videotape recordings within an activity group context to develop a sense of industry and mastery in latency-age children

INTRODUCTION: Van Scoy supports Erikson's belief that children between age six and adolescence—whose activity orientation often obscures emotional turmoil—must develop a sense of mastery or industry. In treatment, however, therapeutic techniques often fail to address the developmental needs of this age group. The activity group can assist in the transition from a play orientation to a sense of industry.

TREATMENT: Participants in the group described here were three eleven-year-old boys and one twelve-year-old boy. All four boys were of average intellectual ability; lived in a residential treatment center; and consistently behaved in a "silly," "immature," "show-offish," "dumb," or "babyish" manner. Thus, the purpose of the group was to reduce the immature behavior by developing more responsible, industrious behavior.

The group met twice a week for five months. There were two adult group leaders, one male and one female. The goal of the group, as presented to the boys, was to make videotape recordings (VTR). The objectives of the therapists for the group were (1) discovery that objects can be used toward a specified end; (2) recognition that a large task is composed of smaller operations; (3) increased self-esteem through mastery of VTR equipment; (4) self-awareness gained from viewing oneself on videotape; and (5) a sense of togetherness, resulting from joint efforts toward the completion of a project.

Meetings were structured with approximately thirty minutes of taping followed by thirty minutes of viewing. Although the boys scheduled to operate the equipment had been encouraged to read the manual, they had failed to do so. The result was a slight delay in the group's ability to proceed; after that, however, the boys were motivated to read the manual. Initially, the boys performed haphazardly. Then, when the group became tired of the constant silliness, one of the boys suggested that they produce and film a movie. The boys were allowed to begin immediately, without planning, and were quickly disappointed by their unorganized efforts. The leaders then helped the group formulate the following steps toward accomplishing their goal: writing a script, securing costumes, constructing scenery and props, applying makeup, constructing titles and credits, rehearsing, and filming the movie. At least six sessions were devoted to writing a four-and-a-half-page triple-spaced script for a seven-act play. After the script was written, the production was quickly completed.

RESULTS: Although Van Scoy admits that the results may have been affected by other occurrences in the treatment milieu, the following beneficial outcomes were reported: (1) a decrease in silly behavior, both at school and at the residence; (2) greater status among peers, due to the mastery of the VTR equipment; (3) discharge of three of the four boys within two weeks of the final session; (4) carry-over of industrious efforts into the residence and school (for instance, initiation of a cleanup schedule, a garden, and a softball team); and (5) an increase in positive feedback, resulting from the decrease in immature behaviors.

COMMENTARY: Van Scoy stresses that the boys involved in activity group therapy, as well as the staff and other boys in placement, viewed the work as interesting and worthwhile, rather than just a play activity. Thus, the activity evolved into a project that the boys were proud to "own." Without staff support, positive results probably would have been minimal, since constructive feedback—which interrupted the cycle of immature behavior, criticism, and resulting low self-image—would not have been provided to the boys.

A second important aspect of the group was the freedom to "plan" activities relatively independent of the adult leaders. Although this approach seemed to help the boys learn planning skills and develop a sense of togetherness, it was not free of risk. That is, when faced with their initial setbacks, the boys might easily have become discouraged and consequently might have abandoned the project. Therefore, the group leaders should carefully monitor the activities and, when necessary, should subtly guide the decisions.

SOURCE: Van Scoy, H. "Activity Group Therapy: A Bridge Between Play and Work." *Child Welfare,* 1972, *51* (8), 528-534.

Additional Readings

Frank, M. G., and Zilbach, J. "Current Trends in Group Therapy with Children." *International Journal of Group Psychotherapy,* 1968, *18* (4), 447-460.

The authors discuss group approaches with children, focusing primarily on activity group therapy (AGT). AGT is described as a noninterpretive approach designed to offer an atmosphere of acceptance, nonretaliation, and nourishment while simultaneously moving its members to resolve conflicts and develop alternate modes of coping. An important prerequisite for success in AGT is the careful composition of the group. The ideal group is comprised of children with a wide range of ego strengths, coping capacities, and problem areas. Thus, the blend of personalities allows children to activate and offset one another. The authors also point out that the AGT "corrective experience" is nonverbal and that activity and action should be differentiated from "acting up," and acting out.

Gunn, S. L. "A Comprehensive Approach to Activity Therapy Programming." *Therapeutic Recreation Journal,* 1973, *7,* 38-41.

Gunn describes a comprehensive system designed to advocate and provide activity therapy programs in inpatient, outpatient, and community-based settings. The clientele included inpatient medical and psychiatric patients, community mental health center outpatients, delinquent youth, aged citizens, students in public schools, adolescent drug abusers, and the physically disabled. Various disciplines (for example, music, recreation, art, occupational, and dance therapy) were represented by the activity therapy staff. This interdisciplinary approach supported the milieu therapy concept and thus enhanced the effectiveness of the therapeutic environment. Finally, the programs were developed around the needs of the patients and not the interests or abilities of a small staff. The author concludes that the approach was therapeutically effective.

MacLennan, B. W. "Modification of Activity Group Therapy for Children." *International Journal of Group Psychotherapy,* 1977, *27* (1), 85-96.

Children's activity group therapy and its modifications to meet the needs of different populations and settings are discussed. The children's developmental stages and problems are seen as influencing the type of group used. The degree of structure and control, the setting and choice of materials, and the behavior of the therapist also affect the group's nature. Degree of group control is affected by member balance, extent of program structure, content of discussions, amount of discussion and interpretation, and number and activity of therapists. The following group types are discussed: diagnostic groups; groups for seriously disturbed, autistic, and schizophrenic children; transitional activity-interview group psychotherapy; play groups; activity groups in the schools; and miscellaneous adaptations, such as a program for intellectually superior children and their parents.

Schiffer, M. "Activity-Interview Group Psychotherapy: Theory, Principles, and Practice." *International Journal of Group Psychotherapy,* 1977, *27* (3), 377-388.

Activity-interview group psychotherapy (A-IGP) is described as a means of achieving derivative insight for emotionally disturbed latency-age children with symptoms of anxiety, guilt, unusual fears, and other intense emotions stemming from neurotic etiology. A-IGP differs from traditional adult-oriented group therapy in that it is less rigidly structured and does not aim at true psychological insight, since prepubertal children lack the ideational capacities, inductive reasoning power, and the need for such insight. A-IGP sessions consist of a period of relatively unstructured play and a time for group discussion. Schiffer recommends that the therapist, when necessary, act as initiator of conversation and make comments based on observations of the children's play; beyond this, the therapist's role should be confined to explanation rather than interpretation.

Soo, E. S. "Premature Terminations in Activity Group Therapy." *International Journal of Group Psychotherapy,* 1979, *29* (1), 115-118.

An attempt to reduce premature terminations of membership in children's group therapy through the collaborative treatment of parents is reported. In activity group therapy—a specific form of ego-oriented group therapy for latency-age children—materials, food, and play are used to help the children achieve emotional reeducation. Before dealing with absences and late arrivals, the therapist must recognize that resistive behavior in the child is a manifestation of the resistance of the parents and that parents have an unconscious determination to replay their past personal traumas through the child. Parents gradually gain insight into this symbolic reenactment of their life history and ultimately work out conflicts that were formerly expressed through the child.

Weinstock, A. "Group Treatment of Characterologically Damaged, Developmentally Disabled Adolescents in a Residential Treatment Center." *International Journal of Group Psychotherapy,* 1979, *29* (3), 369-381.

The use of group therapy and activity group therapy with characterologically damaged adolescents is described. The data presented are from a two-year program involving fifty hospitalized adolescents engaged in group activities and subjected to various therapeutic techniques (including behavior modification). Results indicate that group treatment of this population is feasible. Most subjects developed some capacity for empathy and became supportive of one another. Behavioral improvements were also noted. However, since therapy was conducted in the context of a residential treatment center, it was not possible to evaluate its effectiveness independently of the rest of the treatment milieu.

Guidance Groups

Activity group guidance (AGG) is similar to activity group therapy in that activities are usually followed by discussion periods; however, AGG is typically used in school settings, is more structured than AGT, and the group leader assumes a democratic rather than a permissive stance. Also, the activities are usually more task oriented and are designed to illustrate a predetermined guidance principle (such as cooperation or decision making). Discussions subsequent to the activity further emphasize and illustrate the guidance principle. Key elements used to keep AGG groups on course are structure, involvement, processing, and awareness.

An Activity-Interaction Group for Elementary School Children

AUTHOR: Marilyn Gilbert Komechak

PRECIS: Combining elements from activity groups and verbal discussion groups to provide feedback and to improve the behavior of children within a school setting

INTRODUCTION: Komechak outlines a group approach that blends developmental, perceptual, humanistic/existential, client-centered, T-group, and behavioral theories within the framework of an activity-interaction model. She has used this approach with children in a school setting; follow-up by the child's teacher is expected to maintain and generalize treatment results.

TREATMENT: Groups conducted by the author typically consisted of three to five children within a two-year age range. The activity-interaction groups met weekly in one-hour sessions for eight to twelve weeks. Activity materials included play dough, paint, family dolls, construction paper, glue, felt-tip pens, sketch paper, records, and puppets. In the group sessions, Komechak sought to describe behavior–and to point out its consequences–in a direct and objective manner, avoiding criticism and reprimands. Occasionally, she set and enforced limits but, at the same time, accepted and explored the students' feelings.

RESULTS: The primary therapeutic effects of the activity-interaction approach as outlined by Komechak were as follows: (1) A corrective influence on inappropriate behavior was exerted by the group on its members. (2) The group provided feedback related to an individual's behavior and its effect on members. (3) With Komechak's help and guidance, group members were able to practice giving and receiving from others.

COMMENTARY: Komechak's article illustrates the importance of combining different approaches to meet the needs of the child. The article also shows that school personnel must contribute if treatment is to be successful. That is, while the group may discuss feelings, explore dynamic issues, bolster self-concept, and modify behavior, therapeutic gains are often not sustained unless similar issues are stressed concurrently by school personnel and/or the family system. Thus, any therapist would do well to utilize school resources and work closely with personnel involved in the child's education.

SOURCE: Komechak, M. G. "The Activity-Interaction Group: A Process for Short-Term Counseling with Elementary School Children." *Elementary School Guidance and Counseling,* 1971, *6* (1), 13-20.

Activity Groups Used in Illustrating Guidance Principles

AUTHORS: Bill W. Hillman, John T. Penczar, and Reginald Barr

PRECIS: Learning guidance principles through planning and completing tasks in an activity group

INTRODUCTION: The authors describe activity group guidance (AGG) as an adaptation of play therapy that is suitable for almost all students. In AGG the leader and the group work together to complete a task. Their activities provide experiences that illustrate particular guidance principles (such as solving problems, understanding feelings, or acquiring self-confidence). Discussions following the activity sessions reinforce the guidance principles illustrated during the activity. The authors describe the content, stages, and dynamics of a typical AGG group. Additionally, results of an evaluative study are presented.

TREATMENT: The activities chosen to illustrate guidance principles are limited only by the leader's imagination. They may include arts and crafts, creative drama, creative writing, home economics, physical education, and science. Similarly, the guidance principles illustrated and discussed may be any that the group leader chooses to develop (for example, decision making, cooperation, or the expression of feelings).

The three basic stages for the AGG group include a warm-up discussion period, an activity period, and a follow-up discussion period. During the warm-up period, the leader introduces the guidance principle to be focused on during the activity and follow-up periods. Then the leader and the group agree on specific objectives they want to accomplish during the remainder of the session. The leader also provides clear directions and may even model the necessary skills. Finally, the rules or limits of behavior are reviewed.

The activity period requires more time than any other period. During this period group members work toward completion of the specified project. Group participants may work independently in smaller groups or as a unified whole. The primary objective is for the individuals to experience the guidance principle through working on the activity rather than merely discussing the principle. The group leader is an active participant and may serve as a model. Also, the leader provides feedback to the participants concerning the guidance principle being stressed.

The follow-up discussion period is the key component of AGG. Discussions focus on the participants' thoughts, feelings, and actions as related to the activity and the guidance principle stressed. In addition, the leader helps the group evaluate to what extent goals were reached and makes plans for subsequent sessions.

The authors recommend that groups consist of eight to ten youngsters, representing both sexes and various personality types. Meetings typically are held weekly and last between forty-five and sixty minutes. Male and female coleaders are recommended. Leaders should strive to create an atmosphere of mutual respect, where students are allowed freedom with responsibility. That is, the leader is democratic rather than either authoritarian or permissive. Thus, group members are allowed to make decisions and to experience the consequences (either positive or negative) of their choices.

RESULTS: The authors briefly review a study of the benefits of AGG. All children in three small schools, grades 2 through 6, participated. Approximately twenty-five groups, composed of seven or eight boys and girls, were formed. The coleaders were male and female graduate students majoring in counseling, education, or psychology. Groups met weekly for approximately one hour during the course of a year. Using behavior checklists, the authors assessed the children before and after AGG and conclude that the AGG groups helped to reduce the number of adjustment problems for the participants.

COMMENTARY: Whether used as part of a school's curriculum for "normally" adjusting students or as part of treatment for a psychiatric population, the method described here seems flexible enough to allow numerous applications in a variety of settings and under diverse circumstances. For example, youngsters with adjustment difficulties could be grouped according to presenting problems. Such groups could then design activities and focus discussions on issues related to the presenting problem of the group. Additionally, when used with "normal" students in a school's regular curriculum, AGG has the potential for training students in a variety of skills and for preventing serious emotional problems. However, as the authors suggest, more controlled experimental studies are warranted in order to provide further empirical validation of the technique.

SOURCE: Hillman, B. W., Penczar, J. T., and Barr, R. "Activity Group Guidance: A Developmental Approach." *Personnel and Guidance Journal,* 1975, *53* (10), 761-767.

Additional Readings

Dinkmeyer, D. C. "Elementary School Counseling: An Adlerian-Based Model." *Individual Psychologist,* 1978, *15* (3), 34-39.

An Adlerian approach to elementary school counseling—a developmental approach using group counseling—is described. Because the child is not as free to make choices, parents, administrators, and teachers must also be clients. The roles of significant adults in child development are outlined. The significant adults must recognize that they cannot change others and can only change themselves in order to have an effect on the child's life space. The Adlerian counselor's work is based on the psychological premises of the social meaning of behavior, the individual's choice of roles in the group, the purposiveness of behavior, and the patterns of human personality. Priorities are suggested for the services rendered by elementary school counselors.

Hillman, B. W., and Runion, K. B. "Activity Group Guidance: Process and Results." *Elementary School Guidance and Counseling,* 1978, *13* (2), 104-111.

Activity group guidance (AGG), a developmental approach for working with normal children, is described. AGG is a method through which students can understand, internalize, and apply specific guidance principles while they engage in an entertaining and interesting activity that may be related to any curriculum area. With 120 fifth-grade children of varying ethnic backgrounds as subjects, the authors tested the efficacy of the method. Results indicate that AGG works well with students of differing cultural backgrounds and that AGG increases children's social power. Implications for counselors are discussed.

Kern, R. M., and Hankins, G. "Adlerian Group Counseling with Contracted Homework." *Elementary School Guidance and Counseling,* 1977, *11* (4), 284-289.

Adlerian group counseling, supplemented with homework in the form of contracts, is a viable approach for ameliorating long-term and immediate social and personal adjustment of elementary school children. This study demonstrates that children within a group have resources that they can use to modify their behavior.

Tyra, R. P. "Group Guidance and the SIPA Model." *Elementary School Guidance and Counseling,* 1979, *13,* 269-271.

SIPA (structure, involvement, processing, and awareness) can be used effectively to keep a group on course as group members engage in values-clarification exercises, role-playing situations, and various classroom guidance activities.

Vanderkolk, C. "Popular Music in Group Counseling." *School Counselor,* 1976, *23* (3), 206-210.

The author suggests that contemporary music can reach deep levels of human need and emotions and therefore can be used effectively in group counseling sessions with preadolescents and adolescents.

Verbal Interaction Groups

As children enter into adolescence, their social, cognitive, and verbal abilities increase and mature. Consequently, the appropriate group therapy approach for the adolescent changes from an activity-oriented modality to a verbal modality. Since the adolescent's ability to use reason has increased, the therapist is able to take a more active role in interpreting behaviors and feelings to group members. In addition to feedback from the therapist, the adolescent's peers provide meaningful feedback. Some therapists also have used videotaped feedback in discussion groups. Topics most often covered in these discussion groups are issues and events in the adolescent's life (for instance, dating, school, parents, and physical appearance), problem-solving strategies, and feelings experienced in and out of the group.

Videotaped Feedback with Verbal Therapy Groups

AUTHORS: Billie F. Corder, Reid Whiteside, Mary McNeill, Toby Brown, and Robert F. Corder

PRECIS: Evaluating the effectiveness of videotaped feedback of behavior in a verbal therapy group for adolescents

INTRODUCTION: The authors suggest that the treatment of acting-out adolescents requires the modification of traditional group therapy approaches. Although studies have indicated success in using videotaped feedback with children, similar studies with adolescents have not been conducted.

TREATMENT: The group consisted of ten adolescents with a median age of fourteen. Hospitalized in an adolescent inpatient unit of a state hospital, the adolescents were referred for a variety of reasons, including suicide attempts, aggressive behavior, and psychotic symptoms. Fifty-nine percent of the adolescents were functioning between the "borderline" and "average" ranges of intelligence. The ongoing, open-ended group met during a nine-month period. The frequency of group meetings was not specified. The group was facilitated by two cotherapists.

Each session was videotaped, and alternate sessions served as experimental sessions. The experimental sessions were preceded by a fifteen-minute period wherein the group members reviewed three brief (two-minute) videotaped excerpts selected by the cotherapists from the previous session. The remaining forty-five minutes of each session were devoted to discussions by the adolescents. The control sessions were identical to experimental sessions, except that videotaped feedback was not provided.

During the fifteen-minute analysis periods of experimental sessions, the group first reviewed its goals. That is, the adolescents were reminded that they were there to learn to discuss their feelings, to handle their feelings, and to take control of their lives. The second activity during this period was the review of the previous meeting's videotape. Group members were to acknowledge and verbally reward members who demonstrated success in meeting the group's goals. The third activity was to review the following group rules: (1) No interrupting of peers or cotherapists. (2) Allow everyone to participate. (3) Avoid giving direct suggestions to peers. The fourth activity was the acknowledgment of instances during the taped session where the group rules were followed. Conversely, the fifth activity was the acknowledgment of rule violations exhibited during the session.

RESULTS: Three videotapes of the experimental sessions and three tapes of the control sessions were rated by two judges. Each statement (defined as continued talking by one patient on one topic) was rated according to the following criteria: (1) the content intimacy level (five levels, from "chit-chat" to feelings about intimate areas), (2) the number of direct interactions with peers, (3) the absence or presence of feedback, (4) the absence or presence of content related to the locus of control in others, and (5) the absence or presence of content related to locus of control in one's self. Analysis of the data indicated a significantly higher frequency of intimate statements and feedback by members following participation in the videotaped feedback sessions.

COMMENTARY: The authors conclude that videotaped feedback increases both the quantity and the depth of interactions in a verbal therapy group for adolescents. While these findings offer some evidence for this conclusion, it is unclear whether the differences were attributable to the videotaped feedback or to the other activities unrelated to the videotaping per se. That is, similar results for the control sessions (verbal therapy alone) might have been found if all sessions were preceded by a review of goals, rules, previous successes, and previous inadequacies in group interactions. Thus, while videotaped feedback might be useful, the group therapist might also note improvements in group interactions when sessions are simply preceded by a review of rules, goals, and impressions from previous meetings.

SOURCE: Corder, B. F., Whiteside, R., McNeill, M., Brown, T., and Corder, R. F. "An Experimental Study of the Effect of Structured Video-Tape Feedback on Adolescent Group Psychotherapy Process." *Journal of Youth and Adolescence,* 1981, *10* (4), 255-261.

Transition from Activity Group to Interview Group

AUTHOR: Florence Lieberman

PRECIS: Adapting the format of group therapy to meet the changing developmental needs of group members

INTRODUCTION: Lieberman suggests that the treatment required for prepuberty girls differs from that for either latency or adolescent girls. Activity groups fulfill the needs of latency-age girls, since they provide the required freedom for the development of ego strength and various capabilities. In contrast, the discussion group fulfills the needs of adolescents, since it provides for the intensification of emotions related to ego integration and instinctual problems. In the activity group for latency-age children, the therapist serves as a neutral, permissive parent. In the adolescent discussion group, the therapist is more active and interpretive. With both groups and ages, the therapist becomes a significant object of identification. This article examines the changing nature of a girls' group that began as an activity group but developed into a discussion group over a period of two years.

TREATMENT: The group began with six returning members from a previous activity group. Five of these girls were between the ages of eleven and twelve; one girl was thirteen years old. Another ten-year-old girl was added to the group later. Diagnoses, symptoms, and intelligence levels varied. The girls were from primarily lower-middle-class homes. All families were intact, despite parental difficulties.

The group met once a week in a room designed for a boys' activity group. The therapist remained essentially neutral, although discussions of the girls' feelings and fears related to the following topics were encouraged: friends, school, anger at teachers, appearance, menstruation, and developing physique. Interpretations were also offered by the therapist.

After a summer break, the group returned, and the therapist's role remained basically unchanged. Discussions centered around boys, dating, marriage, changing physiques, criticisms of parents and teachers, and sexuality. During the second year, a faulty heater required the group's movement from the activity room to a conference room. By the end of this session, the group agreed that the "old" activity room would no longer be satisfactory. At this point the group made the transition from activity group to interview or discussion group. The therapist became more active in eliciting discussion and in offering interpretations. Discussions focused on feelings of inadequacy, how to interest boys, whether women can rule men, and babies and intercourse. The therapist observed that the themes revolved around topics more common to older adolescents' groups, although the discussions were perhaps couched in a more tentative manner.

Gradually, the girls took a more active role in discussions and in interpreting one another's statements. Remarks and interpretations by the therapist were carefully tempered, with consideration given to the individual's strengths, problems, and level of development. The therapist indicated that the group served as the greatest therapeutic agent by providing protection, understanding, practice, and acceptance.

COMMENTARY: This article demonstrates the importance of the therapist's sensitivity to the development of the individual members as well as the group as a whole. Since the age group described in this article is subject to rapid developmental changes, the therapist must remain open to changes in dealing with an individual or even the entire group. The change in group format described by Lieberman was coincidental (resulting from a "temporary" room change); however, such an event could be manipulated by the therapist. That is, by an intentional, potentially temporary change in the format or location of a group meeting, the therapist could carefully probe and explore the group's reactions to such a change. If appropriate, more permanent changes and adjustments could then be made in order to meet the needs of the group and its members.

SOURCE: Lieberman, F. "Transition from Latency to Prepuberty in Girls: An Activity Group Becomes an Interview Group." *International Journal of Group Psychotherapy*, 1964, *14* (4), 455-464.

Combining Verbal and Experiential Methods in Group Psychotherapy

AUTHOR: Julianne Lockwood

PRECIS: Using verbal discussions and experiential training to facilitate the accurate labeling of feelings and to develop problem-solving skills

INTRODUCTION: Lockwood begins with the following assumptions: (1) Children are able to retrieve and express feelings in a useful way. (2) Children can become aware of their own needs and emotions—both past and present. (3) Children are able to deal with core conflicts and use experience in an I-you situation. (4) Children are able to use language in labeling emotions and events. (5) Children are able to borrow ego strength from other members of the group.

The general goal of the group psychotherapy described here was to expand the child's modes of problem solving. Specific skills requiring development were (1) the capacity to identify and label problems and (2) the ability to assess and verify one's perceptions of reality. The group provided a safe setting wherein children could rehearse various ways of responding to routine and problem situations.

TREATMENT: The children participating in group therapy (and in the subsequent follow-up interviews) were twenty-five boys and girls, ages nine through thirteen. The 25 interviewers were randomly selected from a pool of 111 outpatients who had participated in group therapy. During their participation in the group, the children received no other adjunctive forms of therapy. The degree of pathology for the children and their families had varied from moderate to severe.

Group sessions lasted for one and a half hours each. The number of sessions attended ranged from six to forty-eight during a period of two to twenty-four months. Variations in the number of sessions were due to early termination or late entry into therapy.

The group was led by cotherapists who encouraged discussion of experiences occurring within and outside the group. Discussions focused on the identification of problems and feelings accompanying these problems. The children were taught to ask themselves the following questions before responding:

1. What is the problem to be solved?
2. How do I label it?
3. What am I feeling?
4. Are my feelings helpful, or are they getting in the way of a good response?
5. What alternatives might I have engaged in?
6. What will be the consequences of problem-solving behavior *X*, as contrasted with problem-solving behavior *Y*?

Additionally, children rehearsed, observed, and modeled alternative methods for responding in routine and problem situations. Methods used were role playing, psychodrama, and real-life interactions.

RESULTS: Interview data were collected by trained investigators who were uninformed of the purpose of the inquiry. All children had terminated group therapy at least six months prior to the collection of the follow-up data. They were rated by parents, school personnel, and their cotherapists. The results indicated that 88 percent were rated as improved by parents, 83 percent were rated as improved by school personnel, and 76 percent were rated as improved by the cotherapists. There were no significant differences with respect to age or sex; however, the number of sessions attended (twenty-five or more over a minimum six-month period) and family involvement were important factors.

COMMENTARY: Although the author acknowledges shortcomings in experimental control, this study provides empirical data regarding the development and maintenance of appropriate behavior outside the group. Additionally, the findings prove that even latency-age children can benefit from groups combining discussion and problem-solving strategies. Finally, since family involvement and the number of sessions attended proved to be important factors, a commitment to treatment on the part of the parents and the child seems essential to the treatment's success.

SOURCE: Lockwood, J. "Treatment of Disturbed Children in Verbal and Experiential Group Psychotherapy." *International Journal of Group Psychotherapy*, 1981, *31* (3), 355-366.

Transformation from Activity Group to Discussion Group

AUTHORS: Carolyn S. Strunk and Lynne J. Witkin

PRECIS: Changing an activity group to a discussion group for latency-age girls

INTRODUCTION: The authors discuss the evolution of an activity group for preadolescent girls. Six girls, all of whom had difficulty with peer relationships, comprised the group. Two girls had been members of a previous activity group. One of these returning group members, Melodie, had serious difficulties in maintaining self-control.

ACTIVITY GROUP: The purpose of the activity group was to examine maladaptive patterns of interaction and the girls' poor peer relationships. The group met for approximately one hour. There was an unstructured play period followed by a discussion period with refreshments. During the activity period, the girls participated in ping-pong, gymnastics, table games, and structured group games. The discussion period was held in a separate room. The girls initially were told that they could behave in any way, as long as they did not hurt themselves or anyone else. The group was facilitated by two therapists, whose roles were to assist the girls in verbalizing their feelings.

In the group's beginning, Melodie was noisy and extremely active. For several weeks the other girls followed Melodie's lead, and the discussion periods were characterized by teasing, name calling, and even physical fighting. After several meetings the therapists met with a consultant and decided to change the emphasis of the group. The activity period was completely eliminated, and the entire session was spent in discussion.

DISCUSSION GROUP: The girls were told that the change was necessary to help them develop more controlled, "grown-up" patterns of behavior, which were expected of them at home, at school, and in the community. The changes were accepted by the girls without any problem; however, Melodie was coincidentally absent from the session.

The group was immediately moved to a smaller room for its meetings. The girls were allowed to decorate the room in order to provide them with a sense of ownership and identification of the "new group." The room had a single door, and one of the therapists was seated in front of the door to prevent members from leaving. The therapists also introduced a plastic symbol, which soon became identified as the "Peace-Love Symbol." Group members alternated from session to session in raising the symbol when the group became too disruptive. Additionally, group refreshments were made contingent on the group's discussion of problems. Each week the girl contributing most to the discussion was "honored" with the privilege of serving the snacks. The girls were informed that they would no longer be allowed to "act like little kids" and that the therapists would receive reports regarding the girls' behavior from parents and teachers.

During the first session, the group performed well, dealing with significant issues such as a father's death, stepparents, and half-siblings. However, the following week Melodie returned to the group. She was loud and disruptive, and in the ensuing weeks a power struggle emerged between the therapists and her. Melodie also insulted the therapists and encouraged the other girls not to talk. As a result of her influence, the group's participation in discussions declined until the therapists were forced to withhold refreshments from the entire group. The therapists reminded the girls that it was the responsibility of each member to keep the discussion flowing despite Melodie's behavior.

Since Melodie continued to disrupt the group, her individual therapy sessions were terminated. When her inappropriate behavior persisted, the therapists initiated a provision for suspension from the group. They told the entire group that anyone who could not maintain self-control would be suspended from group participation. Following the enactment of this rule, Melodie shared for the first time her dissatisfaction with her "special education" placement. Although the suspension rule was invoked twice for Melodie and twice for another girl, the group's behavior began to change. Self-control soon became valued by the group, and the girls provided each other with encouragement and support for their efforts in self-control. The girls discussed their individual improvements in academics and social relationships.

COMMENTARY: This article illustrates the need for matching presenting problems with the type of group used. Although the activity group was initially utilized, it failed to provide the necessary structure for the group. Thus, group therapists might be advised to consider the needs of the children, rather than their own theoretical orientations.

In a related manner, this article demonstrates that a variety of techniques can be combined to maximize the effectiveness of the group. For example, while the group was presented by the authors as a discussion group, they introduced elements of a behavioral group with the implementation of the contingent refreshment period. Additionally, the use of the "Peace-Love Symbol" appeared to provide important nonverbal feedback regarding behavior in the group.

Finally, an important component of the group was the utilization of reports from parents and teachers. If therapeutic gains are to be maintained outside the group context, "linkage" between behavior in the group and behavior outside the group is necessary.

SOURCE: Strunk, C. S., and Witkin, L. J. "The Transformation of a Latency-Age Girls' Group from Unstructured Play to Problem-Focused Discussion." *International Journal of Group Psychotherapy,* 1974, *24,* 460-470.

Additional Readings

Borden, B. L. "Children's Discussion Groups: A Positive Force in Behavior Change." *Individual Psychologist,* 1978, *15* (1), 53-61.

The author describes a five year follow-up study that evaluated children's discussion groups, which were undertaken to explore the children's behavior goals and to utilize their abilities to counsel one another through the guidance of an Adlerian counselor and an assistant. The children often displayed four types of common misbehavior: undue attention seeking, struggle for power, retaliation and revenge, and complete inadequacy. However, since they were primarily normal, functioning youngsters, goal disclosure and alternative behavior patterns were presented to the children at the level of their own understanding. Results support the use of children's discussion groups as a viable positive force in effecting behavioral change.

Walker, A. P., and Sperber, Z. "The Mental Health Professional Without Portfolio on the High School Campus." *Journal of Clinical Child Psychology,* 1978, *7* (1), 25-28.

The development of discussion groups organized to alleviate tensions at two high schools forced to share a single campus is described. The students, who were from differing ethnic and socioeconomic backgrounds, coexisted uneasily. Mental health professionals from the local community mental health facility joined with teachers and counselors at the merged high school and initiated a program of rap groups for the students. Each of the groups was co-led by a mental health professional and a teacher from the high school. Among the most challenging problems was the coleader relationship itself. The patterns of consultation and mutual supervision that evolved are discussed.

Psychodrama Groups

Psychodrama, a therapeutic approach used with a wide variety of children and in a number of different settings, is designed to help children listen to and cooperate with one another; express feelings, fantasies, and reality-oriented concerns; and engage in verbal discussions. Commonly used techniques include puppetry, dramatic games (such as pantomiming and interviews), dramatic plays (writing and producing them), and encounter techniques.

Creative Drama in a Children's Group

AUTHORS: Marilyn Barsky and Gerry Mozenter

PRECIS: Using puppetry, dramatic exercises, dramatic scenes, and encounter techniques to help children listen to and cooperate with one another and identify and deal with their feelings

INTRODUCTION: Barsky and Mozenter suggest that creative drama in group therapy is useful because it helps children express feelings, fantasy, and reality-bound topics that directly concern them. It also leads reluctant participants quickly and "painlessly" into conversations with their peers and therapists. Finally, it provides focus and structure, which are comforting to children, and it allows them to observe the value systems of others. The authors describe the techniques, strategies, and progress of a children's group in which creative drama was used.

TREATMENT: The group, conducted by two therapists over a two-year period, was heterogeneously composed with respect to sex, socioeconomic status, and race. The seven group members, eight to ten years of age, shared the following problems: underachievement at school, behavior problems at home and school, absent or ineffectual fathers, punitive or nagging mothers, and rivalry with siblings.

Sessions were conducted in a room essentially void of furnishings. A puppet theater and hand puppets were accessible, and a few props (such as eyeglasses) were available; however, the supply was deliberately limited, so that the children would be encouraged to use their imaginations.

Before admission to the group, each child was interviewed, and the purpose and procedures of the group were explained. During the initial session, this information was reiterated. In the first few sessions, the therapists frequently discussed concentration, characterization, and pantomiming. Highly structured, simple dramatic games also were utilized during the first year. One game required children to work in pairs as one child pantomimed an action (such as shaving or jumping rope) and the other mimicked this action. This activity required close observation and concentration by the children. In another activity requiring concentration and the use of listening skills, two children interviewed each other and then recalled as many details as possible before the entire group. A third activity required two children to interact, using only the words "yes" and "no." This allowed for a focus on personality styles and feelings, rather than on the content of the dialogue. A fourth technique was the "Magic Shop" game. In this game one of the therapists played a shopkeeper who sold to children various intangibles, such as feelings, new parents, or perhaps some personal ability. Children "purchased" these with other intangibles, such as feelings of anger or inadequacy, that they no longer wanted. Considerable time was devoted to the fifth technique—the production of dramas or "happenings." Therapists occasionally provided help and played a role in a drama if requested; however, the therapists did not impose themselves or their ideas on the group members. As the group progressed, less structure was required and the children were able to work more independently. During the second year, sessions began with discussions of individual and group concerns of the moment. Although the previously mentioned techniques continued to be used, encounter techniques were also occasionally used. For example, during one meeting the group members joined hands to form a circle, and then individuals verbally expressed their feelings about the group and each other.

RESULTS: In the authors' subjective opinions, the use of creative drama in group therapy was a success. The authors' goals of enhanced peer relationships, verbal abilities, creative powers, and ability to deal with feelings were accomplished.

COMMENTARY: Although empirical data would have been useful in determining the success of therapy, this article explains a number of techniques useful in a drama group. These techniques could be easily adapted to a variety of groups utilizing other approaches. However, children involved in such a group undoubtedly need to be carefully screened, and considerable time needs to be devoted initially to exercises that encourage and/or teach children to listen to each other. Without such an emphasis, chaos could easily result.

SOURCE: Barsky, M., and Mozenter, G. "The Use of Creative Drama in a Children's Group." *International Journal of Group Psychotherapy,* 1976, *26,* 105-114.

Drama as Therapy for Adolescent Boys in a Psychiatric Hospital

AUTHOR: Frank J. Curran

PRECIS: Using drama groups with hospitalized adolescents to increase insight

INTRODUCTION: Curran discusses the use of dramatic stories, written and "produced" by patients, as part of the total treatment regime in a psychiatric hospital. The purpose of the drama was to give patients insight into their personal problems, as well as to provide useful information to the treatment team.

TREATMENT: Participants were boys, ages twelve to sixteen, referred from courts, schools, and social agencies. Referral problems included conduct disorders, neurotic symptoms, and psychotic symptoms. The boys were encouraged to spend time daily in writing or rehearsing their stories. They were allowed to create their own stories and to pick their own cast of players—although they were sometimes encouraged to limit the length of their drama, the number of characters, or the use of elaborate stage props. Typically, five to ten boys participated in each play.

Plays were performed before the remaining children on the ward, staff, and patients from other wards. After the play was over and the visitors had left, group members gathered in the room for a sixty- to ninety-minute discussion led by a psychiatrist. The boys involved in the production were first complimented for their efforts, and the group was then asked several general questions. For example, boys were asked what they thought about the play and whether the play was realistic. They were also asked about various characters, and the actors were asked to describe their emotions as they played the parts. The discussions that followed included the following topics: hospital rules, personality problems of the staff or other boys, feelings about school and family problems, and attitudes toward aggression.

RESULTS: The drama group gave patients insight into their problems and helped the staff discover specific problems faced by certain boys. Boys with similar problems later formed smaller groups, which concentrated on their particular difficulties and concerns. Curran suggests that the use of drama groups afforded an outlet for aggressiveness, encouraged advantageous identifications, permitted the atonement of guilt, provided a means for love and acceptance, encouraged the acting out of fantasies, and allowed opportunities to be creative.

COMMENTARY: Although Curran fails to provide empirical data to substantiate the therapeutic claims, this approach seems to offer opportunities not available through other therapeutic approaches. First, it allows children to directly act out their fantasies. Second, it offers a socially acceptable outlet for aggressiveness. Third, it gives children an opportunity to be creative and to receive love and acceptance for their efforts.

SOURCE: Curran, F. J. "The Drama as a Therapeutic Measure in Adolescents." *American Journal of Orthopsychiatry,* 1939, *9,* 215-231.

Psychodrama Groups in Residential Treatment

AUTHOR: Robert L. Geiser

PRECIS: Using psychodramatic techniques to deal with living problems in a residential childcare center

INTRODUCTION: The author describes the use of psychodrama in a foster care agency for dependent and neglected children. Psychodrama was utilized in the following treatment groups: crisis intervention groups, learning problem groups, discharge groups, sibling groups, and leadership groups. In addition, psychodrama was used in some intake groups. The treatment groups usually lasted six to eight weeks. Goals of the treatment groups were to intervene in crises, build egos, aid adjustment, give information, develop empathy for others, and improve impulse control.

TREATMENT: In order to prepare for the use of psychodrama in group therapy, a weekly staff-training group was conducted with selected staff members. Trainees represented the following disciplines: social work, education, childcare, psychiatry, and psychology. After six months of training, the psychodrama groups were begun.

The groups were composed of youngsters between five and fourteen years old. Some groups were homogeneously grouped with regard to diagnoses, while others were not. Two leaders were utilized for each group—usually one male and one female. One of the leaders devoted attention to one youngster, while the remaining leader attended to the rest of the group.

Before participating in a treatment group, youngsters were told that they were to be members of a drama club. The club "produced" plays depicting life in the cottage. Thus, the plays helped them to put their feelings into actions. With time, doubling helped them substitute words for actions.

Since anger was the predominant feeling expressed, the following games were invented to lead to its expression: a yelling contest, an angry word contest, and a mad face contest. Additionally, since most children had experienced deprivation, the sessions were usually terminated with a snack.

RESULTS: The author presents several case studies and indicates that intense transference relationships were formed. Also, the youngsters reportedly were eager to attend the group meetings. Finally, although no empirical data were offered, the author suggests that most children showed positive improvements in cottage living.

COMMENTARY: Although the coleaders abandoned the idea of directing the youngsters' plays, the degree of involvement by therapists in other settings and circumstances could certainly vary a great deal. That is, in certain groups the coleaders could and perhaps should take a more active role in planning and directing. The degree of involvement would hinge on the presenting problems of the individual members, the group composition, the ages of the participants, the setting, and the style of the therapists.

SOURCE: Geiser, R. L. "An Experimental Program of Activity Therapy in a Child Care Center." *Child Welfare,* 1971, *50* (5), 290-297.

Therapy Dramatics in the Classroom

AUTHOR: Emily P. Gillies

PRECIS: Using dramatics to provide insight into the experiences of students and their classmates

INTRODUCTION: Gillies describes the activities that can gradually transform a creative dramatics class into a therapy dramatics group. Groups are conducted with "average" boys and girls (ages six and seven), since, the author suggests, even normal children have disturbed feelings, conflicting emotions, and inner unresolved pulls that they are unable to understand. A knowledge of each individual's family history and a keen sensitivity are required to maximize the effectiveness of such a group. Scenes often dramatized include the following: divorce and separation, sibling rivalry, domineering parents, sexual fantasies, and the impact of "bullies" on other children. By gaining acceptance from others, children in a therapy dramatics group are able to explore the doubts, confusions, and fears that they have in common.

TREATMENT: Gillies recommends that the children begin by dramatizing emotionally neutral nursery rhymes and gradually proceed to more emotionally charged topics. The duration of this transition period may vary, according to the individuals involved, from two to four months. However, individual children should be encouraged to participate only when they are ready. The role of the teacher or facilitator is to bolster the child's confidence and to be acutely sensitive to individual needs.

A topic for dramatization that offers an excellent transition from nursery rhymes to more conflict-laden material is the acting out of parents' occupations. Children are allowed total freedom in planning the drama and may pick volunteers from among other group members to assist in their drama. The dramatization is followed by group discussions facilitated by the teacher.

RESULTS: Gillies says that participation in a therapy dramatics group can give students insight into their own conflicts and those of their classmates. Thus, many children discover for the first time that their fears, wishes, questions, and problems are not unique. By gaining acceptance from others, children are able to feel worthwhile, perhaps for the first time in their young lives.

COMMENTARY: The author does not offer empirical data to

support the subjective therapeutic claims; however, the value of therapy dramatic groups may lie in the preventive nature of the activities. The teacher or facilitator plays the key role in the potential success. Thus, individuals conducting therapy dramatic groups should be sensitive to the needs of the children and should receive adequate professional training.

SOURCE: Gillies, E. P. "Therapy Dramatics for the Public Schoolroom." *Nervous Child,* 1948, *7,* 328-336.

Additional Readings

Carpenter, P., and Sandberg, S. " 'The Things Inside': Psychodrama with Delinquent Adolescents." *Psychotherapy: Theory, Research and Practice,* 1973, *10* (3), 245-247.

The authors describe a psychodrama group for sixteen delinquent adolescents, of both sexes, aged fifteen to sixteen, who had been referred for truancy, drug abuse, fighting, sex offenses, and stealing. The group met weekly for thirty sessions. The purposes of the psychodrama group were as follows: (1) to increase empathy through role playing and role reversal, (2) to teach communication skills, (3) to break through the protective shell preventing depth and intimacy with others, and (4) to encourage acting out in fantasy rather than in real life. Techniques utilized were music, poetry, fortune tellings, drawings, and the Magic Shop (a fantasy exercise wherein individuals can "buy" anything they want). To increase attendance and role participation, a behavior modification system was also implemented. The authors conclude that the approach was successful in bringing about insight and behavioral change.

Crenshaw, D. A. "Teaching Adaptive Interpersonal Behavior: Group Techniques in Residential Treatment." *Child Care Quarterly,* 1976, *5* (3), 211-220.

Crenshaw describes a group therapy program for mildly

retarded adolescents in residential treatment. The purpose of the group program is to help the youngsters return to community life. Techniques utilized include role playing, role training, and structured group exercises. The role-playing activities provide alternate responses to current problems in the residential environment. Childcare workers are used as cotherapists, and Crenshaw describes their contribution as invaluable. Role training provides practice in coping with problems or challenges anticipated after discharge (for example, job interviews). Structured group exercises are used to promote group cohesion by having members share common experiences (such as a most embarrassing situation). The key elements in all these techniques are a high degree of structure, a strong reality orientation, a skill-building approach, and a stimulating and interesting activity.

Godenne, G. D. "Outpatient Adolescent Psychotherapy: Review of the Literature on Use of Co-Therapists, Psychodrama, and Parent Group Therapy." *American Journal of Psychotherapy,* 1964, *18* (4), 584-593.

The author presents an extensive review of the group therapy literature, focusing primarily on the use of cotherapists, the use of psychodrama, and parent groups run simultaneously with adolescent groups. The author found no reports in the literature of groups combining these three aspects (cotherapists, psychodrama, and parent groups).

Godenne, G. D. "Outpatient Adolescent Group Psychotherapy: Use of Co-Therapists, Psychodrama, and Parent Group Therapy." *American Journal of Psychotherapy,* 1965, *19* (1), 40-53.

Godenne describes four outpatient groups in which psychodrama was used within a discussion group format. The groups were heterogeneously mixed with regard to sex and diagnosis and were run by a male and a female therapist. The use of psychodrama enabled adolescents to describe feelings and current life events in such a way that they did not feel as if they were revealing their innermost secrets. However, the author strongly recommends that if psychodrama is to be used during a group's existence, it should be introduced at the initial meeting, so that it will be accepted as a tool and not as a rescue device. Also, simultaneous parent groups are recommended, and the author suggests that different cotherapists conduct the adolescent and parent groups.

O'Connell, W. E. "Action Therapy." *Individual Psychologist,* 1978, *15* (3), 4-11.

The author describes action therapy as a group psychotherapy in which psychodramatic techniques are used for diagnosis, treatment, and training. The goals of action therapy are openness, self-disclosure, and the giving and receiving of feedback. Role reversal is one technique used in the group. The therapist helps group members to act out the part of a particular patient. Self-disclosure by patients is gradually achieved, with the therapist initially modeling this behavior. Patients then present hypothetical self-disclosures of other group members. Finally, the patient discloses her own feelings. In another technique, mirroring, the therapist selects a group member to play the patient. The patient must then interact with "himself."

Arts and Sports Groups

Two approaches with common goals are art therapy groups and sports therapy groups. Both approaches are useful with youngsters who have difficulty expressing themselves. The goals of each approach include enhanced peer relationships and increased self-esteem. In art therapy groups, the leader comments on group process and feelings and serves as an appropriate model. In sports therapy groups, the leader serves as a teacher, providing initial instruction in the specific sport. As maladaptive behaviors appear in the sports group, they are confronted by the group leader.

A Sports Group for Emotionally Disturbed Adolescents

AUTHORS: J. Emmett Dozier, Susan Lewis, Arden G. Kersey, and John W. Charping

PRECIS: Using a sports group as an adjunct or prelude to verbal psychotherapy with emotionally disturbed adolescents in an outpatient setting

INTRODUCTION: The authors summarize findings indicating that some troubled adolescents fail to benefit from "traditional" psychotherapy. These youngsters are unable to utilize verbal communication as a therapeutic vehicle because of previously limited verbal stimulation or because they experience their own aggression as so threatening that they must "keep the lid on" everything, including speech. The sports group, as an alternative mode of treatment, makes use of the developing adolescent's interests to enhance his psychological and physical development. The potential therapeutic aspects of the sports group are as follows: a sense of belonging; positive, intimate relationships with individual peers; enhanced self-concept resulting from learning a sports skill; appropriate channeling of impulses, especially aggressive ones; and an opportunity to come to terms with numerous changes in body structure and function.

TREATMENT: Two sports groups were formed—one composed of females and one of males. Each sports group was conducted twice every week in a small gymnasium. Groups consisted of youngsters, ages twelve to sixteen, who had low self-esteem, poor body images, and poor peer relationships.

Group members learned about and participated in bowling, swimming, boxing, golf, football, and tennis. Each sport was taught in phases, gradually requiring more self-control and autonomy from the participants. As previous maladaptive coping strategies appeared, they were confronted as unacceptable by the group leader and ultimately by other group members. The activities in the sports group were designed to provide a sense of security, purpose, and fun. As a result, youngsters generally became more confident and expressive. Feelings commonly communicated through the sports activities included power, anger, frustration, tenderness (for example, for a hurt teammate), affection, loss, and loneliness.

RESULTS: On the basis of clinical judgment, the authors conclude that the youngsters made significant and lasting gains in personal growth. Additionally, results from a follow-up questionnaire completed by parents indicated that participants had developed more self-confidence and productive peer relationships.

COMMENTARY: Although the authors present a potentially promising approach for treating nonverbal adolescents, their study has at least three shortcomings. First, their conclusions are based on "clinical judgment" and on questionnaires that are inadequately described. Second, although case studies are presented, the actual activities and interactions with the group leaders are not specified. Third, it is unclear whether the group was supposed to serve as an adjunct or a prelude to verbal psychotherapy or whether it was to "stand alone" as a therapeutic approach.

Despite its shortcomings, the article describes an interesting approach to treating the nonverbal adolescent. While puppets or activity groups are useful with younger clients, the sports group may more closely address the developmental and therapeutic needs of the adolescent.

SOURCE: Dozier, J. E., Lewis, S., Kersey, A. G., and Charping, J. W. "Sports Group: An Alternative Treatment Modality for Emotionally Disturbed Adolescents." *Adolescence,* 1978, *13,* 483-488.

An Art Therapy Group for Latency-Age Girls

AUTHOR: Leslie Dashew Isaacs

PRECIS: Using an art therapy group to enhance peer relations, self-esteem, and the expression of feelings in latency-age girls

INTRODUCTION: Isaacs states that her review of the group therapy literature revealed no precedent for a group approach to art therapy with children. Thus, she designed the art group in a similar manner to activity groups: Materials were intentionally in short supply; the group composition was homogeneous with respect to age, sex, and socioeconomic status; and a balance between withdrawn and dominant children was sought.

TREATMENT: Four girls, ages nine through eleven, participated in an art therapy group. Two of the girls were described as withdrawn, and two were aggressive and hyperactive. The girls came from lower- to middle-class homes. Half lived with their natural parents while the remaining half lived either with a divorced parent or a remarried biological parent. All children were also involved in parent-child counseling and/or individual therapy. During the screening interview, the purpose and format of the group were explained to each girl and her parent(s). The following rules were also explained: (1) Sessions were not to be art *classes* where art work was evaluated. (2) There was to be no physical abuse. (3) Individuals were to clean up during the last ten minutes of each session. A six-week commitment to group attendance was secured from each participant. After the first six-week period, however, two girls dropped out and were replaced by two more girls.

The therapist's role was twofold. First, she commented on the group processes and the girls' feelings. Second, she served as a model of appropriate social behavior. She was assisted by a social work student, who observed and recorded the group process during each session.

The activities and art projects were initially structured by the therapist; however, they were progressively less structured as time passed. The therapist intentionally arranged for the limited availability of art supplies. The resulting scarcity of materials served the following purposes: the girls were forced to interact and to share; the therapist was able to initiate discussions about constructive ways to communicate one's need for materials; through joint projects the girls learned to have fun with others, to compromise, to show patience when their needs were not met, and to express expectations and feelings. The girls became increasingly able to disclose their feelings and were provided with feedback from the therapist and other group members. The therapist attempted to relate comments about the girls' feelings and the group processes to similar situations at home and school, thereby leading to the generalization of improvements from the group to the girls' natural environments.

RESULTS: Gradually, the girls' experiences at home and school were no longer avoided or pictured in drawings, but were discussed instead. Also, insults and self-critical comments were gradually replaced by constructive feedback and requests for feedback. Behavioral and attitudinal changes were reported by parents and teachers. Overall, the art therapy group was considered successful in helping the girls become aware of their behavior, understand their impact on others, and learn alternate modes of relating to others.

COMMENTARY: Since all the girls were involved in additional forms of therapy, the relative contribution of the art therapy group in improving behavior is unclear. However, the subjective reports from the therapist, parents, and teachers suggest that the approach was a useful one. Two elements appeared especially crucial to the girls' therapeutic gains. First, the sharing of materials enhanced peer relations and helped the girls express their feelings. Second, behavior and feelings emerging during the group were related to similar situations in the real world, so that therapeutic gains could be generalized and maintained.

SOURCE: Isaacs, L. D. "Art-Therapy Group for Latency Age Children." *Social Work,* 1977, *22,* 57-59.

Music and Art Therapy in a Children's Group

AUTHORS: Kathryn Fleming-Turk and Mary Lou A. Gallam

PRECIS: Using structured, expressive art activities within a group context for children in an outpatient psychiatric facility

INTRODUCTION: The approach described by the authors is based on the developmental therapy model, wherein activities are used to help children develop age-appropriate skills. Music and art activities were combined so that the same problem could be presented in different settings. For example, to teach children the principle of sharing, the therapists would deliberately provide a less than adequate supply of art materials; similarly, group members would be required to cooperate in order to keep an inflated balloon in motion during the playing of music. The approach also utilizes the concept of cotherapists in lead and support roles. That is, one therapist is the leader and is responsible for the explanation and direction of activities. The second therapist assists in the group's management and use of materials. Thus, the lead-support approach provides a model of adults interacting and communicating with each other. Furthermore, it allows for varied adult-child interactions.

TREATMENT: The children participating in the structured expressive arts group were inner-city youths referred to an outpatient psychiatric facility by parents, school officials, medical personnel, and legal authorities. The children were from eight to ten years old and were grouped by their developmental level, not their chronological age. The group averaged six members during the course of the year's meetings. Meetings were held weekly and lasted for approximately ninety minutes. Equal time was devoted to both art and music activities.

During the year the group progressed through five developmental stages, as outlined by M. Wood (*Developmental Therapy,* Baltimore: University Park Press, 1975):

Stage I—Responding to the Environment with Pleasure. In

this stage the therapists' roles were to arouse and satisfy the needs of children, using physical contact, structure and a consistent routine, and a controlled environment. The children were enticed into participation with stimulating activities and were provided a constant routine.

Stage II—Responding to the Environment with Success. The therapists' roles during Stage II were to motivate and direct the children to use their existing behavioral skills to create success experiences. Additionally, the therapists helped to promote success experiences through the structure and consistent routine of the group, through physical and verbal redirection of the children, and through interpretation of actions and feelings of the children. The children were carefully directed in activities that led to success and self-confidence. The group also participated in activities to facilitate self-expression.

Stage III—Learning Skills for Successful Group Participation. The therapists served as models for the group; stimulated and encouraged appropriate group interactions; enforced limits; and reflected and interpreted behavior, feelings, and progress. Techniques utilized by the therapists included redirection, reflection, verbal interactions, and predictable structure. The activities led to cooperation and the forming of friendships under conditions approximating real-life conditions.

Stage IV—Investing in Group Processes. During Stage IV the therapists acted as group leaders, counselors, and reflectors of reality. They utilized interpretations of feelings and behavior, as well as the group Life Space Interviews. The participants determined their activities, which were more reality oriented; for example, group academic learning, role playing, field trips, and competitive activities were utilized.

Stage V—Applying Individual/Group Skills in New Situations. During this final stage, the therapists served as counselors, teachers, and friends. The primary technique utilized by the therapists was the explanation of relationships between feelings, behaviors, and consequences of behavior. Children discussed experiences in "normal" childhood settings.

COMMENTARY: Although the authors present no empirical

data to validate the success of their approach, the potential contribution of this approach appears to be its utilization of a "captivating" method (the integration of art and music activities) within a well-conceptualized developmental model. Thus, the method allows for flexibility and creativity on the part of the therapist and children; moreover, the developmental theory provides a useful structure and progression for all involved.

SOURCE: Fleming-Turk, K., and Gallam, M. L. A. "To Sing and to Draw: Expressive Arts Therapy." Paper presented at meeting of the American Association of Psychiatric Services for Children, Atlanta, November 1978.

Additional Readings

Potts, L. R. "The Use of Art in Group Psychotherapy." *International Journal of Group Psychotherapy,* 1956, *6,* 115-141.

The author presents case illustrations of art therapy used in a group treatment framework. The group consisted of eight young men and women. The meetings were divided into a two-hour painting session and a two-hour group discussion session. The members' art and events transpiring during the group served as focal points of discussion. The group approach provided a variety of attitudes for consideration by each participant.

Powers, P. S., and Langworthy, J. "Art Work: Another Dimension in the Treatment of Psychiatric Patients." *Art Psychotherapy,* 1978, *5,* 71-79.

The authors describe cases illustrating their work in an art therapy group. The group was one facet of a comprehensive treatment program on an inpatient adolescent ward. Each individual's art work reflected his progress in therapy and promoted awareness and therapeutic change, especially in nonverbal patients. The authors suggest comprehensive communication with other treatment team members in order to enhance therapeutic success.

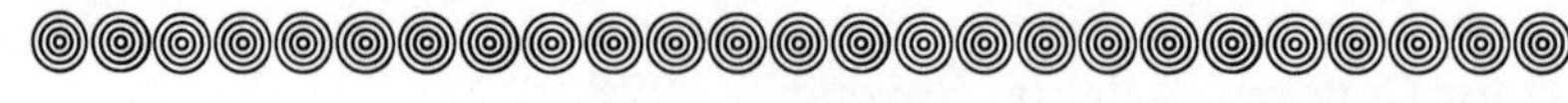

Parallel Groups

In parallel group therapy, children and their parents receive treatment simultaneously. The approach and format of the groups vary according to the presenting problems of the child. In general, however, the parents' groups enable parents of children with a common problem to gain support from one another during a crisis. Group leaders and parents also provide information on child management. Finally, the groups give parents and children an opportunity to explore their own needs and problems.

Psychotherapy for Preschool Children and Their Parents

AUTHORS: Thomas Haizlip, Christine McRee, and Billie F. Corder

PRECIS: Involving parents in either group or individual therapy when their preschool children are in group psychotherapy

INTRODUCTION: The authors describe the need for more services to preschool children, especially within the group therapy context. From a small, informal telephone survey, they concluded that most community mental health clinics do not offer group therapy to preschoolers for the following reasons: (1) There are inadequate numbers of referrals for treatment. (2) Therapists prefer treatment in a therapeutic nursery or kindergarten setting. (3) Theoretical objections to group approaches arise, with preference given to behavioral interventions and/or parent counseling. (4) There is insufficient space. Despite similar difficulties, the authors initiated a group for preschoolers with parallel services to the parents.

TREATMENT: The preschool group was comprised of four five-year-olds. A criterion for inclusion into the group was the child's willingness and capacity to accept limits on his behavior within the group context. Additionally, a preliminary diagnostic session was required to ensure the exclusion of children exhibiting aggressive behavior. Meetings were held in a room regularly used for adult group therapy. Two cotherapists conducted the group while a third individual observed and videotaped the sessions. Children were allowed to play with a variety of toys. When a particular child was observed working on a conflict or issue (as demonstrated by play activities or verbalizations), one of the cotherapists worked with the child individually. The second cotherapist continued working with the remaining group members, reflecting and interpreting their activities. Thus, children were allowed to become more active in the interpretation of issues relevant to themselves.

The child's group therapy was conducted in conjunction with parent therapy. The criterion for inclusion in the parent group was that parents have preschoolers in group therapy. However, this arrangement proved unsatisfactory because this single criterion did not ensure compatibility and group cohesion. Thus, parents later became involved in either individual therapy (one couple) or in other existing parent groups at the outpatient clinic. Parent therapists and child cotherapists met weekly for collaboration and the exchange of relevant information about the family.

COMMENTARY: Although neither objective data nor subjective evaluative comments are provided regarding the effectiveness of this preschool program, this article highlights two important points. First, the number of preschool referrals to community clinics is disproportionately low for the incidence of varied disorders. Although a number of behavior, learning, and adjustment difficulties arise from experiences at school, the outreach by clinics to the preschool population apparently is inadequate. A solution might be referral programs aimed at soliciting referrals from pediatricians, family physicians, nursery schools, churches, and the like. A second important issue is the need for parent involvement when treating preschoolers. Regardless of the theoretical orientation of the therapist, most preschoolers' emotional problems would be amenable to parental involvement.

SOURCE: Haizlip, T., McRee, C., and Corder, B. F. "Issues in Developing Psychotherapy Groups for Preschool Children in Outpatient Clinics." *American Journal of Psychiatry,* 1975, *132* (10), 1061-1063.

Conjoint Group Therapy for Asthmatic Children and Their Parents

AUTHOR: Robert A. Hock

PRECIS: Providing relaxation and assertion training to asthmatic children in conjunction with group psychotherapy for their parents

INTRODUCTION: While a psychosomatic component of bronchial asthma has been acknowledged, the relative contribution of physical and psychological factors remains unknown. In an attempt to maximize the therapeutic effects of treatment, Hock suggests that psychological and medical components be combined to comprise a multimodal approach. By combining relaxation and assertion training for the child with group psychotherapy for the parent(s), Hock sought to enhance the psychosocial functioning of the asthmatic child; increase the threshold for asthmatic symptomatology; ensure that children maintained therapeutic gains while at home; and give parents an opportunity to explore interpersonal, intrapersonal, and marriage difficulties that have exacerbated the child's condition at home.

TREATMENT: Eleven male asthmatics with the following characteristics completed treatment: (1) display of "distinct" psychological problems, (2) evidence of only minimal or slow improvements in previous treatment, and (3) parents who requested psychological help and were willing to participate in group treatment. Parents participating in treatment were predominantly mothers of the asthmatic children; fathers were either absent or unavailable in most instances.

The children's group combined relaxation and assertion training in single sessions. Relaxation training required approximately thirty minutes and consisted of training boys alternately to tense and then relax their voluntary muscles. This was followed by guided imagery, wherein the boys were encouraged to create images of comfort and relaxation. The intent of these activities was to generalize relaxation from the musculature to respiratory activity. Assertion activities included behavioral rehearsal of skills such as making eye contact, initiating conversation, and meeting strangers; structured games such as "What gripes me" and "Trust" (where the group members cooperatively lifted one another); and structured verbal exercises whereby boys were required to provide positive feedback to group members selected at random. Open-ended discussions gradually evolved and dealt with the boys' interpersonal conflicts, feelings, and opinions and appropriate methods of dealing with anger.

The parents' group met concurrently and was involved in open-ended discussions. The following topics were dealt with: concerns regarding their asthmatic children; child management; and interpersonal, intrapersonal, and marriage relationships. The therapists of the children's and parents' groups met regularly to clarify issues and to discuss the development of treatment for both groups.

RESULTS: After approximately one year of treatment, the respiratory function of all eleven asthmatic boys increased significantly (as measured by an objective pulmonary index).

COMMENTARY: Although the medical aspects of the multimodal treatment were not delineated, the techniques described proved effective in increasing pulmonary function. The parents' group appeared especially useful in maintaining these gains. While the specific function of the parents' group was not clear (whether it provided support, education, or resolution of personal conflicts), its use in treatment seems warranted.

SOURCE: Hock, R. A. "A Model for Conjoint Group Therapy for Asthmatic Children and Their Parents." *Group Psychotherapy, Psychodrama, and Sociometry,* 1977, *30,* 108-113.

Simultaneous "Semipermeable" Groups for Mothers and Their Sons

AUTHORS: Theodore E. Hoffman, Kathleen M. Byrne, Kristine L. Belnap, and Margaret S. Steward

PRECIS: Combining elements of activity groups, behaviorally oriented groups, and interpretative groups into simultaneous "semipermeable" groups for mothers and their sons

INTRODUCTION: The authors review the literature suggesting that children raised by the mother alone are particularly vulnerable to behavioral and emotional difficulties. Since the absence of the father appears to be less important than the aloneness of the mother, group therapy was offered to mothers of troubled boys. The group gave mothers support in dealing with their "problematic" sons, information relative to child development and effective child management, and opportunities to explore personal problems as they related to the problem behaviors of their sons.

TREATMENT: Seven boys with the following characteristics were selected for participation in the group: (1) latency age, (2) mild to moderate behavioral or adjustment reaction problems, (3) mothers willing to attend weekly group meetings held simultaneously with the boys' group, and (4) absence of organicity and psychosis in both mother and son. All but two mothers were either separated or divorced.

Ten group meetings were scheduled from the outset. Meetings lasted for one hour, and both boys and their mothers met in one room at the same time. The room was divided by a "semipermeable" boundary (a rope-laced row of chairs), with the boys meeting on one side and the mothers meeting on another. Three therapists were utilized—one for each group and one therapist who regulated any interaction between the two groups.

The boys' group was furnished with tables; a sandbox; a dollhouse; household furniture replicas; hand puppets, toy cars;

paper and crayons; and plastic soldiers, animals, and reptiles. During the course of therapy, the boys' therapist assessed their difficulties; designed interventions focusing on interactions within the group; provided support and reinforcement of positive skills; made educational remarks related to respecting others, sharing, and cooperating; encouraged and modeled the labeling of feelings and behavior; and focused on the issues of separation and reunion with the mother. Thus, the group served to integrate elements of activity, behavioral, and interpretative groups. Additionally, the group activities often brought out behaviors that had been responsible for the boys' initial referrals. The behavior prompted discussion, support, and consultation in the mothers' group. Interchange between the two groups was allowed, although it required permission from the therapists. As the sessions evolved, one mother per session observed and participated in the boys' group for most of the session, returning to the mothers' group to share her observations and impressions.

In the boys' group, much of the time during the early sessions was spent testing the limits; that is, climbing the boundary separating the groups. After four sessions alliances between the boys began to develop, and the testing of the boundary occurred less frequently. As the boys sought to establish contact with their mothers, the concept of negotiated time was introduced, whereby separation was encouraged after gradually shorter periods of contact.

The mothers' group initially was friendly although superficial. In order to relieve the tension and provide information regarding family composition, each mother was asked to draw a picture of and to tell about her family. As the sessions progressed, the mothers shifted the conversations from their problematic sons to former problematic men. The therapist helped them to explore the possibility that their feelings for men might have been entangled with their feelings for their sons. Overall, mothers resisted discussing their personal psychological dilemmas, preferring instead to return to discussions of their sons. When a mother individually visited the boys' group or made observations of behavior from the mothers' group, she was able to view her son's behavior in relation to his male peers. Constructive observations were offered, and mothers often commented that their boys "weren't so bad after all." By the sixth session, most mothers concluded that their boys were behaving better. In the remaining sessions, the group focused on ways to reinforce the child's positive behavior. By the seventh session, mothers began to address the termination of the group; and during the ninth session, the mothers requested feedback from the boys' therapist. Finally, during the tenth session, mothers shared phone numbers for future contact.

RESULTS: The "simultaneous" treatment of sons and mothers was considered a success for the following reasons: (1) The boys' group provided a better understanding of the sources of complaints and stress. (2) The mothers' sense of isolation diminished as they witnessed other families with similar problems. (3) The mothers were able to observe and implement various interventions to effect changes in the behavior of their boys.

COMMENTARY: The simultaneous treatment approach is useful because both therapists and mothers are able to witness the problem behaviors of the children. Thus, the problem of the mothers' "aloneness" is treated in a number of ways. First, mothers receive help and support from the therapists. Second, the other mothers provide support and feedback to each other. Third, they discover that neither they nor their boys are completely unique in their problems. Finally, there is the potential for a support network, which could continue after the group's termination. Although the authors refer to the mothers' efforts to secure phone numbers for future contact, it appears advisable for therapists actively to encourage future contacts and support by mothers involved in such a group.

SOURCE: Hoffman, T. E., Byrne, K. M., Belnap, K. L., and Steward, M. S. "Simultaneous Semipermeable Groups for Mothers and Their Early Latency-Age Boys." *International Journal of Group Psychotherapy,* 1981, *31* (1), 83-98.

Coordinated Group Psychotherapy for Parents of Children in an Activity Group

AUTHORS: Robert O. Pasnau, Miriam Meyer, L. Jeanette Davis, Richard Lloyd, and George Kline

PRECIS: Providing parallel verbal group psychotherapy to parents of children involved in activity group therapy

INTRODUCTION: The authors provide a rationale for group therapy for both children and their parents. For children, the group provides a neutral setting in which they can act out their impulses. Additionally, the activity group provides sublimative activities, reinforcing experiences, group status, and unconditional love and acceptance. The group allows for the gradual reorganization of the child's personality through identification with the therapist as the ideal parent and through identification with group members as siblings.

While the child's group may symbolically represent the ideal family, the actual family usually requires its own restructuring and reorganizing. Thus, a parallel parents' group is useful for the following reasons: (1) It helps parents recognize and deal with their own ambivalence, hostility, and guilt feelings toward their child. (2) It helps parents realize that activity is the child's means of communication. (3) It helps parents gain increased awareness of their contribution to the child's difficulties.

TREATMENT: This project lasted for approximately one year. Children participating in activity group therapy were boys between the ages of seven and nine, "psychoneurotic," not retarded, and of parent(s) willing to participate in a parallel parent group. The criteria for parent involvement were initially vague; however, after several months it was stipulated that both husbands and wives must attend the parents' group. Every week the parents' group and the children's group met in different rooms at the same time. Both groups were led by a male and a female therapist. Cotherapists met after the group meetings for consultation and discussion of the developments within the groups.

The first several months of the children's group were marked by adjustments and transition. By the third month, there was more interaction among the boys, resulting in the formation of a group identity. Activties during the fourth month were characterized by themes of giving and receiving. During the fifth month, group members were preoccupied by the advancing pregnancy of the female cotherapist and her ensuing departure from the group. The boys' fear and anger surrounding these circumstances were discussed, as well as their fear that the male therapist might also leave. During the sixth month, the female therapist was temporarily absent, and the group was characterized by more lively activity, hide-and-seek games, the testing of limits, and the boys' insistence on leaving early. By the end of the seventh month, the female therapist had returned, and there was a new readiness to deal with dynamic issues. During months eight through ten, the group functioned as a cohesive unit. Additionally, there were more problem-solving activities, more peer interactions, and improvements in individual members of the group. The last few months were spent dealing with separation.

The members of the parents' group were initially curious about one another's children. Additionally, some parents denied problems in their children and/or themselves, while others looked to the cotherapists for answers concerning their children's symptomatology. The group was instrumental in helping parents accept both their positive and negative feelings toward their sons. Finally, the group eventually focused on how parent-child and parent-parent relationships affected the child's behavior.

COMMENTARY: The authors' recollection of events that transpired in the parents' group highlights an advantage of parallel groups for parents. That is, such a group allows parents gradually to shift their focus from the identified patient (the child) to themselves. This process allows for the discussion of marital conflicts by parents in such a way as to reduce the potential threat of such conversations. Thus, the parallel parents' group serves as an extremely useful adjunct to individual and/or group therapy for children.

SOURCE: Pasnau, R. O., Meyer, M., Davis, L. J., Lloyd, R., and Kline, G. "Coordinated Group Psychotherapy of Children and Parents." *International Journal of Group Psychotherapy,* 1976, *26,* 89-103.

Parallel Groups for Autistic Children and Their Parents

AUTHORS: Rex W. Speers and Cornelius Lansing

PRECIS: Providing group psychotherapy to autistic children, their mothers, and their fathers

INTRODUCTION: The authors assume a psychodynamic formulation for the condition of autism. They describe group therapy offered to autistic children and their parents as part of a total treatment approach.

TREATMENT: Four children, ages three and a half to four and a half, comprised the original group. The clients were diagnosed as exhibiting childhood psychosis with autistic features. The primary symptoms included language deficits; absence of bowel and bladder control; sleeping and eating disturbances; fascination with twirling objects; repetitive, stereotyped behaviors; and severe tantrums with self-destructive behavior. After five months a fifth child entered the group. In the year to follow, four additional children were added to the group. Mothers were also seen regularly, and after nine months, a fathers' group was formed.

Children met for three one-and-a-half-hour sessions per week. Two of the three weekly sessions were conducted on a single day. Mothers were seen for a single one-and-a-half-hour session every week. The children were provided with various toys, a pan of soapy water, percussion instruments, drawing materials, play dough, and food. After several sessions group members began to interrupt one another's autistic behavior. The resulting "panic reactions" were characterized by crying, screaming, shaking, and kicking. As the sessions proceeded, the cotherapists designed and arranged the activities in order to keep the group together. For example, only one pan of soapy water or one sheet of paper was provided, thereby promoting contact and sharing among the children. The fifth child served as a catalyst to unify the group against a "common enemy"—an intruder. The new child's aggressively exhibitionistic behavior made withdrawal by the remaining children difficult. The group retaliated by "ganging up" on her, trying to eliminate her from their environment. Thus, much of the cotherapists' time was spent restraining the aggressors. Soon her behavior was modeled by other children, resulting in similar acts of aggression among group members. It was at this point that the authors reported the first evidences of group formation as each child began to respect the retaliatory powers of the group.

Within the context of play activities, the cotherapists—via interpretive comments—dealt with the autistic withdrawal, "sibling rivalry," and the violation of property rights. With increased interaction, the process of separation-individuation became more evident. As the process continued, children spontaneously used pronouns correctly, and after eighteen months children were communicating with one another. When the four new children entered the group, they too exhibited panic reactions similar to those by the original group members. The experienced group members served a therapeutic purpose, introducing the new children to their visual images as reflected in a mirror. These efforts by the original children reduced the anxiety of the new ones. After over eighteen months of treatment, the following improvements were noted in the original group members: (1) All five were capable of following directions. (2) All five could sit attentively for as long as twenty minutes. (3) Communicative speech was present. (4) All five were toilet-trained. (5) Four attended kindergarten the following year.

The mothers became intensely involved in treatment, with a resulting strong group cohesion. Mothers were advised early in treatment to employ "nannies" to aid in the daily care of their autistic youngsters. Although this provided the mothers with some respite from their demanding children, jealousy of the nannies soon became evident. Additionally, the mothers related to the therapist as an all-giving mother. The eventual "sibling rivalry" between mothers and the jealousy of the nannies provided material for group discussion and interpretation by the therapist. Role playing was also utilized to work through their own narcissistic and dependency needs. Therapy continued to focus on problems of displacement ("bad self" becoming the "bad child"), and the theme of depreciating males and husbands soon surfaced.

At this point the fathers' group was initiated. Responding to the changes in the mothers, most fathers entered into treatment, albeit reluctantly. Generally, the men had used isolation techniques to prevent emotional relationships in the past. Similar withdrawal tendencies reappeared, and sessions were marked by physical absences and emotional isolation. At the time this article was submitted, the men were beginning to deal with their intense anger toward their wives.

COMMENTARY: Parallel groups for autistic-involved families fulfill a variety of needs. As part of the child's total treatment plan, the group increased interaction and individuation by the child. Additionally, mothers were provided a vehicle for support and a mechanism through which they could explore their own unmet needs. As mothers began to change, a need for the fathers' group followed. Although the final results of the parallel groups for parents were not presented, the efforts of the authors represent a substantial attempt to meet the needs of the entire family.

SOURCE: Speers, R. W., and Lansing, C. "Group Psychotherapy with Preschool Psychotic Children and Collateral Group Therapy of Their Parents." *American Journal of Orthopsychiatry,* 1964, *34* (4), 659-666.

Additional Readings

Epstein, N. "Brief Group Therapy in a Child Guidance Clinic." *Social Work,* 1970, *15* (3), 33-38.

The author describes the efforts of a child guidance clinic to provide brief group therapy to parents and their children. The purpose of the groups was to develop and enhance competence in parents and children. The author focuses primarily on the clinic's work with parents' groups. Parents were usually seen as couples and were homogeneously grouped with respect to the age of the children and presenting problems. A crucial premise of the group therapy was that parenthood is one of the most difficult tasks encountered by people—one for which people receive virtually no training or education. Thus, much of therapy involved the offering of advice and suggestions regarding parent-child relationships. An important aspect of the training/therapy was the therapist's availability for follow-up after the six weeks of group therapy.

Roberts, J., Beswick, K., Leverton, B., and Lynch, M. A. "Prevention of Child Abuse: Group Therapy for Mothers and Children." *The Practitioner,* 1977, *219,* 111-115.

The authors describe a group therapy project designed to aid families with childrearing problems that might lead to abuse. Two groups, one for mothers and one for children, met weekly for six months. The seven members of the mothers' group were characterized by a lack of self-esteem, social isolation, and unrealistic expectations of child and family, all of which were alleviated to some extent by the therapy. Members of the children's group suffered from separation problems, inhibited behavior, delayed maturation, and aggressive behavior. The children showed progress in the areas of independence, social skills, and overcoming inhibitions. The effectiveness of the program is asserted, but it is cautioned that the program is inadequate in cases where one or more of the participants is suffering from a severe psychiatric disorder.

Part Two

Group Therapies for Specific Problems

The prescriptive approach to therapy seeks to refine therapeutic methods so that one can eventually say what specific remedy or therapeutic technique is most effective for a specific problem or disorder. Instead of forcing a child into one "all-purpose" therapeutic mold, then, group therapists are trying to individualize, to fit the group approaches to the needs of the individual child. Ideally, this prescriptive approach will result in maximum therapeutic effectiveness in the briefest time period.

It is important for child group therapists to keep abreast of the progress that has been made in adapting group techniques to meet the needs of children with specific disorders or who are "at risk" to develop psychological problems. Chapter Three describes the use of prevention groups for "at-risk" children, while Chapter Four contains specific group interventions for particular disorders of children.

3 Prevention Groups for Children and Youth at Risk

Children at risk of developing serious emotional problems if left untreated are those who are having difficulty adjusting to a severe stress or trauma, such as the children of divorced parents, and those who are having difficulty accomplishing developmental tasks, such as withdrawn children and children with gender identification problems or identity confusion. Group therapies offer the support and understanding these youngsters need to cope with stressful situations such as divorce. These therapies also provide a safe, accepting environment in which youngsters can experiment with peers in resolving developmental crises. Such preventive group interventions are likely to prove inexpensive compared to later costs in personal and family suffering, delinquency, institutionalization, and lost manpower.

Many of the interventions reported in this chapter utilize a developmental, educative approach that focuses on teaching coping skills to deal with current and future problems. This approach stresses education and positive enhancement, as opposed to removing behavioral abnormalities or promoting deep insights into behavior. For this reason, paraprofessionals and educators can be adequately trained to deliver *some* of these programs without the financial burden of continuous involvement by professionals as group leaders.

Children Experiencing Developmental Problems

Every youngster must master a sequence of predetermined developmental tasks to grow into a mature, fulfilled adult. Failure in mastering any of these critical stages of development has serious effects on the growth and psychological adjustment of the individual and can lead to serious psychopathology. Therapeutic groups that target specific developmental tasks provide the child or adolescent with the opportunity to talk with others who experience similar feelings and problems. The youngsters develop coping skills that they can use in future situations to continue their positive development. In the therapies in this section, the therapist is an important role model. With children, therapy is generally activity oriented and promotes interactions that help the group members learn appropriate social and developmental skills. With adolescents, therapy is discussion oriented and promotes mastery through insight and understanding.

Preventing School Adjustment Problems in High-Risk Schoolchildren

AUTHOR: Joseph A. Durlak

PRECIS: Activity therapy reinforcing target behaviors for second graders with potential school adjustment problems in later years

INTRODUCTION: The Rochester Primary Mental Health Project (PMHP), a program for the early detection and prevention of school adjustment problems, utilizes nonprofessionals (housewives) as helping agents with identified children. This article describes a similar program, except that volunteer teachers and college students are used as helping agents and the children are treated in a group rather than one to one.

TREATMENT: The program was conducted in two American schools in West Germany with enrollments of 1,100 and 1,400, respectively, and an average class size of 26 students. The AML, an eleven-item quick questionnaire, was used to screen the entire second-grade class in both schools. This questionnaire, filled out by the teachers, yields a score for acting out (A), mood (M), and learning (L). The children who scored in the top 10 percent were considered a potential high-risk group. For those children, the teachers then filled out the Teacher Referral Form (TRF), which provides more detailed information about the children's adjustment problems. Parental contact was limited to obtaining consent for the child's participation in a treatment group. Fifty-six children were placed in the treatment groups.

The sixteen group leaders were volunteer teachers, school counselors, and several upper-level college students majoring in psychology. They attended three one-and-a-half-hour training sessions that emphasized the strategies, procedures, and goals of a group reinforcement system; observed two children's therapy groups where a token system was used; and were given relevant reading material. A senior psychologist did the training and supervised the leaders in weekly one-hour sessions. He also observed the groups in session and gave leaders specific feedback about their handling of activities and reinforcement procedures.

The children were assigned to groups that included five to seven children and represented a mixture of problems and behaviors. They were seen weekly for one hour over a period of eight weeks. The goal of the group meetings was to increase the frequency of the children's target behavior via positive reinforcement. For example, shy and withdrawn children who did not participate in social interactions were rewarded for "talking to others" or "working with others"; children who were severe management problems–who constantly moved about, got into fights, and talked out inappropriately–were rewarded for "waiting your turn" or "working on your own"; children who had poor work habits and could not follow directions or finish a task and had short attention spans were rewarded for "working on a task" or "following directions."

The children were told that they would have special tasks to do in the group for which they could earn chips (poker chips). Chips could be used to buy small items at the school store, either at the end of the meeting or at the end of the week if they saved them. Reinforcement in the form of poker chips was paired with verbal praise and attention. Shaping, prompting, and various forms of intermittent reinforcement schedules were used to assure that each child earned a minimum number of chips in the first two meetings. The average schedule of intermittent reinforcement was 60 percent the first week, gradually tapering off to 20 percent in the seventh week. No tokens were given during the eighth week, but contingent verbal reinforcement was continued.

During the program, each child had a colorful chart with his or her name and target behaviors listed. At the beginning of each meeting, the children marked how many chips they had earned the previous week on their charts. The children's progress was praised liberally, and the relationship between the chips and the child's behavior was explained each time.

The leaders selected activities that would provide the children with opportunities to perform their target behaviors. Activities typically were arts and crafts, group games, and listening to and discussing stories.

RESULTS: According to teachers' ratings, the children in the group treatment improved in classroom adjustment following the eight-week program and on a seven-month follow-up study. The author concludes that this form of treatment is economical and efficient in preventing school adjustment problems. He states that the program also alerted the primary-grade teachers to early signs of maladaptive behaviors that predict later school problems and provided them with skills to reverse the dysfunction.

COMMENTARY: The school is a major part of the child's life, and school adjustment has serious implications for developing adequate self-esteem, peer relations, and adult relations. Early intervention programs aimed at transition points—that is, at the beginning of primary, junior high, and high school—can orient the youngster to the new situation, prepare him to handle anticipated problems, and show him that his feelings and reactions are normal. The early intervention can also encourage the youngster to become actively involved in the school—for instance, through participation in student government and clubs—so that the youngster identifies with the school and classmates from the beginning.

SOURCE: Durlak, J. A. "Description and Evaluation of a Behaviorally Oriented School-Based Preventive Mental Health Program." *Journal of Consulting and Clinical Psychology,* 1977, *45,* 27-33.

Parallel Group Therapy with Feminine Boys and Their Parents

AUTHORS: Richard Green and Marielle Fuller

PRECIS: Parallel groups–for feminine boys, their mothers, and their fathers–instituted in an attempt to reorient the boys' sexual identification

INTRODUCTION: According to the authors, boys who act like girls are at high risk for sexual adjustment problems, transsexualism, and/or homosexuality as adults. Those who seek behavioral reorientation as adults will find that such reorientation is extremely difficult and often unsuccessful. Consequently, mental health professionals attempt to intervene during boyhood.

This article describes an intervention strategy used with seven boys whose parents were concerned with the boys' feminine behaviors. All the boys dressed in women's clothes or improvised if such clothing was unavailable; they strongly preferred girls as playmates; they insisted on playing female roles in fantasy play; they preferred playing with girls' toys; they displayed feminine gestures and sometimes said that they wished they were girls.

TREATMENT: The seven boys in the group ranged in age from four to nine, and they met in weekly one-hour sessions with a male therapist. The seven mothers met biweekly for one hour with male and female cotherapists. There were four fathers, and they met biweekly with the male therapist while the mothers met with the female therapist. Bimonthly the parents all met together with both therapists.

The boys met in a recreational area and were verbally reinforced for "masculine" behavior, such as climbing high on the monkey bars, running, kicking a ball, and plunging head first down the slide. Masculine nouns were emphasized: "That's a good *boy*." "Come on, *guys*." The boys were initially resistant to participation but gradually developed enthusiasm and initiated their own games. The therapist made negative comments about feminine gestures or role taking, such as "Don't run like that" and "You don't look like a stewardess; you look more like a pilot." The boys also began criticizing each other's feminine behavior.

The group enabled the boys to recognize and criticize feminine behaviors in other boys and, ultimately, to recognize the same behavior in themselves. It also provided the first adult male "authority" figure for three boys who did not have fathers in their homes, and it provided the first male playmates that two of the boys had ever had.

Similarly, the mothers were able to see the faults in other mothers' approaches to their sons' behavior and were given opportunities to share their concerns with other mothers and to rehearse ways to handle feminine behavior in their sons.

An important aspect of the group experience for the fathers was the discovery that other fathers also did not relish playing ball with their sons after working all day or sacrificing the Sunday TV football game to take the boys fishing. The recognition that other fathers were reluctant to spend time in father-son activities appeared to ease the intense feelings of guilt the fathers were experiencing. One father reluctantly joined the Indian Guides with his son and was amazed to find that he enjoyed it. His enthusiastic reports of his activities with his son helped the other fathers get over the hurdle and be more involved with their sons.

RESULTS: The parents reported a variety of changes in their sons, including a reduction in cross dressing, feminine gestures and speech, female role taking, and statements expressing a desire to be a girl. The parents also rated the father-son relationship as closer.

COMMENTARY: The authors cannot state which treatment components were responsible for the behavioral changes in the boys. They note that further research is needed to determine whether this method is more effective than individual therapy or a token economy intervention. We believe that all three groups were important and helpful for the participants, and it was probably this total-systems treatment approach that produced the positive results. This systems approach appears to be the treatment of choice because it attempts to (1) change the child's inappropriate behaviors, (2) change parent behaviors that may be reinforcing or contributing to the problem, and (3) teach the parents ways to manage the problem behaviors and thus maintain the behavior changes seen in treatment sessions in situations of daily living.

SOURCE: Green, R., and Fuller, M. "Group Therapy with Feminine Boys and Their Parents." *International Journal of Group Psychotherapy,* 1973, *23,* 54-68.

Adolescent Identity Crisis

AUTHOR: Arnold W. Rachman

PRECIS: Group therapy as treatment of choice for resolving identity crisis of adolescents

INTRODUCTION: The author proposes that contemporary adolescents, in increasing numbers, are suffering from identity confusion, the negative stage of the search for a personal identity. An integral part of the adolescent's ego identity is peer group identity, since an adolescent evaluates himself in much the same way as his peers evaluate and respond to him. The adolescent gives meaning, direction, and support to the peer group, and the peer group fulfills the same functions for its individual members. As a defense against identity confusion, many adolescents naturally turn to their peers and group membership to enhance their self-esteem. Group therapy channels the adolescent's interest in peer group membership and acceptance in a positive, corrective direction.

TREATMENT: The group follows a discussion format and incorporates encounter and marathon techniques. The basic aim is to establish group processes that bring about identity crisis resolution. The therapist encourages group members to develop alternatives to conflicts and problems and to make decisions. She uses role-playing and encounter techniques to promote free role experimentation, psychosocial play, and free elaboration of fantasy. By exploring fantasy and dream material, adolescents reduce their guilt toward impulses expressed in the dreams, and they side with the developing ego elements in the dream, such as those aspects that show positive direction and a sense of mastery.

As therapy progresses, the therapist becomes a meaningful authority figure. As the adolescent confronts the therapist and works with her in the group, he learns to relate in a reciprocal and more equal fashion with adults, which fosters his independence from infantile ties with parental figures and new ways of relating to them.

Rachman presents several case examples of group therapy with adolescents experiencing identity confusion, including a boy with neurotic and borderline symptoms, a delinquent boy, and an adolescent abusing drugs.

COMMENTARY: Rachman argues that most of the problems seen in adolescents are related to identity confusion. Therapy must therefore help them form a positive self-identity by providing direction, organization, and support. An adult model with positive, meaningful ideologies also must be provided. The group fosters separateness from the family and new ways of relating to the family and peers.

SOURCE: Rachman, A. W. "Group Psychotherapy in Treating the Adolescent Identity Crisis." *International Journal of Child Psychotherapy,* 1972, *1,* 97-119.

Additional Readings

Althof, S. E., and Keller, A. C. "Group Therapy with Gender Identity Patients." *International Journal of Group Psychotherapy,* 1980, *30,* 481-489.

Group treatment was used with adult patients requesting sex-change operations. All were in various stages of gender transition; several were postsurgical patients. The authors observe that 84 percent of the patients seeking gender reassignment had "serious character pathology," and all the patients had disturbed developmental histories. Persons with gender identity problems are generally not successfully treated as adults. More successful intervention occurs when the problem is identified and treated in childhood.

Apolito, A. "Primary Prevention: A Breakthrough in Sight." *American Journal of Psychoanalysis,* 1978, *38,* 121-127.

The author reviews primary prevention approaches to mental illness and suggests that group therapy, family therapy, and transactional analysis can educate children to deal with threatening psychological forces before serious psychological injury results.

Muro, J. J., and Engels, D. W. "Life Coping Skills Through Developmental Group Counseling." *Journal for Specialists in Group Work,* 1980, *3,* 127-130.

A developmental group counseling approach is described that helps members know themselves; develop self-acceptance, self-direction, decision-making abilities, and sensitivity to the needs of others; and master developmental tasks. The authors note that the skills required for overcoming developmental tasks are the same skills needed for coping with daily living.

Zimet, C. N. "Developmental Task and Crisis Groups: The Application of Group Psychotherapy to Maturational Processes." *Psychotherapy: Theory, Research and Practice,* 1979, *16,* 2-8.

Therapeutic groups are proposed that would deal with critical stages of the maturational process, including identity development, adolescent social skills, sex role development and identity, vocational decision making, generativity and childbirth, parenting, the empty-nest stage, unmet career expectations, and the variety of adaptations required in old age. This preventive approach would reduce psychological dysfunction—before the problem escalates to psychopathology—by providing support for individuals facing common problems in everyday living.

Hospitalized and Physically Disabled Children

The relationship between physical health and psychological adjustment has long been recognized. There is a growing interest in the medical establishment in utilizing pediatric psychology to treat a variety of problems that interfere with optimal medical treatment. Group therapies have been an integral part of this movement in treating the "whole" child. Relaxation and discussion groups have been used with asthmatic youngsters and youngsters with severe muscle spasms. Behavior therapy and play therapy have been used with youngsters with psychosomatic illnesses. Guided group activity is used with children facing surgery or chronic illness, to reduce anxiety and enlist their cooperation with treatment and aftercare. Discussion groups have been instituted with terminally ill and physically handicapped children, to help them cope with the complex problems they face in daily living.

Group for Chronically Disabled Adolescents

AUTHOR: Sadi Bayrakal

PRECIS: Group therapy with seriously handicapped teenagers to help them establish meaningful relationships

INTRODUCTION: Bayrakal reports that chronically disabled children are twice as likely to suffer from psychiatric disorders as normal children. Seriously handicapped children are isolated from the mainstream of social life and have difficulty in finding meaningful interpersonal relationships. Many of them also face the reality of impending or early death. With few exceptions, these youngsters exhibit a similar emotional profile of apathy, poor school achievement, poor self-image, social isolation, chronic dependency, and chronic depression. Because of their physical limitations and fragile ego identities, disabled youngsters tend to remain isolated even from similarly handicapped peers.

The author, a psychiatric consultant for a school for disabled children, instituted a therapeutic group with adolescents to provide them with an opportunity to share common concerns and feelings, and to relieve some of the isolation they experience.

TREATMENT: Eleven adolescents, ranging in age from fourteen to seventeen and suffering from muscular dystrophy, participated in the group. Muscular dystrophy is a genetic disease that strikes in early childhood (when the child is four to seven years old) and progressively cripples the victim, who usually dies ten to fifteen years after the initial appearance of the symptoms. All the children were of average to above average intelligence. All were confined to wheelchairs and required help for even simple routine functions.

The group met weekly for about an hour and a half over a period of nine months. Bayrakal ran the group with a traditional psychoanalytical approach, making comments and interpretations related to transference, defenses, intragroup dynamics, the group's relation to outside groups, and affective components of the sessions. The group went through six phases, each involving different moods and content within the sessions.

During the first phase, dependence-flight, the group members searched for a group goal, warded off anxiety by discussing neutral subjects, and defended against feelings of dependency by criticizing caregivers and teachers. Two boys left the group. In the second phase, the group members began to show their independence from the therapist. They questioned his presence and his role, and then ignored him or showed open hostility toward him. One of the most disturbed members took the role of leader, and the group then progressed into the regression phase. In this third phase, the members discussed muscular dystrophy and their frustration with their wheelchairs. They experienced sadness when a favorite teacher died, then denied sadness when a classmate died a few weeks later. The destructive wishes and fantasies were given full expression, encouraged by the leader. One member of the group became the target for many attacks. A sense of disintegration and anomie dominated the sessions, and the therapist was "reduced to being just another member of the group."

In the fourth stage, the interdependent stage, a female member began to demand that the group members take more action toward resolving real issues that concerned them. The group members expressed discontent with their teachers, their caregivers, and also themselves. They began moving away from the sick leader to the persistent female member. With the new leader, they developed a new goal, which was to raise money for a recreation room. For the first time, they became enthusiastic and worked together on the project. The members interacted more intimately than ever before, and the project was a success.

During the fifth phase, the disenchantment phase, the main preoccupations of the group were issues of friendship, love, boy-girl relationships, sex, marriage, and family life. The mood became one of anxiety as the lack of meaningful relationships became obvious. There was a warm atmosphere in the group as members shared painful thoughts and feelings and tried to draw close to one another. However, they were unable to respond to each other's appeals for intimacy and friendship, and the effort to achieve emotional closeness failed.

In the resolution phase, members changed moods appropriately according to the topic under discussion. They were aware of their involvement with each other and were able to talk freely and show genuine interest in each other's thoughts, feelings, and plans for the future. The therapist was dropped from conversation almost completely, except when the group wanted assurance that the group would be continued the following year.

RESULTS: The author and others involved with these teenagers reported significant improvement in the attitudes and functioning of the group members at the end of the nine-month group experience.

COMMENTARY: In this article one gets the sense that the therapist was more an observer than an active participant in the group and that the group never achieved the emotional closeness the members desired. Perhaps a more actively involved therapist would provide the emotional support that the handicapped children were not able to give to each other and would serve as a model to help them become more supportive of each other or find support from outside sources.

SOURCE: Bayrakal, S. "A Group Experience with Chronically Disabled Adolescents." *American Journal of Psychiatry,* 1975, *132,* 1291-1294.

Group Therapy on a Pediatric Ward

AUTHORS: Dorcas C. Cofer and Yehuda Nir

PRECIS: Group sessions held on a pediatric ward to reduce children's anxiety and resistance to hospital procedures and to correct distortions

INTRODUCTION: Hospitalized children—separated from their parents; placed in a strange and restrictive environment; subjected to pain and immobilization and uncomfortable diagnostic procedures—can develop moderate to severe depression and anxiety, manifested by regression, withdrawal, resistance to hospital routines and procedures, aggressive and disruptive behavior, sleep disturbances, and increased somatization.

Cofer and Nir describe various techniques used in hospitals to reduce the psychological stress placed on these youngsters, such as rooming in of mothers, staffed ward playrooms, and play therapy. Younger children are encouraged to operate on dolls and to tell stories to each other. Adolescents are encouraged to participate in making ward decisions, to socialize, and to vent their emotions in times of stress.

The use of group techniques with hospitalized children has grown out of research with adult and terminally ill patients. This research suggests that group therapy sessions and preparatory communications help patients accept their illness and adjust to hospital procedures and postoperative stresses. It has also shown that seriously ill children manifest less withdrawal and regression when adults around them adopt open attitudes toward illness and help the children freely express their feelings and concerns.

The authors describe a group approach instituted to ameliorate the negative effects of hospitalization in children. They refer to their method as theme-focused therapy because content of the sessions was limited to two aspects of the hospital experience: (1) the lack or distortion of factual information and (2) fantasies, fears, and anxieties regarding hospitalization.

TREATMENT: The group sessions were held three times a week on the pediatric ward, usually in a patient's room. Two therapists were present. Participation was voluntary but strongly encouraged, and attendance ranged from three to ten members. Patients were excluded if they were markedly retarded or emotionally disturbed to the extent that they would disrupt the group. In addition, since children are experiencing different developmental tasks at different ages, it was occasionally necessary to exclude a youngster who was significantly older or younger than the mean age of the group.

After the therapists explained the purpose of the group, the children introduced issues of concern, usually questions about medical procedures. The therapists encouraged the children to answer each other's questions, finding that information provided by peers is more convincing than that provided by adults. For example, a child who has "survived" anesthesia is a more valid source of reassurance for a child about to undergo surgery than the therapist is. The therapists found that the children's lack of information intensified their distortions and fears. One child, for example, worried that frequent blood taking would deplete the body's supply; another feared that the metal plate in her head would attract lightning if she stood near a window during a storm.

Children often use denial in relation to their illness, and the group was helpful in confronting a child's pathological denial. It also provided support and modeled acceptance of illness, which helped other children express repressed concerns. A case example was presented in which a diabetic youngster, who was admitted to confirm his diagnosis and regulate his diet and insulin, was cheating on his diet. The doctors did not know it and were having difficulty regulating his condition. The group confronted him with his cheating and found that he was denying the seriousness of his illness because he was afraid of becoming a "junkie." The therapists discussed legal and illegal use of drugs, which helped the child accept his illness.

Concerns of the children were age dependent, with younger children expressing separation fears and school-age children expressing fears of medical procedures and mutilation.

Sexual concerns were sometimes raised; but because of the anxiety-producing aspect of this subject, the discussion was refocused unless the sexual concerns were related to specific medical procedures.

The therapists' roles are to be supportive and to model by verbalizing negative feelings about hospitalization. They attempt to bring into the children's awareness repressed feelings that are responsible for impaired psychological functioning. The therapists also serve an educational role by providing factual information to correct distortions, and they reduce anxiety by eliciting peer support among participants. The authors caution that the therapists must also bring closure to issues raised in each session, since many of the members may be discharged before the next group meeting.

COMMENTARY: The theme-focused group offers children an opportunity for cathartic expression of fears and complaints and to gather factual information in an atmosphere of mutual support. The environment itself, in which the children live together and share the common experience of a medical crisis, facilitates a group bond, quicker interaction, and sensitivity to therapeutic support that would not be possible with strangers. The hospital benefits because the children are more cooperative with treatment and exhibit less anxiety, hyperactivity, and aggression. The existence of the group raises the consciousness of the medical personnel to mental health problems of the patients and provides information on how they can help the children adjust to a situation that is frightening for them.

SOURCE: Cofer, D. C., and Nir, Y. "Theme-Focused Group Therapy on a Pediatric Ward." *International Journal of Psychiatry in Medicine,* 1975, *6,* 541-550.

Support for Hospitalized Children

AUTHOR: John L. Frank

PRECIS: Psychodynamic group therapy sessions to help hospitalized children master the anxiety inherent in the hospital experience

INTRODUCTION: The author discusses the multiple sources of stress that make hospitalization a major psychological event for children. These children suffer from the physical and emotional discomforts of illness, injury, or altered bodily function; separation from loved ones; dependence on strangers to meet basic needs; invasion of privacy; real and unreal fears of pain and mutilation associated with medical procedures; uncertainty about the future; and "the ever present threat of stimulated internal strivings, such as passive dependency wishes," that are awakened by hospitalization. The child's ability to adjust to so many new and difficult changes in such a short time depends on his medical condition, ability to handle stress in the past, progress in solving the normal inner conflicts of his age, and the quality and availability of support for the child from parents and from the hospital staff.

This article describes a weekly group meeting for pediatric patients to help them adjust to the hospital experience as a part of the comprehensive care of children at an innovative hospital. It was felt that a group would help the children by allowing them to express their feelings and fears openly and to work through their fantasies and by correcting misunderstandings and distortions of information.

TREATMENT: The group meetings were held in the hospital conference room and were led by the child psychiatrist on the unit. A play specialist from the pediatric unit was present to take notes, and other interested medical and nursing personnel were permitted to sit in on meetings, but no more than three or four visitors were allowed per group. Children were strongly encouraged but not required to attend, and some meetings were held in the rooms of patients who were interested but could not attend because they were immobilized. Attendance ranged from five to fifteen youngsters. The children represented a diverse population. Half of them came from low-income areas and were admitted for problems such as chronic lead poisoning, shigellosis, gonorrhea, failure to thrive, and abuse by parents. The other half came from middle-class families and presented problems related to respiratory, gastrointestinal, endocrine, or hemotological diseases.

After asking each child to introduce himself, the leader introduced himself. Once the ice was broken, the children began complaining about the hospital food, the length of their stay, their loneliness for family and friends, and the rigors of their daily routine. When they saw that the leader listened to their complaints with interest and without criticizing them, they began expressing feelings and concerns about medical procedures, revealing many distortions and fantasies about medical treatment. For example, injections were likened to "being stabbed with a knife," and doctors were likened to vampires, who will remove so much blood that a child's insides become drained. Often the leader asked one or two of the more active members to elaborate on their ideas, believing that all the children would benefit from the supportive atmosphere of the group and from listening as problems were worked through.

Frank presents four clinical cases, showing that many children use the group as an audience to act out and work out their personal dramas. For instance, a ten-year-old boy with leukemia acted up in the group whenever someone mentioned an illness or operation. It became clear that he wanted to know more about the disease in his body but was afraid of what he might find out. Later the psychiatrist found that his mother was afraid of her son's disease and could not talk about it without becoming overwhelmed with anger and fear. After the mother was helped to become open and supportive with her son about his illness, he was able to adjust to it and to the tests and treatments he needed.

RESULTS: The children liked the group very much and often

did not want to end the meeting. They asked for more frequent meetings and said that the meetings were helpful. The group was also helpful to the staff, by exposing the psychiatrist to more children and their problems than he normally could reach; training residents in normal and pathological child development and adjustment to stress; and improving the relationship between the psychiatric and pediatric disciplines within the hospital.

COMMENTARY: Therapy groups on children's hospital wards are generally designed to alleviate children's anxiety by correcting distortions and rumors, providing factual information, demonstrating the staff's concern and support, and modifying ward policies that may be unnecessarily stressful for the children. These group meetings provide informal advantages, often not recognized by group leaders, such as orienting new patients to the ward, reducing the patients' feelings of isolation, and developing positive attitudes.

The author observed some areas of concern for the practitioner developing a similar group. First, children were not very talkative and their moods varied widely between sessions. The practice of allowing three or four visitors per session, primarily medical staff, may have caused this in part. The children may have been reluctant to express their true feelings for fear of alienating their surrogate caregivers or because there was less group cohesion when strangers attended the meetings. Second, younger children, ages six through nine, were more anxious and excited by the hospital experience than the older children. We can hypothesize that younger children are more confused and disoriented by the hospital situation and suffer more serious separation anxiety than older children; thus a group targeting this younger age group would seem to have more value than one for older children. Finally, a group that meets two or three times a week would provide more support and foster more group identification than a group that meets only once a week.

SOURCE: Frank, J. L. "A Weekly Group Meeting for Children on a Pediatric Ward: Therapeutic and Practical Functions."

International Journal of Psychiatry in Medicine, 1978, *8,* 267-283.

Use of Coping Techniques to Reduce Anxiety in Hospitalized Children

AUTHORS: Lizette Peterson and Carol Shigetomi

PRECIS: Combining cognitive coping strategies with information and filmed modeling to reduce anxiety in children hospitalized for elective tonsillectomies

INTRODUCTION: Peterson and Shigetomi present a brief review of studies designed to reduce anxiety in hospitalized children by providing them with information or with filmed models. These preparation techniques may have been less than optimal for the following reasons: (1) Children and parents often have viewed the *effects* of coping skills without learning the actual skills. (2) Modeling and information techniques failed to provide for the continuing emotional support of the child throughout hospitalization. (3) Preparation techniques have typically excluded parents from active participation. (4) Preparation techniques have seldom provided strategies that could be used to reduce pain. Thus, a purpose of this study was to provide specific coping techniques and to determine whether such techniques are more effective than information and modeling alone.

TREATMENT: Subjects were thirty-five girls and thirty-one boys, ages two and a half to ten and a half, from middle-class homes and hospitalized for elective tonsillectomies. Treatment groups included children receiving information only; information plus modeling; information plus coping; and information, modeling, and coping combined. Twenty-four groups, composed of two to seven children, were used in the study. Each group was taken on a guided tour of the following hospital areas: the admitting office, the laboratory, the operating room, the parents' waiting room, the playroom, and the patients' rooms.

Information was provided at "Big Bird's Ice Cream Party," to which the children and their parents were invited by the pediatric surgeons. Typical hospital experiences were explained while "Big Bird" assumed the role of the child.

Modeling was provided by a film, which showed the preparation, hospitalization, surgery, and recovery of a seven-year-old white male.

Coping skills included cue-controlled deep muscle relaxation (that is, children were taught to stretch, tense, and then completely relax their muscles, using deep breathing and the cue word *calm*), distracting mental imagery (children were asked to imagine the temperatures, smells, sights, and sounds of scenes that were quiet and made them feel happy), and comforting self-talk (phases such as "I will be all better in a little while" and "Everything is going to be all right").

RESULTS: Physiological records, observations, and self-reports supplied by children, parents, nurses, and experimental observers were used to assess the anxiety of the children in the various groups. The results suggest that children who received coping and modeling preparations were calmer and more cooperative than children receiving any of the other treatments (information alone, information and modeling, or information and coping).

COMMENTARY: This study provides an example of how a number of behavioral approaches may be utilized within a group context to reduce anxiety in hospitalized children. The principles described would also be useful in individual treatment or with children exhibiting other adjustment difficulties.

SOURCE: Peterson, L., and Shigetomi, C. "The Use of Coping Techniques to Minimize Anxiety in Hospitalized Children." *Behavior Therapy,* 1981, *12,* 1-14.

Additional Readings

Flanagan, C. "Children with Cancer in a Therapy Group." *Archives of the Foundation of Thanatology,* 1979, *7,* 22.

Group art therapy was provided to enhance expression of affect and to give ego support for children and adolescents with malignant neoplasms. Information obtained in the group was used to increase appropriate parent and medical/nursing support.

Sheridan, M. S. "Talk Time for Hospitalized Children." *Social Work,* 1975, *20,* 40-44.

A discussion group was developed to encourage children to share their fears and fantasies of the hospital experience. The leader presented realistic information to resolve unrealistic fears. The group was effective in eliciting the children's cooperation with medical procedures and was used as a training device to teach hospital personnel more about pediatric patients.

Sheridan, M. S., and Kline, K. "Psychosomatic Illness in Children." *Social Casework,* 1978, *59,* 227-232.

To determine whether a child's illness may be psychosomatic, a worker should evaluate the following symptoms: (1) physical changes related to a child's emotional stress, (2) conversion reactions, (3) tissue changes or organic disease resulting from long-standing emotional problems, and (4) physical diseases or problems which themselves cause emotional stress. Recommended approaches to treating the psychosomatic child include family therapy, parent discussion groups, behavior modification, individual therapy, and play therapy.

Children of Divorce

Currently, 1.2 million families a year are being dissolved through annulment and divorce, affecting an average of one child per divorce, or 1.2 million children a year. Many parents are so emotionally drained by the divorce and the changes it has produced in their lives that they are unable to give adequate attention and support to their children. Extended families and friends view the children's problems as something the family will take care of and something the child must adjust to. Thus, children who cannot adjust to the divorce often cannot get help through their normal support systems. A number of group treatment programs have been instituted to support these children and help them work through their feelings and problems related to the separation and loss surrounding parental divorce. To overcome the resistance of parents toward treatment and to avoid stigmatizing the children in any way, most of the programs are conducted in the schools. The programs are generally developmental and teach coping skills. The success rate of the programs reported here was found to be highly dependent on the attitudes of the parents toward the program. Several of the programs developed parallel parent groups at the request of the parents of the children involved.

Situation/Transition Group in the School

AUTHOR: Dorothy W. Cantor

PRECIS: A school-based group designed to provide crisis intervention and ongoing emotional support

INTRODUCTION: Some children under eighteen whose parents have been divorced show marked behavior changes, particularly in school. These children, who make up a disproportionate number of referrals for children's psychiatric evaluations, may display angry, acting-out behaviors; fears and phobias; and feelings of deprivation, sadness, and/or loneliness. Despite the pervasive, disruptive effect divorce has on children, many parents do not seek outside help to support their children through the crisis. Parents may not be able to afford individual therapy and may be resistant to or ignorant of mental health services available, or there may be a lack of services in their community.

Cantor, a school psychologist, suggests that the public or parochial school is a logical place to provide supportive services to youngsters experiencing such a stress. She notes that the schools have trained mental health workers on staff, including school psychologists, social workers, and guidance counselors, whose services should include preventive programs. The school also is an important social institution, second only to the family in affecting children's lives. Most of the children affected by divorce are of school age, and many have school problems. Finally, the children are already in school, and it could provide instant crisis intervention and emotional support ten months of the year.

Cantor describes a situation/transition group developed for children of divorce. In this model the group provides emotional support, catharsis, and an opportunity for children to share information relevant to the stressful experience.

TREATMENT: The group leader asked teachers of the third- through sixth-grade classes in the schools to submit names of children whose parents were recently separated and who were exhibiting behavioral anomalies in the classroom. Parents of the children were contacted and asked to give their permission for their children to participate. The parents were also invited to meet with the psychologist prior to the program to discuss goals and concerns. Of sixteen names submitted, three were already in therapy privately and ten were given permission to participate. The children were given the option to participate or not, and one child chose to drop out after the second meeting.

Nine children and the leader met for ten sessions, ending at the close of the school year. Although specific methods and exercises are not given, it appears that they used a group discussion format to cover such topics as their feelings about the divorce, problems encountered in having to choose between parents, the experience of loss, relationships with stepparents, and problems with visitation. The group also provided crisis intervention for another child in the school whose parents split up suddenly. The group allowed him to join them and provided information and support to the child, alleviating much of his anxiety.

RESULTS: Although the teachers perceived little change in classroom behavior, the children enjoyed the group and asked to extend it over the next year to provide ongoing support. Parents unanimously supported the project. A group for first and second graders also was planned.

COMMENTARY: This article demonstrates that many schools are taking the initiative in treating children of divorced parents because the parents, for a number of reasons, do not follow up on the school's request that parents seek community or private mental health services for their children.

SOURCE: Cantor, D. W. "School-Based Groups for Children of Divorce." *Journal of Divorce,* 1977, *1,* 183-187.

School-Based Group for Children of Divorce

AUTHOR: Anne Kurtzman Effron

PRECIS: A group for public school children with problems related to difficulties surrounding their parents' divorce

INTRODUCTION: The author, a school social worker, developed a therapy group for children when it became apparent that many of the referrals for service were children whose parents were in various stages of separation and divorce. She asked fourth-, fifth-, and sixth-grade teachers to refer youngsters who might benefit from a counseling group for children coping with separation and divorce. Through the group she hoped to help children accept the loss of their parents as a couple; understand the forces leading to the problem, instead of viewing themselves as the cause; and develop self-awareness and self-esteem.

All the youngsters referred had difficulties in concentrating, and their performance at school had declined. They also had poor peer relationships, since they were overaggressive and immature or showed signs of depression, hypermaturity, and isolation. The aggressive and immature children were not socially isolated, since they gained a certain popularity by teasing and other acting-out behaviors. The hypermature children were socially isolated, since their constant search for teacher approval hindered them from making friends and they were perceived by peers as 'teacher's pets.' Both of these reactions, in the social worker's view, reflected an unresolved mourning process.

A prerequisite for group selection was an ability to talk about one's life situation. Denial and retreating into fantasy were contraindications for inclusion in the group. A youngster who insisted that his parents were happily married was referred to a community mental health center for more intensive treatment than the school could provide.

Parents were notified by letter and a follow-up phone call about the proposed program. Most of the parents knew that their children were having trouble in school but rarely attended parent-teacher conferences. The counselor presented the parents with the positive message that the children could be helped to deal with the divorce better. The parents were passively accepting of the group.

TREATMENT: Eight children between the ages of ten and twelve were involved in the group, five boys and three girls. The children were interviewed individually to explain the purpose of the group, assess personal conflict areas, and develop goals for each group participant.

The twelve-week program utilized role playing, affective education techniques, and creative writing to stimulate discussion and self-awareness. Each of these concrete activities recreated different life situations, which were then discussed.

The author provides examples of scripts used for role playing. Several sessions focused on children's reactions to parental separation such as: fantasies of reconciliation, attempts to help parents by taking on more responsibilities, and feelings of guilt or abandonment. The role playing began with an example and an inappropriate response; then members were asked to face the reality of the situation and find new and creative solutions, which were then acted out.

Affective education techniques included games and audiovisual materials aimed at helping youngsters understand their feelings better. One film used, *Hurt, Anger, and Sharing* (Educational Films, 1975), shows the problems of a boy whose dog dies and depicts the emotions of people experiencing loss: denial, anger, depression, and sadness in recalling shared memories. In this session the leader interpreted divorce as a loss to the children and helped them compare the two losses through structured discussion. The leader also explored positive aspects of divorce, such as less fighting.

Other suggested materials include *The Sky Is Falling—A Program for Children of Divorce* (Port Washington Union Free School District, Port Washington, New York), which combines film and behavior modification techniques, and *Me and Dad's New Wife* (Time-Life Films, 1977), about a twelve-year-old girl who has difficulty accepting her divorced father's new wife.

Educational games include "Photography and Feelings," in which the children bring in favorite family photographs and are asked questions to help work through their loss, and "Pie of Life," in which children divide a circle into pie slices that show how much time they spend in daily activities (school, with friends, with family, and so on) and then discuss whether it reflects their real desires or what they might change.

Creative writing projects allowed the children to express personal concerns that could later be discussed individually with the social worker or brought up in general terms to the group for discussion. The children suggested such topics as being caught in a custody fight, anticipating a visit from a parent who has been away for a year, extra responsibilities of living in a one-parent home, and establishing a relationship with a parent's new boyfriend or girlfriend. The children were also asked to write about previously discussed topics, so that the social worker could see how well they were assimilating the ideas presented.

RESULTS: The program received positive reactions from the children, the teachers, and the parents. In fact, parents who had previously been uninvolved with the school participated more in parent-teacher conferences, and three families became involved in family therapy at a local mental health clinic when it became clear that the short-term group was not enough for the children.

COMMENTARY: Besides the direct services the group provided for the children, the program also served as a bridge to their families, who became more involved with the school and with community services such as Big Brothers, which they learned about through the school. Parents also expressed interest in a companion group for parents that could meet at night, and this will be added in future programming.

SOURCE: Effron, A. K. "Children and Divorce: Help from an Elementary School." *Social Casework,* 1980, *10,* 305-312.

Multimodal Approach to Counsel Children in Groups

AUTHOR: Barbara J. Green

PRECIS: A multimodal method of counseling to ensure comprehensive attention to the many changes that divorce produces in children

INTRODUCTION: The acronym HELPING is used to describe the seven modes or fundamental elements used in multimodal counseling. Each mode is a necessary element of human development and interacts with the other modes in this theoretical framework. The counselor's role is to assess the deficits and provide treatment for each and every mode.

The *H* is for health. The counselor helps the children recognize how their health affects their emotional and perceptual experiences. The *E* represents emotions; that is, being able to experience joy and express feelings in a nonjudgmental environment. Treatment in the *E* mode may include stress inoculation, anger control, and fun training. The *L* is for learning. In this mode the counselor may encourage involvement in extracurricular activities, tutoring, or bibliotherapy. *P* is for people and positive interpersonal relationships, and treatment may focus on communication skills, how to make friends, and involvement with a Big Brother or Boy Scouts. The *I* stands for images and interests; that is, a positive self-image and a variety of interests or hobbies. *N* is for need to know; that is, self-awareness and knowledge of one's attitudes and beliefs. Treatment here involves correcting negative or irrational attitudes and may include self-talk training. Finally, *G* represents guidance of behaviors. The treatment techniques used in this mode may include behavioral rehearsal, behavior contracting, problem-solving skills, and accepting responsibilities and consequences.

The multimodal approach provides a systematic way for the counselor to explain treatment to parents and to children in the group. For example, children of divorcing families may have poor eating habits and sleeping problems (H); feelings of anger, depression, guilt, loneliness, and rejection (E); declining school performance (L); social network changes, resulting from a move to a new neighborhood (P); loss of identity (I); irrational thoughts about self or parents (N); and changes in behavior (G).

The counselor serves as a guide as the group explores divorce through the HELPING perspective. Multimodal divorce groups have the following objectives: to facilitate interaction and support among participants; to provide realistic facts pertaining to divorce; to promote recognition, clarification, and understanding of emotions stemming from the divorce; and to help participants confront and cope with problems arising from divorce, deal with family and peer relationships, develop positive self-images, broaden their range of interests, and replace maladaptive behavior patterns with more positive behaviors.

TREATMENT: The program consists of eight weekly sessions, each comprised of an icebreaker, a stimulus activity, and a closing time.

In session one, youngsters are given 5 X 7 cards and pens to write their names and several specific things about themselves, such as a favorite thing to do, a favorite TV show or star, favorite foods, or favorite colors. The children then break into pairs and use the cards to interview each other. The group then reconvenes, and the dyads introduce each other to the group. The stimulus activity is a group discussion to develop group goals. The closing time is used to discuss issues of rules and confidentiality. Children are assigned their week for sharing time, and each child is given a copy of *The Boys and Girls Book About Divorce* by Richard A. Gardner (New York: Bantam, 1970) and asked to read as much as he can by the next meeting.

In session two, "Divorce and Feelings," the children begin by talking about the person with whom they identify most, the feeling with which they identify most, or the behavior with which they identify most. The main activity is a discussion of the book, with emphasis on the feelings that come with divorce. The group members then make a poster depicting the feelings; and each person fills in "feeling gauges," which indicate how much of the relevant feelings–such as sadness, guilt, and anger –the person has experienced during the divorce. In the closing time, the rest of Gardner's book is assigned, one child leads sharing time, and refreshments are served.

Session three is "Divorce and What to Do About It." In the icebreaker the children divide paper into four spaces and write or draw something they like to do alone, something they like to do with friends, something they like to do with their family, and something they like to do with one parent. They share this information with the group. In the stimulus activity, the rest of Gardner's book is discussed, with special emphasis on recognizing and admitting one's feelings. Next, the children generate some problems in divorce. They then brainstorm possible solutions and role-play some if there is time. The leader discusses the importance of "regulating their emotions and lives through proper sleep, daily exercise, and nutritional food." Finally, they practice expressing their feelings to other children in the group, using sentence stems such as "One way I can make myself feel better is . . . ," "When I feel angry I . . . ," and "If someone is lonely he can. . . ." The closing time is the standard sharing time and refreshments. As a homework assignment, the children are asked to tell another person, at least once every day, how they feel.

Session four is "Talking About Divorce." Children draw a self-portrait for the icebreaker. The stimulus activity is the "Acting, Feeling, Choosing Game," in which cards (containing sentences such as "What do you do when you're upset? What else can you do?" "What makes you mad about the divorce?" "If you had a choice of parents to play with, which one would you choose?") are used to promote discussion and role playing of various aspects related to divorce. In the closing time, each child is given three blank cards and is asked to make additions to the "Acting, Feeling, Choosing Game" for homework.

In session five, the children list positive statements about themselves on the portraits they made the previous week. They share these with the group, and the group can add to each child's list. The "Acting, Feeling, Choosing Game" is used again as the main activity, starting with the new cards by the children.

For homework, the children are asked to increase their lists of positive self-statements and to say something complimentary to another person each day.

Session six begins with each participant drawing a family portrait and describing it to the group. The filmstrip *Understanding Changes in the Family: Not Together Anymore* (Guidance Associates, 1973) is shown. The children take turns role playing the parts in the filmstrip, including possible solutions to problems depicted in it. The leader then discusses the benefits of sharing personal concerns with friends and family members. Homework for this session is for each child to share his divorce experience with a close friend.

In session seven, the children write positive statements about their families on the back of their family portraits and discuss how it feels to be a part of a family. The program *Breakup* from the *Inside-Out* series (National Instructional Television Center, 1973) is shown. In the discussion that follows, the leader writes down the children's ideas on how to cope with divorce. For homework, each child is to talk to at least one family member about the divorce.

In the final session, the children make posters of the HELPING symbol by writing down their ideas, words, or symbols for each of the letters. Each child shows his poster to the group, and the leader points out how each is unique. The stimulus activity is a round-robin discussion in which each member responds to statements such as "I learned . . . ," "I feel . . . ," "I wish I could . . . ," "Divorce makes life different by. . . ." The session closes with a party.

COMMENTARY: This multimodal program is accepted well by parents and the children because it is treated as an adjunct therapy to the classroom, in the same way speech and hearing therapy are. Most of the school programs for children of divorce use this matter-of-fact approach.

The article provides a detailed description of each session, making it an informative and practical resource for the therapist who does not have much group experience. The HELPING acronym is useful in designing educational or developmental groups that address other problem areas because it assures that all aspects of the problem are included in treatment.

SOURCE: Green, B. J. "Helping Children of Divorce: A Multimodal Approach." *Elementary School Guidance and Counseling,* 1978, *12,* 31-45.

Client-Centered Education-Support Group

AUTHORS: Louise Guerney and Lucy Jordan

PRECIS: A community-based and community-sponsored education-support group formed to help children adjust to their parents' separation or divorce

INTRODUCTION: Recognizing that parents going through a divorce or separation are often emotionally exhausted and unable to provide emotional support for their children, community service groups felt that the children of these parents, whether or not they appeared to be exhibiting adjustment problems, should be provided with support to prevent or resolve conflicts arising from the crisis. A preventive, developmental approach was utilized to convey support and personal growth and avoid any implication of pathology. The goals of the group were to help the children develop "realistic appraisals of their own situations" during and following divorce; problem-solving skills in relation to conflicts evolving from divorce; and a positive self-image and a positive image of their parents. The target population was children ten to twelve years old who volunteered to participate.

Group leaders were volunteers who had master's degrees in human behavioral areas and experience in working with children. They were given four training sessions of two and a half hours each, in which a client-centered discussion-leading model was presented. Sessions included extensive role playing. In their role as leaders, they were supposed to "present information, respond empathically, offer nondirective leads, use consensus-reaching techniques, and assist children in generating . . . problem-solving methods."

TREATMENT: The group consisted of nine children, ages nine to thirteen. All the children were living with their mothers, and an average time of one and a half years had elapsed since their parents' divorce. Most of the participants were referred through the local Parents Without Partners. There were two leaders, a male and a female. The group met for six one-hour sessions.

The first half of the opening session consisted of two icebreakers. The second half consisted of generating rules for the meetings, with issues of confidentiality being the main focus. Each member was also given the *The Boys and Girls Book About Divorce* by Richard A. Gardner (New York: Bantam, 1970) with suggested home reading assignments.

Sessions two through five followed a general format of an opening warm-up game, followed by a stimulus film or game and a discussion of the material presented. The stimulus materials included were a grab bag of feelings, which the children acted out and discussed; the filmstrip *Understanding Changes in the Family: Not Together Anymore* (Guidance Associates, 1973); the film *Breakup* from the *Inside-Out* series (National Instructional Television Center, 1973); and cards related to divorce issues from the "Thinking, Feeling, and Doing Game" by Richard A. Gardner (Creative Therapeutics, 1973). The assigned readings from *The Boys and Girls Book About Divorce* were also discussed in relation to the children's own experiences. Refreshments were served after each session.

The final session was primarily an evaluation session, in which the children gave feedback in a structured discussion.

COMMENTARY: The leaders perceived the children as surprisingly open about discussing their feelings—possibly because two members, who were quite verbal and adjusted to their parents' divorce, acted as models for the rest of the group. Thus, if one can control placement, it would be helpful to include a couple of children who are in advanced stages of adjustment to serve as models for the children. The leaders also observed that most of these children had accepted their life situation and used the group to integrate their thoughts and feelings rather than for actual problem solving.

Community organizers of the program found that, despite a recognized need for this type of group, it was underutilized by the community. Because of schedule conflicts, some parents who had made initial contacts did not have their children participate. To circumvent this problem, perhaps community organizers need to motivate parents more, or perhaps meetings could be held at school, so that parents would not have to provide transportation. The community organizers were planning to develop a speakers bureau and public education services to sensitize the general public to the needs of children of divorce.

SOURCE: Guerney, L., and Jordan, L. "Children of Divorce—A Community Support Group." *Journal of Divorce,* 1979, *2,* 283-294.

Process and Technique of Counseling Children of Divorce

AUTHORS: Mary Sonnenshein-Schneider and Kay L. Baird

PRECIS: A program for elementary school counselors to use with groups of children whose parents are divorced

INTRODUCTION: The authors offer guidelines on developing group counseling sessions for school counselors. First of all, they suggest that the counselor have individual meetings with parents to secure permission for the child's participation in the group and to gather relevant facts about the divorce. The counselor can use this information later to verify the child's stories and confront fantasies. The authors state that most parents willingly relinquish their child for therapy, since they feel drained by the divorce but are aware that the child needs support in adjusting to the new situation. Almost every child affected by divorce desires group membership and will work hard to convince a reluctant parent to let him participate.

The authors recommend that any child whose parents are divorced or separated should be allowed to participate. The group should not be restricted to those showing overt problems, since it has a preventive as well as a remedial effect. All children experience bad feelings about divorce and are faced with the new knowledge that their parents are not perfect; thus, all of them can profit from the group.

The group should last twenty to thirty minutes, which allows enough time to discuss one subject but does not overtax the children's attention span. For younger children (grades one and two), fifteen to twenty minutes is recommended.

TREATMENT: In conducting sessions, the counselor structures group interaction for Piaget's Concrete Operational Stage, during which understanding is achieved through the interaction of the conceptual and the concrete. The counselor presents an initial stimulus to introduce the topic for the discussion. For example, drawings of the family or a filmstrip may be used to generate discussion. The initial stimulation period should be brief and to the point; it is not a lecture but a stimulus for discussion.

The counselor should be flexible in facilitating discussion. For example, the counselor may hand a child puppets to act out a situation that is distressing. When a group member expresses a problem, the group should brainstorm possible solutions. The children then use puppets or role-play to rehearse the act of asking for what they want. For example, one boy was unhappy because, when he visited his father, his father's girlfriend was always there. The first solutions presented by the children were empathic fantasies filled with revenge. They suggested poisoning the girlfriend or introducing her to a handsome young man.

(According to the authors, this is a healthy, therapeutic digression that should not be halted by the counselor.) The group finally decided that the boy should bring up the problem with his father and ask for a certain amount of time alone with him, such as two hours. They then rehearsed the scene. Later the boy reported that the idea worked and that his father was impressed with how maturely he had handled the situation.

The authors suggest a variety of techniques, such as movies, storybooks, art projects and writing projects, that can make the discussion more concrete.

COMMENTARY: The authors discuss what processes practitioners should expect from children, how to set up a group, how to deal with issues flexibly, and how to set realistic goals and expectations. They present a group model in which the therapist provides little formal structure and helps the children help each other by guiding their verbal interactions. This model allows children to deal with divorce issues they are concerned with; it promotes self-discovery and autonomy from adults as the children learn problem-solving skills and peer support skills.

SOURCE: Sonnenshein-Schneider, M., and Baird, K. L. "Group Counseling Children of Divorce in the Elementary Schools: Understanding Process and Technique." *Personnel and Guidance Journal,* 1980, *59,* 88-91.

Children's Divorce Groups

AUTHORS: Gary S. Wilkinson and Robert T. Bleck

PRECIS: A detailed description of an eight-session group therapy program for children whose parents are divorced

INTRODUCTION: The authors developed an eight-session program for school counselors to use with small groups of children meeting for an hour to an hour and a half a week. They give a detailed description of the activities of each session and suggest statements to use with the children during different activities. The program attempts to help the child clarify his feelings about the divorce, realize that others are experiencing similar feelings, gain a realistic picture of the divorce experience, and learn new ways of dealing with the feelings associated with divorce.

TREATMENT: The counselor begins session one with a warm-up exercise in which the children repeat as many of each other's names as they can remember. Next, the counselor leads the children in developing group rules, including taking turns, raising hands to talk, and keeping certain things confidential. Then, to help the members become better acquainted with each other, the counselor asks the children to write down a secret on a piece of paper. The counselor models several responses. The secrets are collected and read by the counselor, who discusses similarities and differences.

The second session is designed to help the children feel comfortable talking to each other. The themes are nonstressful and focus on self-awareness. The children draw an animal that is like them in some way, and again the counselor models a response. They then share their pictures and give reasons why they selected a particular animal. In the last half of the session, the group makes a list of pleasant feelings and unpleasant feelings.

The third session begins with the filmstrip *Understanding Changes in the Family: Not Together Anymore* (Guidance Associates, 1973), which presents many of the feelings children experience in relation to their parents' divorce. In a discussion that follows, the counselor guides the children in recognizing the feeling-behavior-consequence sequence by asking, "What did that feeling make you do?" and "What happened as a result of what you did?"

In the fourth session, the children are given a piece of paper shaped like a shield and instructed to draw four pictures on it: a picture about a good time they had with their families, a picture about an unpleasant time they had with their families, a picture of why they think their parents got divorced, and a picture of something they would like to see happen to their families in the next year. The counselor asks for volunteers to share their pictures and uses the pictures to discuss concerns and fantasies the children associate with divorce.

In the fifth session, the children are directed to brainstorm and list problems related to divorce. They then rank the problems and decide on two or three that are most important to the group. The counselor then structures role playing of the problem situations. The group members discuss the characters, and the counselor focuses on the characters' feelings, behaviors, and consequences. In the following meeting, the group uses puppets to act out the situations role-played the week before and new ones. Group members suggest alternative ways of dealing with the problems being played out.

In the seventh meeting, the counselor discusses positive aspects of divorce, such as less fighting in the home, getting to know parents better, and being able to invite friends over without being embarrassed by their parents' fighting. The children use magazines to cut out pictures that represent positive aspects of divorce and make a collage. The group then discusses the situations portrayed in the collages. In the eighth and final session, the counselor defines feedback and leads the group members in giving positive feedback to each member, such as a feature or behavior that they like about the child. Each member is then asked to relate things he has learned in the group. The counselor summarizes and leads a discussion on ending the group.

COMMENTARY: The advantage of a developmental approach to a group of this type is that it is preventive in nature and does not stigmatize the children as having a problem. In fact, the group dispels stigmas the children have about divorce and shows them that their situation is not unique. The children also learn new ways of coping with the problems and feelings associated with divorce.

SOURCE: Wilkinson, G. S., and Bleck, R. T. "Children's Divorce Groups." *Elementary School Guidance and Counseling,* 1977, *11,* 205-213.

Court-Mandated Group for Children of Divorcing Parents

AUTHOR: David M. Young

PRECIS: Preventive-educational workshop for adolescents of divorcing parents

INTRODUCTION: The family court in an Indiana community was concerned that, despite the rising divorce rate over the last several years, there were no community support services for the children of divorcing parents. Because the family and friends of these youngsters try to protect them from the situation and refuse to discuss it honestly and openly, many children of divorcing parents are later referred to mental health agencies in the community for problems related to their parents' separation. The court mandated that the children of parents seeking a divorce through the court attend a predivorce workshop designed to prepare the children for coping with the emotional aspects of their parents' separation. The focus of this preventive program was to sensitize the adolescents to their emotional and social reactions to the divorce and to help them understand the needs and problems their parents were experiencing.

A program was developed for seven- to eleven-year-old children and another for twelve- to seventeen-year-olds. This particular article describes the program for the older children.

TREATMENT: The half-day workshop was mandatory for adolescents aged twelve to seventeen. There were approximately seven participants and one leader in the group. There was no fee charged to participants.

The leader began the day's activities by having each member fill out a name tag and introducing himself and the day's agenda. He acknowledged that, since the group was mandatory, many of the members probably did not want to be there and that these feelings were natural. To build group cohesiveness, the leader asked the group members to identify themselves and tell what they liked to do for fun. The leader modeled a response to the task with his own response and asked each person questions related to his stated interests.

The leader then led a group discussion based on three questions: "(1) Why do you think you're here? (2) What do you think divorce is? and (3) How do families and people change when there is a divorce?" In this twenty-minute discussion, the leader called on only those participants who were willing to be involved and facilitated the discussion by raising issues and providing examples.

The next activity was a fifteen-minute film about the problems of a girl, Andy, whose parents were divorced. The leader introduced the film to the participants and warned them that it might provoke strong feelings. He added that these feelings were normal and would be discussed after the movie. The film was *Family Matters (What Is a Family)* (Agency for Instructional Television, 1975). After the film the following questions were discussed: "(1) If you were to tell a friend about the film, what would you say? (2) What is the most important message? (3) Should Andy have invited both her parents to the swim meet [an important conflict in the film]? (4) How did Andy and each of her parents handle the divorce, and what could each of them have done to make things better? (5) Compare the divorce in Diane's family to the one in Andy's family. How did the two girls help each other? (6) What needs did Andy have that were not being met, and how did she try to meet them? Was she successful?" The discussion lasted fifteen to twenty minutes. At this point there was a ten-minute break for refreshments and informal conversation.

The next phase was a didactic presentation by the leader

on the variety of feelings and reactions to parental separation based on Richard A. Gardner's *The Boys and Girls Book About Divorce* (New York: Bantam, 1970). Eight reactions were presented: "(1) experiencing loss of control over parents' behavior, (2) feeling sadness, (3) being disappointed in parents, (4) feeling ashamed, (5) feeling that parents will stop loving you, (6) being angry, (7) feeling guilty (self-blame), (8) blaming one parent." When presenting each feeling, the leader noted that the feeling is common for young people and parents to experience, that it is okay and natural to experience those feelings, and that it is important to talk about ways of sharing and dealing with those reactions under discussion. The leader encouraged questions and presented problem-solving strategies for each of the eight emotional reactions presented.

COMMENTARY: Preworkshop questionnaires indicated that most of the adolescents had negative or neutral feelings about attending the workshop, with older youngsters being more resistant than the younger ones. The strongest indicator of the participants' feelings about the workshop was their report of their parents' attitude toward the workshop. Thus, it may be helpful for anyone developing a similar group to enlist the cooperation and support of the parents. The pretest also indicated that those children who were most worried about their parents' divorce were also experiencing more feelings of guilt and self-blame than those who were less worried. Despite their initial attitude toward the workshop, the majority of the adolescents reported that the workshop was useful, particularly because of the supportiveness of the group.

SOURCE: Young, D. M. "A Court-Mandated Workshop for Adolescent Children of Divorcing Parents: A Program Evaluation." *Adolescence,* 1980, *15,* 763-774.

Additional Readings

Hancock, E. "The Dimensions and Meaning of Divorce." *American Journal of Orthopsychiatry,* 1980, *50,* 18-28.

This article describes the pervasive impact of divorce on adults and children. It provides valuable insights into parental behavior and personality changes that affect children. Though the effect of divorce on children changes with developmental level, Hancock notes that divorce causes identity confusion in children because their identity, roles, and sense of meaning and belonging are dependent on the family social unit. This article is recommended reading for anyone involved in therapy of divorced adults or children of divorce.

Schofield, H. A. "Divorced Kids' Group." *Children in Crisis,* 1981, *1,* 7.

A self-help support group where high school students affected by divorce can discuss their feelings and problems has been operating for several years. Members of this group go to other schools to help them start groups and to community meetings to sensitize the public to facts and myths about divorce. Assertiveness training exercises are used to develop coping skills.

Shy, Withdrawn Children

Shy children have a high incidence of school adjustment problems, including poor peer relations, poor self-concept, and poor relations with adults. In individual therapy these children may defeat their therapist through overcompliance and constriction. In group interaction, however, the youngster is thrust into varied situations where his anger is provoked and can be expressed more easily and directly without fear of an adult. Group therapy exposes the youngster to the positive aspects of socialization and provides safe opportunities for interaction. The child learns by watching others and discovers that he can receive social rewards by initiating action and making decisions. He learns and experiments at his own pace. Even the most shy youngster responds to the group contagion involved in play projects.

Token Reinforcement with Shy, Withdrawn Boys

AUTHORS: Paul W. Clement and D. Courtney Milne

PRECIS: Improving social approach behaviors of shy, withdrawn boys through token reinforcement in group play therapy

INTRODUCTION: This article describes a research study instituted to determine the therapeutic effects of group play therapy. The authors, themselves therapists, attempted to answer the following questions: (1) Within the context of group play therapy, what combination of experiences produces the largest number of changes in behavior and in emotional state? (2) Will an approach that includes tangible rewards for reinforcement of preselected behavior lead to more change than an approach where tangible rewards are excluded?

The authors ran three groups of boys referred for socially withdrawn and maladjusted behavior, and proposed that behavioral group therapy would increase productivity in school, improve self-concept and social adjustment, and decrease problem behavior.

TREATMENT: Eleven boys between eight and nine years old with IQs ranging from 80 to 123 participated in the study. They had been referred by their teachers at the request of the authors, who administered psychological tests to determine whether the boys needed treatment. Mothers were a part of the screening and were seen in guidance groups while their boys were seen in therapy.

The boys were randomly assigned to three groups. The Token Group, with four members, met with the therapist for play group therapy once a week for fifty minutes. They received verbal reinforcement and brass tokens for social approach behavior, either walking toward a boy or talking to a boy. The tokens could be exchanged for candy, trinkets, or small toys at the end of the therapy hour. Initially, verbal interactions were shaped by giving tokens for single words; in the middle of therapy, the child had to speak short phrases to get a token; and in the final weeks, the child had to say complete sentences to be reinforced. A variable-interval reinforcement schedule was used throughout treatment.

The four boys in the Verbal Group received the same treatment and verbal reinforcement that the Token Group did, but they received no tangible reinforcers. The Control Group included three children who met weekly in a playroom with no therapist and received no treatment.

RESULTS: At the end of fourteen weeks of treatment, according to ratings by observers, the Token Group showed more improvement in social approach behavior than the Verbal Group, and the Verbal Group showed more improvement than the Control Group, which showed no change. The Token Group also showed a decrease in problem behavior. All the groups failed to show any change in productivity, anxiety, and psychological adjustment. However, the group had met for only a short time, and the boys were not overanxious to begin with and were apparently working up to their abilities in school before treatment began.

COMMENTARY: It is not surprising that no differences were found in anxiety, psychological adjustment, or productivity, since play therapy by its very nature is more long term than the fourteen weeks of this study. The boys might have improved in these areas if the authors had run the groups longer, although the improvement in social approach behavior is certainly an accomplishment after only fourteen hours of treatment.

According to the authors, the mothers rated their sons as more improved in all areas than did teachers or observers. Although the mothers may have rated their sons higher because they knew they were in treatment, as in the Hawthorne effect, this knowledge may also have sensitized them to noticing more positive behaviors in their sons. Also, the involvement of the mothers in a guidance group may have made them feel more effective as mothers and less critical or less easily upset by the boys' problem behaviors.

SOURCE: Clement, P. W., and Milne, D. C. "Group Play Therapy and Tangible Reinforcers Used to Modify the Behavior of 8-Year-Old Boys." *Behaviour Research and Therapy,* 1967, *5,* 301-312.

Activity Therapy for a Withdrawn Girl

AUTHORS: John C. Coolidge and Margaret Galdston Grunebaum

PRECIS: Treatment for a withdrawn and school-phobic child in individual and activity group therapy

INTRODUCTION: Although mental health clinics commonly use individual therapy to treat latency-age children, Coolidge and Grunebaum suggest that a group approach might be more useful for these peer-oriented youngsters. In the peer group, the child senses more tolerance for trial-and-error learning of new skills and regression than with adults. Also, the child is immediately rewarded for giving up inappropriate behaviors by closer bonding with the group. The authors describe a case in which individual therapy alone could not break through the defenses of a withdrawn girl.

TREATMENT: Ellen, a five-and-a-half-year-old child, had school-phobic symptoms of vomiting and nausea, was dependent on her mother, and had no friends. Her parents had emigrated from Europe following war experiences. Neither was a secure person, and both had had unhappy relationships with their parents. While pregnant with Ellen, the mother developed severe toxemia, and a hemorrhage at seven months had necessitated a caesarean section. The three-pound Ellen was in the hospital for seven weeks and was hospitalized repeatedly for anemia in the first few months of life. She had had feeding and sleeping problems since infancy, and both had become sources of arguments between mother and child. The parents kept Ellen away from other children as a child for fear she would catch germs. By four, she had not played with other children, and at that time her brother, Jonathon, was born.

Both mother and child were seen in individual therapy. Mrs. C., the mother, gained much insight into her own behavior through therapy, revealing that her own mother had been restrictive, that she herself had never been socially adept, and that she had had the same symptoms of nausea and vomiting coming to therapy that her child manifested on school mornings. As she progressed, she was able to allow Ellen more freedom. As a result, Ellen became confronted with her peer problems more often.

In two years of therapy, Ellen became less anxious and restricted and more able to express some of her angry feelings through play. Her school attendance improved, and therapy was discontinued with both mother and child. A year later, Mrs. C. returned and reported that Ellen was listless, complained about school, and had no friends. Ellen was again seen in individual therapy. Although she did not reveal her conflicts in play or verbalization, the therapist concluded that she wanted to have friends but was afraid of peers and unable to risk losing her overdependent relationship with her mother. She was placed in activity therapy, in the hope that group interaction might mobilize conflictive material that she would bring back and discuss in individual therapy.

Once she was in the group, her behavior did begin to change. However, since she did not bring any material into individual therapy, it was discontinued and she remained in group therapy.

The group had five other girls in it, and the members' problems were counterbalanced. For example, Ellen's rigid defense patterns were chosen to off set the impulsivity of another girl. For the first time, Ellen was entering a continuing social situation where she would be in close proximity to a group of girls. She was so anxious that it took her weeks to learn their names. Ellen tended to play by herself with crayons and paper, but she closely watched the other girls, who were more active in testing the leader and expressing conflict with each other. Ellen learned vicariously through the actions of others, and they soon drew Ellen into the group. The therapist counted on this tendency of the group to draw a peripheral member into it.

RESULTS: Ellen made clear progress during the group therapy: at first withdrawing from the group when she became angry, then being aggressive with play materials, and eventually being able to confront other girls and demand that they comply with the rules. She became more casual and less restrictive in her behavior, was able to negotiate for what she wanted, and made friends with girls in the group and elsewhere.

COMMENTARY: The authors conclude that group therapy is useful for children like Ellen, whose emotional trauma is preverbal in origin and who are unable to verbalize the anxiety they experience. Individual therapy does not improve such a problem, but the group provides a nonthreatening atmosphere where the child can learn at her own pace and by observing others.

SOURCE: Coolidge, J. C., and Grunebaum, M. G. "Individual and Group Therapy of a Latency Age Child." *International Journal of Group Psychotherapy*, 1964, *14*, 84-96.

Assertiveness Training of Shy Children

AUTHORS: Susan D. Leone and Jim Gumaer

PRECIS: Assertiveness training for socially isolated, withdrawn youngsters to improve their relations with peers and decrease their anxiety

INTRODUCTION: Although teachers and counselors are quick to recognize the classroom adjustment problems of acting-out youngsters, they often fail to address the needs of shy and passive youngsters because such youngsters are not a problem in the classroom. The authors note that socially withdrawn children also have adjustment problems, with low self-esteem and high levels of internalized anxiety. This article describes a program that the authors developed to improve these youngsters' assertiveness, self-esteem, and social status in the classroom and to decrease their anxiety.

TREATMENT: Teachers were asked by the school counselor to refer children to the group who did not initiate discussions with others, did not ask for help, and did not participate in class discussion. Eleven children were selected and agreed to participate. Their parents were notified of the group, and all agreed to their children's participation. The children were divided into two groups and were seen in eighteen weekly forty-minute sessions. Specific plans consisting of objectives, structured activities, and recommended counselor responses were used in each session.

The first session was used to get acquainted and review the goals of the group. Members were then asked to draw their favorite animal and write their name on the animal. They were asked to introduce themselves to the group and discuss their reasons for choosing that animal. As expected, children were reluctant to participate verbally and needed encouragement from the counselor. The counselor posted the pictures on the board in the meeting room and ended the session by reviewing the purposes of the group, stating that they were all there to learn to work and play better with other children. They could learn these things, he said, by talking about their thoughts and feelings in the group; therefore, at the next meeting they would receive candy each time they made verbal contributions in the meeting.

The children were given a small piece of candy and verbal reinforcement every time they made an appropriate verbal response. As they interacted more, a variable-ratio schedule of reinforcement was introduced in session four. By session eight, the use of candy to reinforce interaction was phased out.

In sessions two through twelve, the meetings began with an audiotaped relaxation exercise followed by a guided fantasy. The tapes were used to help the children learn to relax and be comfortable in the group and to become more aware of their thoughts and feelings. In one guided fantasy, for example, the children were instructed to imagine they were a ball, lying in the grass. Children come and pick the ball up, throw it high in the air, and finally put it down in the grass and go inside. With each instruction, the counselor encouraged the children to be aware of how they felt as the ball, being held, thrown in the air, then left alone. Following the guided fantasy, the children discussed their thoughts and feelings about the fantasy.

In session three, the counselor discussed how one's own behavior affects the behavior of others, with some outcomes that are pleasant and some that are unpleasant. The counselor then asked the children what behaviors they might want to change. He said that behavioral contracts might be useful in the group to help members change their behavior. The behavior contracts drawn up focused on the children's assertiveness with parents, teachers, and classmates. To complete the contract successfully, a child had to perform the behavior—such as asking parents' permission for a special favor or activity, asking a teacher for help with schoolwork, or asking a classmate to play with him—and have the appropriate person sign the contract. Children who successfully completed their contracts were awarded ten minutes of free time after the session; children who were unsuccessful returned directly to their classroom after the session.

In sessions four through six, the children saw videotapes of children modeling assertive and nonassertive interactions. They discussed assertive and nonassertive behaviors and feelings of the models. In the next three sessions, the children role-played the same situations they had seen on the tapes and were encouraged to interpret and act the underlying feelings in the tape, such as anger and rejection. As a result, the children began disclosing similar feelings and experiences. In sessions ten and eleven, the children were taped as they role-played the situations, reviewed the tapes, and compared their behavior with the models.

By session thirteen, it was no longer necessary to plan activities to stimulate discussion, since the children were introducing their own topics and problems to role-play and discuss. They asked to continue the relaxation tapes and behavior contracting through the rest of the meetings.

RESULTS: The results showed that children in the groups perceived themselves in a more positive way and were rated by teachers as being considerably more assertive in class. The children's popularity with peers also improved. Their overall anxiety was reduced, but not significantly. The authors propose that the activities of this peer group—exploring new skills of relating to people and talking about personal feelings—were anxiety producing; therefore, even if their anxiety remained high, it seemed encouraging that the children had learned to relax enough to try new ways of behaving.

COMMENTARY: Assertiveness training can be an effective method of teaching shy children the skills necessary to interact successfully with peers and adults in the school setting. This method is less threatening to these children than individual counseling and can reach more children cost-effectively. Also, the schools can identify and remediate children in the school for problems that the parents may not be concerned with or may not be able to seek professional help for.

SOURCE: Leone, S. D., and Gumaer, J. "Group Assertiveness Training of Shy Children." *School Counselor,* 1979, *27,* 134-141.

Activity Group Therapy with a Socially Isolated Boy

AUTHORS: Leslie Rosenthal and Leo Nagelberg

PRECIS: Using activity group therapy to help a shy youngster express repressed hostilities and tensions that interfered with building age-appropriate friendships

INTRODUCTION: Henry, a socially isolated boy of eight and a half, had academic difficulties, refused to go outside to play, would not greet relatives, and preferred to play with girls younger than himself. At camp, just prior to referral, he was described as extremely infantile, provocative, withdrawn, and enuretic. After three weeks at camp, he still had not learned his counselor's or bunkmate's name.

Henry was born prematurely, at six months into the pregnancy, and was incubated for two months. The mother, a rigid, domineering person, had overprotected Henry all his life. She underplayed Henry's difficulties and blamed them on the school. His father worked late hours as a waiter and spent little time with the boy.

TREATMENT: Henry was referred to activity group therapy because it offered a nonthreatening, growth-producing atmosphere and provided needed opportunities for masculine identification. His mother was seen in individual therapy.

In initial sessions Henry behaved provocatively—for instance, mimicking another member of the group—but was unable to defend himself against the attacks he elicited. He would walk close to the wall of the room, as if guarding against attacks. However, he expressed intense liking for the group and marked all his meetings on the calendar for a year in advance. At the close of the first season in therapy, he was still provocative and infantile; he did not work constructively, leaving projects half finished and smearing paint instead.

By the end of the first year, he had made one friend and expressed interest in going to camp. He had also fought with another boy and told his mother she bossed him too much. At this point, because the treatment supervisor believed that he was exhibiting schizoid behavior, Henry was enrolled in individual therapy. He did not like it and stopped going, but continued his involvement in the group. Psychological testing revealed that he had normal intelligence but preferred to act four years younger than his age.

In the second year of treatment, Henry sought the help of the therapist on arts and crafts projects, and also tested his permissiveness. Since the therapist remained calm and neutral, Henry developed a strong positive transference with him. He continued to remain on the periphery of the group but began to engage in short periods of aggressive, masculine play, such as batting and King of the Mountain. His smearing of paint ceased. He began to accept invitations to play games with others. At camp he introduced his mother to his friends. At home he went to the playground by himself and greeted relatives by name. Henry was able to relate to others in a variety of situations; but he still tended to act withdrawn, was unable to defend himself physically, and when frustrated or anxious would destructively pound on the walls, tables, and doors with saws and hammers.

By his fourth year in treatment, at age thirteen, he appeared to have reached a plateau. His school performance had improved; his resentment of authority was gone, and he had good relationships with teachers and relatives; he relinquished infantile play for age-appropriate masculine games; and he had a better self-concept. However, he still manifested a detached quality in peer relationships; he remained introverted and destructive of materials in the group; when under pressure he sought refuge in a make-believe world; and he had paranoid fears. The group leaders felt that his powerful regressive drives could be resolved only in interpretive therapy. Therefore, he was referred for individual therapy with a diagnosis of character disorder with schizoid or borderline features.

COMMENTARY: Activity therapy was not completely successful for Henry because he was more disturbed than the therapist had realized initially; yet he did make vast improvements in the group. The authors note that Henry's ambivalent feelings toward the group—liking it intensely but acting provocatively—reenacted his need to repeat his premature expulsion from the womb and his ambivalent feelings toward his mother of dependence-independence strivings. The therapist's understanding of this phenomenon prevented the enactment of negative countertransference feelings in working with Henry.

SOURCE: Rosenthal, L., and Nagelberg, L. "Limitations of Activity Therapy: A Case Presentation." *International Journal of Group Psychotherapy,* 1956, *6,* 166-179.

Community-Based Treatment of Withdrawal

AUTHORS: Joseph C. Solomon and Pearl L. Axelrod

PRECIS: Activity group therapy for socially isolated, neurotic girls who were resistant to individual therapy

INTRODUCTION: This paper describes a therapy group for withdrawn, anxious girls who, Solomon and Axelrod propose, were unable to form appropriate relationships with peers because serious disturbances in their home settings consumed all their emotional energy. The girls were considered emotionally disturbed but had refused individual treatment. The group was designed to help members make more adequate social adjustment by providing structured, supportive experiences in interpersonal relationships.

TREATMENT: Eleven withdrawn, neurotic teenage girls participated in the group. They all presented the common symptoms of "being nervous, socially shy, hermitlike, and unable to make friends." They exhibited various neurotic habits, such as obsessiveness and overcompliance with adults, and all had problems in adjustments with family members. They ranged in age from thirteen to fifteen, and their IQs ranged from 85 to 115.

The group was led by a female caseworker. A leader of the same sex was chosen because these girls had problems with basic social relationships and family relationships, and the use of a therapist of the opposite sex might stir heterosexual feelings that would complicate the group process. A male psychiatrist acted as consultant, and a female recreation assistant provided technical advice. The hour-long sessions were held once a week in a local community center.

The girls were initially interviewed by the leader, who described the activity group for shy girls and invited them to participate. All the girls expressed an interest to join in order to overcome their withdrawal and improve their social relationships. The leader obtained information on the girls' interests and a background history.

At the first meeting, craft materials and simple games were provided, and the girls were told they could do as they pleased. For more than thirty minutes, no one spoke; then, when conversation did take place, it was limited to individual contacts between the girls and the therapist. There was a sense of competition as all the girls worked on craft projects and wanted to gain praise from the therapist. At the second meeting, one girl asked another what school she attended, and the therapist was able to draw others into this conversation. By the eighth meeting, the girls began clustering together in groups of two or three, but they still worked on their projects individually and had minimal conversation. They asked to meet for a longer period of time, and the sessions were extended to ninety minutes.

For five months the girls worked on crafts; then they gradually shifted to play small-group games. They began to have discussions in the group. The girls decided to have a party and wrote a play to present to the therapist. The play involved inhuman creatures such as zombies and a lot of aggression.

The girls began discussing adolescent problems such as insecurity with boys, dating, and makeup. The therapist interpreted information related to the immediate group process but avoided interpretations regarding an individual's personal problems. When a girl's personal problems caused problems in the group and needed to be resolved, the therapist made secret appointments by sending a note in the mail and meeting the girl at her office in a clinic.

After six months of meetings, the girls discarded crafts and games entirely in favor of social activities. They spent two weeks together at camp. When they returned, they formed a club and chose a club name, song, and colors. They worked hard to redecorate and paint their meeting room with the club colors. They began to invite visitors to club meetings, and they voted two new members into the group. Most of the girls also became involved in extracurricular activities at school; and they attended parties and double-dated together. When the girls requested more evening activities, the leader suggested that her part in the group was over and that they were ready to transfer to a recreation worker and continue their own interests at the community center. The girls readily agreed to this change.

RESULTS: By the end of eight months of treatment in activity group therapy, all but three of the girls had made significant progress and were considered normal, well-adjusted teenagers.

COMMENTARY: In this group the craft activities gave the girls ego satisfactions and provided a distancing factor, so that they could observe each other and begin to interact at their own pace. The permissive attitude of the leader and positive acceptance by other members gave the girls a sense of belonging and security that they had never experienced before, even in their own families. The opportunity to discuss adolescent problems with peers was also a first for most of the girls. The therapist provided a positive female role model for the girls, several of whom had psychotic mothers and had not formed normal identifications. The interest of some of the girls in their personal appearance motivated less tidy girls to pay more attention to their appearance. Finally, the girls who had resisted individual therapy for fear of the close interpersonal contact with a therapist were given an opportunity to observe adults who were permissive and supportive. These members were then more comfortable with occasional private sessions with the therapist to discuss their personal concerns.

SOURCE: Solomon, J. C., and Axelrod, P. L. "Group Psychotherapy for Withdrawn Adolescents." *American Journal of Diseases of Children,* 1944, *68,* 86-101.

Additional Reading

Soo, E. "The Impact of Activity Group Therapy upon a Highly Constricted Child." *International Journal of Group Psychotherapy,* 1974, *24,* 207-216.

Activity group therapy was provided after individual therapy had failed with a neurotic, effeminate, highly constricted boy. The experience produced symbolic acting out of repressed fantasies and impulses, which released emotional tensions and made more psychic energy available for appropriate ego functioning. Activity group therapy improved the child's peer relations and fostered male identification with the therapist and group members.

Foster and Adopted Children

Foster and adopted children suffer stresses that children from intact families do not experience—stresses that may interfere with their ability to master developmental tasks. Because they are not with their natural families, for whatever reason, they often feel rejected and worthless. The resulting poor self-images and insecurity of these youngsters make it difficult for them to accept and bond with their new parents. Even those foster and adopted children who have adjusted to their new families may suffer from identity confusion. Foster children often react to their situation by adopting an "I don't care" attitude and acting out their frustration, thereby disrupting their placement and their adjustment to school. Adolescent girls in foster care often act out sexually in an attempt to find someone who cares. Some even have babies so that someone will love them. In addition, the unstable, chaotic, and sometimes abusive backgrounds of many foster and adopted children further affect their self-image and ability to trust adults. Group therapy can help these youngsters realize that their situation is not unique. The group provides them with an opportunity to discuss and resolve their mutual concerns and helps solidify positive identifications with their families.

Group Therapy for Foster Children

AUTHORS: Bonnie Burke Ludlow and Norman Epstein

PRECIS: Group sessions instituted by a foster care agency to cope with the counseling needs of foster children

INTRODUCTION: Children in foster care constantly fear their uncertain future and worry about their control over life situations caused by the absence of natural parents and consequent subjection to unpredictable bureaucratic forces. They have vague and amorphous self-images and are hesitant to trust the adults around them. Caseworkers at foster care agencies are often overloaded with cases and barely have time to fill out required reports, much less to provide counseling and emotional support to the child in crisis in the foster care system. Some of the children in the agency described in this article did not have basic information. They did not know why they were in foster care, where their brothers and sisters were, and what social workers do. The agency began group meetings to resolve questions that were causing confusion and anxiety in the children; to acquaint the children with the agency and its services and help them trust the agency; and to permit the children to express their feelings and experiences, so that the agency could get to know the children better. The program was geared toward preadolescents (ten to twelve years old), to prepare them to face the normal storms of adolescence.

TREATMENT: The group consisted of eight members who were relatively free of emotional problems. There was a trained group leader and a coleader, who was being trained to assume leadership later. The group met for eight weekly sessions that were an hour to an hour and a half long.

The agenda was flexible, with a plan to cover certain issues but with no schedule. The children generally introduced the topics they wanted to discuss, and they focused on talking about their natural families, visitation, reasons for placement, and questions about legal issues.

The children did not want to be adopted but did not know how to tell that to their foster parents. Although sympathetic with the problems of foster parents, they were also critical and hostile about the role of the natural children in their foster homes. The children in the group were sensitive to and supportive of each other and formed friendships. When one member was absent, the other children were worried and read disaster in the unknown.

RESULTS: As a result of the group sessions, the children had a better understanding of what they could do and what they could not do vis-à-vis the agency and foster parents, and what they could expect in the future. Because the children were able to share information, problems, and experiences, the trauma of foster care apparently was lessened. Foster parents reported that withdrawn children began to open up and be more assertive at home. Foster parents were also warned about acting-out behavior by some children and were told how to deal with it, and several children were identified as needing more intensive therapy.

COMMENTARY: This group filled an obvious gap in the agency's services and provided a short-term method of alleviating the children's unrealistic worries and preventing later adjustment problems. The group met at the agency's offices, which gave the children greater access to their social workers, who in turn showed more interest in the children and their problems. The children were enthusiastic about the meetings, and the agency discovered that a member's absence was often related to concerns by a foster parent or caseworker that the agency was checking up on him through the children's meetings. The concerns of the foster parents were addressed at later groups.

SOURCE: Ludlow, B. B., and Epstein, N. "Groups for Foster Children." *Social Work,* 1972, *17,* 96-99.

Parallel Groups for Adopted Children and Their Parents

AUTHORS: Reuben Pannor and Evelyn A. Nerlove

PRECIS: Parallel therapy groups instituted for adopted children and their adoptive parents to discuss their concerns and feelings about adoption and improve communication and the relationship between the two groups

INTRODUCTION: The normal storms and stresses of adolescence are magnified and more problematic for adopted children and their adoptive parents. The child's search for identity necessarily leads to the past, making him curious about his natural parents and more vulnerable to feelings of rejection, albeit from people the child never knew. In turn, the adoptive parents often perceive the adolescent's search for his "real" parents as rejection of them. These parents are more anxious than natural parents and less capable of dealing with the stresses of adolescence. They also have great difficulty in accepting their child's independence, perhaps because it reawakens their infertility distress.

The program described in this article was started by the local child welfare service after numerous requests (from adoptive parents, adoption agencies, private therapists, and adopted children) for help with problems related to adoption and adjustment, such as acting-out behaviors, intense identity crisis, and conflicts with adoptive parents and the natural children in the family. The children's group was primarily supportive, providing an opportunity for the children to see that their situation was not unique and that they could express common concerns and feelings without upsetting their adoptive parents. The parents' group was established to help the parents develop insights and self-awareness that would improve their way of relating to the children, to help them see that their situation was not unique and gain support from each other, and to educate them to differentiate the normal problems of attaining independence in adolescents from problems attributable to adoption. The overall goal was to improve the communication between parents and adoptees.

TREATMENT: Eight families with twenty-three adopted children were included in the therapeutic groups. Of the twenty-three children, fourteen were adopted and nonrelated, one was adopted and related, and eight were born to the mothers and adopted by their fathers. They ranged in age from twelve to nineteen. A male and a female therapist met with the parents for the first four weeks. The female therapist met with the parents for the next four weeks while the male therapist met with the children. There was then one session with everyone meeting together, and a final summing-up session for the parents.

In the parents' group, one therapist encouraged participation, promoted an atmosphere of warmth and honesty, and probed for insights and self-awareness. The other therapist provided research data and related his experiences with reunions of birth parents and adoptees. The parents introduced topics of concern for group discussion—topics divided almost evenly between problems of adoption and everyday problems of childrearing. The parents were intensely interested in what might happen to them and their children if the children were reunited with their birth parents. Many of the adoptive parents expressed concerns that the children would prefer their birth parents to them. The therapists reassured the parents that the children were not seeking different parents but simply knowledge about themselves and their origins.

The adolescents also divided their discussion between problems related to adoption and more general concerns about adolescence, such as parent-child problems and how to prevent pregnancy. The therapist attempted to bring out feelings about adoption that the children had not been able to discuss with their parents or other natural groups. It became apparent that the children, sensing that their parents would be upset by their concerns, never talked about them with anyone. They were especially concerned about why they were adopted, what their natural parents looked like, and whether their adoptive parents had any information about their natural parents. Although the adolescents agreed that it was better to be adopted than live with a neglectful or abusive parent, most did not favor the idea of giving a baby up for adoption, which revealed their own feelings about having been given up for adoption.

In the multifamily session, the adolescents made supportive statements to their parents about adoption and asked serious questions about their adoptions. The parents were more comfortable telling the adopted children about their backgrounds and felt less threatened by the birth parents and the childrens' curiosity about them.

COMMENTARY: The authors state that this short-term, educative group experience, which focused on the vulnerability of adoptive families during the adolescence of adoptees, proved helpful to both the adoptive parents and the youngsters. The article suggests a service need for these families that have a high risk of experiencing adjustment problems when the adopted child reaches adolescence. Adoptive agencies generally do not address this need. When counseling new adoptive parents, adoptive agencies could utilize the comments and concerns of adoptive parents in this article and thereby prevent some of the problems that the parents in the group experienced.

SOURCE: Pannor, R., and Nerlove, E. A. "Fostering Understanding Between Adolescents and Adoptive Parents Through Group Experiences." *Child Welfare,* 1977, *56,* 537-545.

Additional Reading

Lee, J. A., and Park, D. N. "A Group Approach to the Depressed Adolescent Girl in Foster Care." *American Journal of Orthopsychiatry,* 1978, *48,* 516-527.

Lee and Park describe a mutual-sharing, problem-solving group for adolescent girls in foster care. The population they treated were black youngsters from poor, unstable neighborhoods in New York City. The main characteristic of the girls was pervasive depression. The anger the girls felt toward their dead or deserted mother was turned inward, resulting in depression and feelings of rejection and worthlessness. The authors observe that many adolescents act out their anger in self-destructive ways by misbehaving in school, not doing work they are capable of, and rejecting even the most loving of foster homes by running away or misbehaving until they are ejected.

The girls in the group were fifteen to eighteen years old and—with the exception of varying degrees of depression and identity confusion related to foster placement—fell within the "normal" range of adolescent adjustment. The group was voluntary, and only girls who were very immature or had more serious psychopathology were excluded. The group met weekly during the school year. The therapist was the girls' social worker. Her role was that of a nurturant mother substitute. She facilitated mutual problem solving among the members by confronting when appropriate, challenging them to find alternatives, directing feelings in the appropriate direction, labeling feelings, and bolstering defenses when discussions got too painful.

A group ego emerged that consisted of the girls' pooled strengths, so that when one member had a problem coping, another was able to provide direction. The group gave the girls an opportunity to think out their ideas with each other and get advice from the group before proceeding. Self-pity and impulsive acting out were replaced by notions of achievement, career planning, and an ability to enjoy life. The group itself gave the girls a feeling of love, sisterhood, and support that made their lives less confusing and more manageable.

4

Intervention Groups for Specific Problems

Problem behaviors in this chapter are more pathological and enduring than those described in the previous chapter and require active involvement and intervention by the therapist(s). Generally, the therapeutic goals are to foster identification with the therapist, so that group members will incorporate the prosocial values the therapist represents. Improved peer relationships, improved self-awareness and awareness of others, an ability to empathize with others, improved problem-solving skills, and improved reality testing are expected to occur as a result of the therapeutic group process.

Since many of the problem behaviors presented here are not clearly delineated in clinical practice, the reader should consult a variety of related sections when considering treatment alternatives. For example, most of the children in this chapter have poor peer relations in conjunction with academic or impulse control problems, and the therapist must decide which approach is more characteristic in the targeted treatment population.

Poor Peer Relations

A crippling deficit for many children is their social ineptness. Learning social skills is a basic developmental task that normally occurs as the child begins to separate from the family group and identifies with his peer group. Forming relationships and resolving conflicts in the peer group prepare the child for responsible involvements in the social groups that are an integral part of adult life at home, at work, and in the community. Social ineptness correlates highly with school maladjustment and childhood emotional difficulties and is predictive of emotional difficulties in adults. The socially inept youngster is unable to compromise or cooperate with peers, lacks flexibility, and is unable to make or keep friends. Although most socially inept youngsters are provocative and aggressive, some are quiet, passive, and withdrawn, with only occasional explosive outbursts. Poor peer relations can develop from overprotective parents who did not allow the child to freely explore his world and become involved with peers, or from an inadequate and chaotic home situation that prevented the child from feeling secure and able to trust others, or from unresolved sibling rivalry conflicts. Group therapy is the treatment of choice for these youngsters, since it is the peer group that the child must ultimately adjust to. The therapy group provides a safe atmosphere in which members learn and practice new skills and are confronted by peers for inappropriate behavior. The group members together develop alternative social behaviors for each other's problem behaviors.

Teaching Social Skills to Socially Inept Youngsters

AUTHORS: Richard P. Allen, Daniel J. Safer, Ronald Heaton, Alice Ward, and Marlene Barrell

PRECIS: Socially ineffective fourth and fifth graders given tangible reinforcers for performing graduated social behaviors

INTRODUCTION: The authors describe socially ineffective children as having "ineptitude in peer relations, inability to make or keep friends, and a lack of ability to compromise with peers." Clinicians have used a number of therapeutic approaches with these children, including behavior modification, modeling, training teachers to promote socialization, and nondirective counseling. The authors' approach makes use of behavior reinforcers and a group forum where children can practice social skills, gain confidence, and transfer the newly learned skills to situations outside the group.

TREATMENT: Youngsters in the fourth and fifth grades of two schools were screened by means of a sociogram. Children who received one or no selections by peers on the sociogram were then rated by their teachers for lack of interpersonal flexibility and lack of ability to cooperate and compromise with peers. A group parent conference was held with the parents of targeted children, to explain the program and obtain consent. Groups with eight members each were formed, and they met weekly for fifty-minute sessions over a period of thirteen to seventeen weeks. The sessions were directed by a school guidance counselor and a mental health technician.

Small plastic chips were used as reinforcement tokens and were given to the children at the end of a timed period. The periods were two to seven minutes long at the beginning and four to nine minutes long in later sessions. The children were told at the beginning of the period what behaviors would be reinforced. They saved their chips in clear plastic cups that were conspicuously mounted in the group meeting room. At the end of the meeting, the chips could be used to purchase small toys or candy.

The first meeting was a free-play session in which the leaders observed and recorded social interaction. The children were given ten tokens each, so that they could sample the reinforcers. The program itself consisted of three phases, each focusing on different and more demanding social skills. In the first phase, children were reinforced for the following behaviors: playing simple games in groups of two, then three and four; changing small-group membership as directed; choosing leaders; acting as leaders and winners; setting rules for games or interactions; competing with other groups; and communicating between groups and a referee. Usually two or three behaviors were targeted for each session and were intermixed over time periods. At the end of each time period, children who were engaged in the behavior received a token.

In the second phase, the youngsters were reinforced for more imaginative, less structured play, such as charades and telling jokes and riddles. They were trained and reinforced for presenting jokes and charades in actual classrooms for other children. They continued to be reinforced for choosing leaders and rules and being leaders. This phase was designed to develop social poise and flexibility in a group situation.

The final phase was designed to transfer the social behaviors learned in the group to situations outside the group. In this phase, tokens were awarded in the group for playground interactions observed by the teacher.

Throughout treatment, children also earned tokens for performing positive, spontaneous group behaviors above the level expected for a particular child—for example, making room in a group for a child sitting by himself.

RESULTS: Sociogram retests showed that 75 percent of the children were more popular with their peers. Also, as indicated by an analysis of a thirty-minute free-play session, the children no longer played by themselves, whereas prior to the treatment they had played by themselves 55 percent of the time. Follow-up studies made five months and twelve months after treatment showed that the children's social progress had persisted.

COMMENTARY: Social ineptness interferes with a child's academic adjustment, keeps him tied to his family, and reinforces a negative self-image. The authors point out that children referred for psychiatric services are three times more likely to be socially ineffective than the incidence found in a regular classroom. A group treatment approach seems the natural method to teach social skills, since it enables the child to practice these skills in a structured, nonpunitive social environment where immediate social reinforcement is given for appropriate behaviors. The participants usually form friendships that endure outside the group.

SOURCE: Allen, R. P., Safer, D. J., Heaton, R., Ward, A., and Barrell, M. "Behavior Therapy for Socially Ineffective Children." *Journal of the American Academy of Child Psychiatry,* 1975, *14,* 500-509.

Seriously Disturbed Latency-Age Boys

AUTHORS: Marv Clifford and Terry Cross

PRECIS: Using play therapy group methods to help seriously disturbed boys in residential treatment improve peer and staff relationships

INTRODUCTION: A therapy group at a residential treatment center enabled group members to improve impulse control and peer relationship skills and to express repressed anger. Play was used as a means of expression, and psychotherapy was used to promote the natural elements of peer group involvement.

TREATMENT: Four boys diagnosed as behavior disordered and one boy diagnosed as borderline psychotic participated in the group. They ranged in age from seven to eleven. They meet weekly for fifty-minute sessions for a period of six months. There were two therapists, the authors. The focus of therapy was on specific "behavior change contracts" for each child. Since the children demonstrated their peer problems in each play session, ample opportunities arose for the therapists to use the group members and the group process to confront the child with the behavior and develop options for change. For example, one boy showed negative behaviors with peers and had few friends. When he encountered peer rejection during group play, the members pointed out why he was rejected and presented options for more positive behavior.

The children developed their own rules: "(1) Don't physically harm another person or yourself. (2) Don't leave the room without permission. (3) Don't swing from the overhead pipes in the room. (4) Don't intentionally break toys, furniture, or the windows. (5) Don't talk about what other children did in the group or said." There was also the "Stop and Go" rule, in which a child or a therapist could tell a youngster to "Stop" if he was breaking a rule or showing inappropriate social behavior, such as taking a toy away from another child. The second child would have to return the toy, and they could resume play when both agreed the incident was over by saying "Go." If a child was unable to stop and control himself after a verbal command, the therapist would hold the child until he calmed down and could resume play. These immediate interventions and discussions with peers raised each child's awareness of how his behavior affected others and gave the therapists cues for other interventions.

RESULTS: The authors conclude that many of the goals were reached. Two boys who had not been making progress in individual therapy began to bring out material stimulated by the group in their individual sessions. One child used the group to work through his anger toward his parents and stimulated similar behavior in others. The boys were able to use the problem-solving skills learned in the group with peer problems that arose in their cottages.

COMMENTARY: The "Stop and Go" technique is a powerful method to use with children, since they can immediately confront a child who is interfering with their play. As the authors note, it also alerts the therapist to problems as they arise. The rule also gives the children a sense of fair play and protection.

SOURCE: Clifford, M., and Cross, T. "Group Therapy for Seriously Disturbed Boys in Residential Treatment." *Child Welfare,* 1980, *59,* 560-565.

Improving Social Skills Through Guided Interaction with Adjusted Peers

AUTHORS: Josephine R. Hilgard, Donald C. Staight, and Ursula S. Moore

PRECIS: A therapeutic summer camp where adolescent boys with major problems relating to people participated with well-adjusted boys

INTRODUCTION: Research has demonstrated the success of using well-adjusted peers to develop social skills in the less adjusted. The inclusion of more integrated peers adds ego strength to the group that counters and controls the impulsiveness of the less well-adjusted members.

The authors describe six severely withdrawn boys who had been enrolled for two years in "affiliative therapy," where they had developed strong, positive relationships with college students. The boys had made marked progress in relating to adults but were still unable to build relationships with peers.

Therefore, the authors devised an eight-week summer program that would bring these boys in contact with well-adjusted peers to develop their social skills.

TREATMENT: Two types of "adjusted" peers were selected: the first was a clear-cut leadership type who excelled in all sports, was friendly, and had a sense of humor; the second was a friendly type who was less skilled in sports but willing to try and also had a good sense of humor. Two of each of the two types were included with the group of six withdrawn boys.

The purpose of the group, as explained to the boys, was to study how communication can be developed among individuals who are quite different. No distinction was made between adjusted and unadjusted boys, and all were paid to participate in the group, which they thought was a college research study.

The ten boys met three times a week with two college leaders and a group therapist. The sessions were three hours long. The first hour was spent in activities such as swimming, baseball, and volleyball. After a fifteen-minute refreshment period, there was a discussion divided into two periods: a "fishbowl" discussion period and a general discussion period.

In the fishbowl technique, the boys were divided into two subgroups. The first group of boys was assigned a topic to discuss, while the others observed the discussion and reported their observations. The roles were then reversed. In later sessions, the boys in one group were assigned a particular boy in the second group to observe. This experience taught the boys to give constructive feedback to each other and made them pay attention to positive and negative behaviors in group interaction.

The boys also completed rating scales on themselves and each other, rating interpersonal skills such as humor, capacity to speak interestingly, and ability to listen to others. The scale helped the boys see which interpersonal skills were valued.

RESULTS: The poorly adjusted youngsters all made marked progress in the group. Reports from their parents and an independent psychologist demonstrated the boys' improved ability to relate to others appropriately.

According to the authors, several features of the program were responsible for the therapeutic effectiveness of the group activities. First, the boys engaged in spontaneous and free play, and the enthusiasm and carefree fun of the situation contagiously affected all the boys. Second, the formal requirements of observing and rating others made the boys more aware of their behavior and the social behavior of others. In several instances, boys' behavior changed dramatically when the group role-played their behavior and they realized how inappropriate it was. The boys were able to identify with the leaders and imitate their behaviors. The identification with the group was also an important aspect; that is, the boys realized for the first time that they had friends who could be counted on, and they took pride in belonging to such a "swell" group of people. Finally, when other members were absent, and during the last week of meetings, the boys were able to talk about their feelings of closeness with each other and their sense of separation and loss.

COMMENTARY: A therapy group composed of both ill-adjusted and well-adjusted individuals has an advantage over a therapy group of patients who all suffer some deficiencies. The well-adjusted individuals act as models for the less adjusted. Moreover, in this kind of group, the stigma of being "sick" is reduced. As a result, the members with problems can begin to identify in a productive manner with well-adjusted members, instead of identifying themselves as poorly adjusted.

SOURCE: Hilgard, J. R., Staight, D. C., and Moore, U. S. "Better-Adjusted Peers as Resources in Group Therapy with Adolescents." *Journal of Psychology,* 1969, *73,* 75-100.

Multiple Therapy Approach

AUTHOR: Sigmund Løvåsdal

PRECIS: Combining play therapy and group discussions to help boys with poor peer relations learn new social skills

INTRODUCTION: Løvåsdal developed a therapeutic group that combined the advantages of play therapy and group therapy. That is, concrete examples of behavior from the play time furnished material for the discussion period. The children were told by the therapist and peers about the consequences of their behavior in a constructive and nonjudgmental way. They discussed ways of solving interpersonal problems and suggested new ways of behavior to use in the group and in situations outside the group. The children were encouraged to express their feelings to help them understand why they behaved as they did.

TREATMENT: Four boys, ranging in age from nine to thirteen, participated in the group with one therapist. Two of the boys were concurrently enrolled in individual therapy. All had poor peer relations. Three of the boys were aggressive and provocative, and one boy was withdrawn and preferred to play alone.

At the first session, the therapist told the boys that they would play in the playroom for thirty minutes and then meet together to discuss situations from the play session. While the boys played, the therapist took careful notes of interactions between group members. His role was that of an observer, and he did not engage in play or structure activities; however, if serious trouble arose, such as a fight, he did stop the action and reviewed the rules. The boys picked up the toys at the end of the play time and went into another room for fifteen minutes of discussion. Changing location had the benefit of calming the children down and helping them make the transition to verbal discussion. The therapist then presented one or more specific events that had occurred during the play time, such as a quarrel, to focus the boys' attention on the problem behavior. The group together clarified what went on in the interaction, what caused it, and how it was terminated. The boys involved were encouraged to verbalize what they were feeling at different points in the interaction. The group then discussed alternative ways of solving interpersonal problems.

For example, one boy in the group, Nils, was annoying to the others because he interfered with their activities. Nils was astonished to learn that the other boys did not want him to touch their play materials. Up to this point, Nils said he did not know why other boys didn't like him. His social improvement in the group was marked, and he learned to play more appropriately. Another boy, Kjell, played by himself, was overweight, and was not accepted by peers. Although he tended to play alone in the group, he was quite verbal in the discussions and gained peer acceptance through his sensitive and independent behaviors and statements.

The therapist ended each session by shaking each boy's hand, a gesture to communicate that the boy's participation was appreciated and to communicate aspects of trust and acceptance.

COMMENTARY: This multiple therapy approach provided a positive group experience for the children and also provided therapeutic peer influences toward more positive social interactions and a place to try new social behaviors. The author contracted with the children and their parents every ten weeks to decide whether they would continue or terminate. This, however, was not an integral aspect of treatment, and individual therapists should use their clinical judgment in determining how long the group should continue.

SOURCE: Løvåsdal, S. "A Multiple Therapy Approach in Work with Children." *International Journal of Group Psychotherapy,* 1976, *26,* 475-486.

Additional Readings

Clement, P. W. "Children as Behavior Therapists." In A. M. Mitchell and C. D. Johnson (Eds.), *Therapeutic Techniques: Working Models for the Helping Professional.* Fullerton, Calif.: Personnel and Guidance Association, 1973.

Children from the target child's natural environment were used as active therapeutic agents. In the classroom, at home, and in the neighborhood children can be trained to observe the child's behavior and carry out specific interventions. The intervention usually is some form of contingency management, in which specified reinforcers (tokens) are administered after identified target behaviors are performed. Clement describes several methods that he has used. In one commonly used method, he taught social skills to shy, withdrawn children by showing them videotapes of peer models performing a variety of social tasks. In another method, one child in a small group was identified as "Chief" for the session; the "Chief" wore a bug-in-the-ear microphone, and the therapist sat behind a two-way mirror and instructed the "Chief" when to give group members tokens and verbal praise for socially appropriate behavior. In another method, the target child was asked to help the therapist or teacher with other children who had similar behavior problems. By helping to modify the behavior of others, the target child learned appropriate behavior. In a group contingency method, the other children in the class or in the family became supportive of change in the target child's behavior when they all received rewards for the child's performance of desired behavior.

Savin, H. A. "Multi-Media Group Treatment with Socially Inept Adolescents." *Clinical Psychologist,* 1976, *29,* 30-39.

Group therapy was instituted to modify the behavior of withdrawn, passive, and socially inept adolescent boys at a residential treatment center. Treatment focused on improving the following communication skills: eye contact, physical posture, verbal following, and expression of feeling. The boys watched videotapes of peer models performing positive and negative examples of the communication skills. The boys role-played social situations and were taped themselves. The videotapes provided valuable information on how they looked to others, what they needed to improve, and what progress they had made.

Anxiety and Fear

Group therapy has proved effective in treating fears and phobias in adults and children. The most successful methods incorporate the desensitization techniques of having the group relax and visualize progressively more anxiety-producing events, followed by a group discussion. Group discussions add the therapeutic effects of interpersonal identification and support to the behavioral methods. Students who were desensitized commonly reported improved self-confidence and a sense of competence because they perceived the treatment to be a coping skill that could be mastered and applied to other problem situations in their lives.

Group Desensitization

AUTHORS: Gordon L. Paul and Donald T. Shannon

PRECIS: Using desensitization techniques and group discussion to reduce test anxiety and public-speaking anxiety in college students

INTRODUCTION: After reviewing the research on treatment of anxiety problems, Paul and Shannon concluded that systematic desensitization is the most effective method of treating phobic disorders and reducing maladaptive anxiety. Their short-term procedure for anxious college students combines the anxiety-reducing effects of desensitization with the therapeutic interpersonal support and identification found in intensive group therapy.

TREATMENT: The program was conducted at a university where all students were required to take a public-speaking course. To obtain subjects, the authors tested on several anxiety scales 710 students enrolled in public-speaking courses the first semester. Males who scored high on the scales were invited to participate in the treatment/research described here. Part of the students were treated individually in the first semester, and part of the students were treated in groups the second semester. The results were then compared.

Of the students receiving individual treatment, some were seen in insight-oriented psychotherapy, some in individual desensitization, and some in an attention/placebo group. In the insight-oriented approach, the therapist attempted to reduce anxiety by helping the student gain understanding of and insight into his problem. In the individual desensitization approach, the therapist trained the student in deep muscle relaxation, using a technique of tensing and relaxing major muscle groups. The student constructed an anxiety hierarchy of low to high stressful events related to public speaking. The therapist then counterconditioned the events on the hierarchy by directing the student to imagine the events while deeply relaxed. In the attention/placebo approach, the student was given a "fast-acting tranquilizer" (placebo) and then performed a stressful task. The therapist explained that this was a method of training people to think and work under stress. All students participating in these three individual approaches received five one-hour sessions of treatment.

In the second semester, ten anxious students were divided into two groups. They met for nine weekly sessions of group desensitization. The desensitization procedure was similar to that used in the individual sessions. A portion of the sessions was reserved for discussion, in which the therapist focused on improving confidence, skills, and awareness of the effects of interpersonal behaviors by emphasizing similarities between the problems, emotions, and experiences of group members. The therapist referred questions to the group and pointed out problems in communication in the group. The sessions were held in a 9′ × 12′ room with five overstuffed chairs placed in a semicircle facing the therapist.

In the first session, the therapist presented the rationale and course of treatment. The students were told that they could learn appropriate reactions to stressful events by repeatedly visualizing these events while deeply relaxed. Members chose to target anxiety in public-speaking situations, which they all found stressful. During the last thirty minutes, they received training in progressive relaxation, tensing and then relaxing gross-muscle groups throughout the body. The last ten minutes were used to correct any problems or misconceptions related to the relaxation. The students were instructed to practice relaxation twice a day for fifteen minutes.

In the second session, the group constructed a hierarchy related to public speaking. Only items that all members could relate to were used, and the items were geared toward the most anxious member. The fifteen-item hierarchy began with "You are discussing your approaching speech with friends two weeks before it is due" and ended with "You are standing in the center of the auditorium and presenting a speech to a packed house." The last twenty-five minutes consisted of relaxation practice and training in imagery to see if all the students could imagine stressful situations.

The remaining sessions consisted of discussions of problems related to relaxation or the hierarchy, followed by relaxation and working through the hierarchy. Both groups successfully completed their hierarchy by the sixth session, so they constructed new hierarchies related to test anxiety. This new hierarchy was completed in the ninth session. The end of the last session was used to bring closure to the group.

RESULTS: Pre- and posttest measures, self-reports, and grade point averages were used to evaluate the effects of treatment. Both the group and individual desensitization methods increased extroversion and reduced overall anxiety and anxiety in interpersonal interactions. Students treated in the group desensitization method also showed a gain in grade point averages, while a control group showed a decrease of almost one full grade point. Participants reported improvement and confidence in their ability to talk with friends and relatives and in social groups. They also reported improvement in personal problems, general self-confidence, general composure, and general tension.

The group desensitization method had certain advantages over the individual method. First, members became aware of others with similar problems and were able to practice the social skills they felt deficient in. Second, the group provided immediate positive reinforcement for members as they improved. Primarily, however, the group desensitization method required only 1.8 hours of therapist time per client, while the individual treatment required 5 hours of therapist time per client.

COMMENTARY: This treatment was effective in reducing college students' test anxiety and fear of public speaking. The self-reports of reduced anxiety were confirmed by the increases in grade point averages. According to the therapists, group members approached the desensitization treatment as an active mastery technique that they could apply to other stressful situations. Thus, the treatment not only overcame their academic-related anxieties but gave them confidence in generalizing their problem-solving abilities.

SOURCE: Paul, G. L., and Shannon, D. T. "Treatment of Anxiety Through Systematic Desensitization in Therapy Groups." *Journal of Abnormal Psychology,* 1966, *71,* 124-135.

Animal Phobias

AUTHOR: Brunhilde Ritter

PRECIS: Using vicarious and contact desensitization procedures to treat snake phobia in preadolescent children

INTRODUCTION: Ritter notes that the most frequent and intense fears of children are related to animals. Furthermore, a survey of adults showed that these phobic reactions persist into adulthood. In this article the author compared vicarious desensitization (in which children watch a therapist and peer models fearlessly interact with the phobic object) and contact desensitization (in which the children watch peer models and then touch and handle the phobic object) in the treatment of snake phobia. Since contact desensitization had been found useful with college students who were afraid to dissect animals, Ritter decided to test the method in treating phobic children.

TREATMENT: The participants were twenty-eight girls and sixteen boys, ranging in age from five to eleven years old, who were afraid of snakes. Their snake avoidance had been assessed on a twenty-nine-item performance test that required increasingly more direct interactions with a harmless, four-foot-long gopher snake. Item 1, for example, required the child to stand in a room fifteen feet away from the snake, who was in a closed cage; Item 15 required the child to hold the snake within the cage with a gloved hand for five seconds; and Item 29 required the child to hold the snake on his lap for thirty seconds. The children were assured the testing would be stopped immediately if they became too frightened to continue. The children rated the amount of fear they experienced with each task as "not afraid at all," "a little afraid," or "very afraid." Only children who could not perform Item 15 were included in treatment. The forty-four children were randomly assigned to the contact desensitization treatment, the vicarious desensitization treatment, or a control group. In both treatments, the children participated in two thirty-five-minute sessions spaced a week apart. The children were treated in groups of seven or eight.

In the vicarious desensitization treatment, the children entered a room where five peer models were seated in chairs around the caged snake. The therapist told the children they would not be asked to touch the snake but were to watch the peer demonstrators. The therapist took the snake, Posie, out of the cage and petted it. The demonstrators also petted and handled the snake. The fearful children then took turns being "teachers" and commanded the demonstrators to perform various tasks from the twenty-nine-item performance test. The same procedure was used in the second session.

In the contact desensitization treatment, the therapist sat near the children and petted the snake. The therapist encouraged interested children to put on a glove and said that she would help them pet the snake. The child put his gloved hand on the therapist's hand while she stroked the snake. The child then petted the snake unaided, and finally with a bare hand. As soon as several children had touched the snake, the others also became interested in playing with the snake. The children then took turns being "teacher" and "demonstrator" in performing tasks from the original performance test. Hesitant children were assisted by bolder peers.

RESULTS: After only two treatment sessions, 80 percent of the children in the contact desensitization treatment completed all twenty-nine items on the snake avoidance performance test. In contrast, 53 percent of the children in the vicarious desensitization treatment completed all the items, and none of the control children completed the items. On a fear inventory administered before and after treatment, the children in both desensitization groups showed decreases in other fears, such as fear of thunder and fear of being ridiculed by peers, but the difference was not statistically significant. The author concluded that contact desensitization was more effective than vicarious desensitization and that this treatment of phobias was cost-efficient, since twelve children were successfully treated with only 140 minutes of therapist time.

COMMENTARY: These children did not necessarily have a true, debilitating phobia, since they could easily avoid the feared object (snake) without interference with daily activities. They were fearful because they lacked experience with the object, rather than because they had had a previous traumatic experience. We believe that this method could be easily and successfully used with other animal phobias, including those associated with trauma, such as a dog phobia resulting from a serious dog bite. For such a situation, however, the treatment would likely require more therapy time with more gradual progress made toward direct interactions with the animal.

SOURCE: Ritter, B. "The Group Desensitization of Children's Snake Phobia Using Vicarious and Contact Desensitization Procedures." *Behaviour Research and Therapy,* 1968, *6,* 1-6.

Additional Readings

Babbitts, R. M. "Cognitive and Autonomic Group Procedures with Speech-Anxious Children." *Dissertation Abstracts International,* 1980, *40* (12), 5789-B.

School children, ages twelve to fourteen, who demonstrated anxiety in speaking in front of the class received one of the following treatments: rational-emotive therapy that addressed issues specific to speech anxiety, rational/emotive therapy that addressed issues related to general anxiety, or progressive muscle relaxation. The specific cognitive procedure was superior to both the general cognitive procedure and the relaxation procedure in reducing speech anxiety in the adolescents.

Cohen, R. "The Effects of Group Interaction and Progressive Hierarchy Presentation on Desensitization of Test Anxiety." *Behaviour Research and Therapy,* 1969, *7,* 15-27.

Group desensitization treatment is more economical than individual treatment, and group interactions enable members to learn with others who have similar problems. College students exposed to guided group discussions in conjunction with desensitization reported more test-anxiety reduction than students treated in a group with minimal group interaction. The students whose test anxiety was reduced said that they had become more aware of different aspects of anxiety and had developed self-confidence, self-esteem, and self-control through understanding and mastery of their test anxiety.

Deffenbacher, J. L. "Group Desensitization of Dissimilar Anxieties." *Community Mental Health Journal,* 1976, *12,* 263-266.

Group desensitization treatment for individuals with a similar anxiety cannot be used in most mental health clinics because clients with similar anxieties do not request treatment at the same time. More frequently, several persons request treatment for a variety of anxieties. This article describes modifications in group desensitization that make it possible to treat these diverse anxieties in a single group. The first two sessions are similar to standard techniques, in that rapport is established and visual and relaxation training is conducted. In the remaining sessions, individual members develop their own individual hierarchies and print the individual items from the hierarchy on 5″ X 8″ index cards. Members then place several sequential cards from their hierarchy on a music stand next to them. The group as a whole is relaxed, and members are then asked to visualize the scenes on their own cards.

Donner, L. "Automated Group Desensitization—A Follow-Up Report." *Behaviour Research and Therapy,* 1970, *8,* 241-247.

Female college students with test anxiety were treated in

group desensitization. The therapist's verbalizations were taped throughout the sessions. A second group of students were treated in an "automated" group where the tapes of the previous group were used. Members of both groups reported less test anxiety and had improved grade point averages. While both groups continued to improve over the six-month follow-up period, the group where the therapist was present showed more dramatic progress than the "automated" group. The implications of the therapist's presence versus his absence are discussed.

Kondos, O. "Reduction of Examination Anxiety and 'Stage-Fright' by Group Desensitization and Relaxation." *Behaviour Research and Therapy,* 1967, *5,* 275-281.

Common fears among schoolchildren are the fear of failing examinations and the fear of giving reports in class; 44 to 90 percent of sixth graders, for example, report such anxieties. Prior to tests, these children experience excessive tension and excitement, which generally improve their performance on the test. However, approximately 18 percent of the children deteriorate in performance because the anxiety interferes with their ability to perform. These children were labeled as having stage fright. Group desensitization, which has been found effective in reducing test anxiety in college students, was conducted with test-anxious schoolchildren in grades six through nine. The method was successful in reducing their anxiety, and these effects were more successful and enduring than relaxation training alone.

Autistic and Psychotic Behavior

Some diagnosticians regard childhood schizophrenia and childhood autism as two distinct disabilities; others believe that these disorders exist on a continuum. Some believe that psychosis is the result of a physiological defect or damage; others believe that it results from emotional disturbances early in life. Not surprisingly, therefore, therapists practicing group therapy with this population differ in choice of treatment. Some therapists provide a permissive environment, such as activity group therapy, to resolve primary conflicts and to improve social skills. Other therapists stress a more structured approach, such as verbal discussion and behavior modification, to reduce inappropriate behaviors and verbalizations and replace them with more appropriate communication and social skills.

Confrontational-Educational Group for Autistic/Schizophrenic Adolescents

AUTHOR: Norman Epstein

PRECIS: Using a highly structured approach—including rules, behavior labeling, rewards, and penalties—to teach appropriate social behaviors

INTRODUCTION: A therapy group was developed in a school for emotionally disturbed children within a psychiatric center. These twelve- to fourteen-year-olds behaved bizarrely. Their verbalizations were often irrelevant and betrayed primary-process thinking patterns. They behaved hyperactively and seemingly without purpose. A prominent feature of the group was the lack of social contact among the children. Individual therapy had proved unrewarding, unproductive, and frustrating. Consequently, the group format was devised to provide on-the-job (that is, in-the-school) training in appropriate behaviors and communication skills to aid in learning.

TREATMENT: The six group members were all from the same school class and were the oldest children in the school. With a therapist and the teacher present, the group discussed schoolroom behaviors. The therapist's goal was to teach sufficient appropriate behaviors in the group meeting so that a small amount of communication could take place. These groups were highly structured. Ground rules defined and prohibited crazy behaviors. Immediate confrontation followed any crazy behavior by a child. Initially the therapist alone confronted, but eventually the members of the group cooperated with him in identifying and disapproving of inappropriate behaviors and impulsive verbalizations. The atmosphere was nonpermissive, and the therapist imposed order—often repeating the verbal commands and prohibitions many times.

In addition to punishing behaviors that worked against communication, the therapist also taught and rewarded constructive behaviors by hugging, verbal praise, applause, and tickling. The children, for example, were taught to think about whether what they were about to say made sense or not, thereby providing an intermediate step between thought and impulsive verbalization. Also, the children were taught to establish eye contact and listen to someone else speaking.

Although two cases are briefly described, the case of Martin seems best to convey the flavor of the experience. Martin grew up in front of the television set. By keeping him there, Martin's parents avoided having to deal with his needs for physical warmth, attention, and socialization. Although his speech made no overt sense, it reflected a preoccupation with television reality. The therapist made Martin responsible for being coherent by stopping him when he started to ramble but allowing him to relate the plots of his favored medical stories. During a discussion of what each member wanted to be when he grew up, Martin said he wanted to be a doctor so that he could care for the therapist in his old age. Martin then began to wander—describing the therapist as an old man and himself as a doctor taking the therapist into the operating room. The therapist stopped short Martin's lapse into incoherency by forcefully interrupting him and holding him by the shoulders. Martin asked what he had done wrong. The process was examined point by point. He was told that he had drifted into fantasy after making sense and expressing beautiful thoughts. This led to a group discussion of the need for control over one's verbalizations if one is to avoid being treated as crazy by other people. This control was defined as not only desirable but also possible under circumstances where meaningless speech is not tolerated and where one thinks before speaking. Martin became more coherent and relevant.

RESULTS: The children developed a repertoire of communication and supportive skills that permitted some coherent social intercourse. The approval of the therapist, especially in the form of hugging and tickling, was a crucial motivator in getting the children to cooperate in identifying inappropriate behaviors of their peers.

COMMENTARY: The author believes that this program was

beneficial in heading off long-term institutionalization for these youngsters. There is, however, no real evaluation of the effects of the group. Also missing is a discussion of the potential for the use of these confrontational techniques (for example, labeling as crazy) by one child in cruelly teasing another.

SOURCE: Epstein, N. "Group Therapy with Autistic/Schizophrenic Adolescents." *Social Casework,* 1977, *58,* 350-358.

Group Therapy with Psychotic Children

AUTHORS: Laurent Gratton and Adolfo E. Rizzo

PRECIS: Limited progress in a year-long observational group for nonverbal autistic and schizophrenic children

INTRODUCTION: Gratton and Rizzo cite the difficulties of working with young psychotic children, who are nonverbal; have highly symbolic play, which is difficult to interpret; and make slow progress, if any. The authors developed a group approach to treating psychotic children, assuming that the group would stimulate conflict material, which would then be expressed in play.

TREATMENT: Seven children, five boys and two girls, were included in the group. They all came from intact families. Four of the patients were diagnosed as suffering from infantile autism; three were labeled childhood schizophrenics and had been psychotic for over two years. Only one child had a minimal degree of speech; the others were nonverbal or had lost acquired speech. All had normal electroencephalograms, and none showed positive neurological signs.

Three therapists met with the group. For the first month and a half, they met three times a week; for the next nine and a half months, they met five times a week. The sessions were a half hour to an hour long, depending on the "tolerance of the patients and the therapists." The sessions were held in a 9′ X 12′ room that was bare except for chairs and some permanent bookshelves. No toys were provided; however, children who brought objects that they were attached to were allowed to keep them. The therapists were nondirective and did not require the children to play. They did attempt to stimulate the children by holding them or touching them or by encouraging them to crawl.

The children were initially fearful of human contact and would panic if the therapists even looked at them. They resisted coming to sessions and would climb on the bookshelves to isolate themselves. Some of the children completely denied the world around them; they would not blink if something came close to their eyes, and they showed no startle response to sudden loud noises. They did, however, appear to know what was happening in the room, even though their response was odd. For example, if one child attacked a therapist, the other children grew silent and waited.

The authors noted that these children behaved, on the whole, like contented infants. They made cooing sounds, reacted to stimulation with their whole bodies, and frequently moved their hands to their mouths. Few of them were mature enough to engage in symbolic play. One boy was preoccupied with holes and crevices and, later, the therapist's ears, nose, and mouth. Another would urinate on the floor and slap the wet floor with his hands, saying "Glasses." After the therapists told the boy that all this might have something to do with his father, who wore glasses and abused him, the boy appeared less anxious, and the behavior ceased.

By the second month, the children came passively to therapy and occasionally had minimal interactions. By the third month, they clustered around the therapists and would touch each other, usually in odd ways such as banging head against head or mouthing and smelling each other. They actively explored the room and the therapists by biting, licking, poking, and smelling.

By the fifth month, they sought support from the therapists and competed for their attention. They appeared more in contact with the group. At six months, they came eagerly to therapy and were upset if it started late or was canceled. They interacted more and left their objects behind. Their formerly dull, expressionless look became more lively and appropriate, and occasionally they smiled.

The program was ended after one year because of funding problems. The children remained nonverbal.

COMMENTARY: The authors state that progress was slowly made, which suggests that autism is not irreversible. They estimate that some autistic children may reach more normal levels of functioning with four or five years of daily therapy.

SOURCE: Gratton, L., and Rizzo, A. E. "Group Therapy with Young Psychotic Children." *International Journal of Group Psychotherapy,* 1969, *19,* 63-71.

Latency-Age Psychotic Children

AUTHORS: Janice Kay Haaken and Frederick B. Davis

PRECIS: Group treatment for psychotic children, with emphasis on verbalization, free expression of feelings, and interaction

INTRODUCTION: Therapy groups for psychotic children are usually activity groups that provide highly structured activities, under the assumption that children will grow emotionally through being productive and learning to socialize within the structural requirements of the group. The authors developed a less structured, more spontaneous type of group, where free expression and direct communication, rather than communication through materials, were encouraged.

TREATMENT: Three therapists worked on a rotating basis, so that two therapists were always present in the group. The size of the groups ranged from five to eight and averaged seven members; girls outnumbered boys by about two to one. The children, who ranged in age from six to twelve, were diagnosed as psychotic, atypical, or borderline schizophrenics. The groups met daily, Monday through Friday, for half-hour sessions in a bare room.

One goal of therapy was to make the children aware of their behavior and its effect on others. For example, during a discussion about aggressive feelings, one passive boy wet his pants. The therapist commented that some children cannot discuss anger openly and therefore express it in other ways, such as wetting when anxious. Within days this youngster was more active in the group and participated in punching-bag activities with the others. When a girl hallucinated, the other children became quite anxious. The therapist stated that when one child gets "spacey," others become frightened. The children were then able to verbalize how scary it was to observe or experience hallucinations.

The therapists initiated fantasy play—asking the children, for instance, to pretend they were animals—to help the children become more spontaneous and less rigid. The children enjoyed expressing aggressiveness in animal play, and some of the children turned it into monster play. The therapists helped passive members participate by suggesting that each child take turns being a monster. The children could immobilize a pursuing monster by saying "Be still" if they became too anxious during the playing.

The authors note that these children have a "crippling deficiency" in being unable to ask others to satisfy their needs for warmth, attention, and closeness. The therapists initiated much physical contact by rubbing each child's back and talking to him or her in a close, personal way, holding and rocking a child who cried, and rubbing the neck or back of an anxious child. The children soon began asking to be held or touched by the therapists and then each other. They also became comfortable sitting close to each other and touching while they talked.

A related problem was the children's sense of isolation and alienation. The therapists used experiential techniques commonly used with adult groups to develop group cohesiveness and feelings of closeness. For example, they used the "breaking-in" technique, in which the group forms a tight circle and "rejects" one person. The person on the outside must figure out how to get back into the circle. Another member became the "rejected" member's coach to help him get back in.

The therapists took an instructional role to discuss impulses such as aggression and sexuality, to help the children understand that such feelings are natural but must be expressed in acceptable, controlled ways. For example, when a boy and girl engaged in "sexual explorations" in the bathroom, the therapists discussed more appropriate ways of expressing their interest in each other. The group atmosphere stimulated impulses and provided many opportunities to recognize and discuss appropriate ways to deal with impulses rather than act them out.

The therapists began the sessions, which initially were fragmented and chaotic, by finding a common theme or mood that the children were expressing. If the mood was anger, punching bags might be brought out; if there was a problem with control, time out might be used more frequently. When one child was about to leave the institution, the therapists provided punching bags, and the children expressed their anger and sadness about his leaving.

The therapists taught the children problem-solving skills by interpreting inappropriate behaviors as problems to be solved. For example, when the children were arriving late for sessions, the therapists pointed out that the group needed to solve the problem of lateness and its disruption to the group. When one youngster tried to push her way into interactions and was repeatedly rejected, the therapist commented that her method was not working, and she was able to try alternative ways of achieving contact with others.

COMMENTARY: The authors do not report the results of the intervention; they imply, however, that the children made progress in behavior control and group cohesiveness and were able to take responsibility for the functioning of the group away from the therapists. The therapists used their own feelings as "barometers of group feeling and tolerance." In other words, if the therapists became uncomfortable about behavior in the group, they would interpret it or intervene, and the group anxiety level would drop.

SOURCE: Haaken, J. K., and Davis, F. B. "Group Therapy with Latency-Age Psychotic Children." *Child Welfare,* 1975, *54,* 703-710.

Play Group Therapy with Psychotic Adolescent Girls

AUTHORS: Dorian M. Rose, M. Catherine Butler, and Florence L. Eaton

PRECIS: A therapeutic play group instituted for hospitalized psychotic girls who were not improving optimally and showed interest in play equipment

INTRODUCTION: The authors developed a nondirective play therapy group for severely disturbed girls who were not responding to hospital treatment. Individual therapy, the traditional form of treatment, was not appropriate for the girls because of their poor communication skills and their lack of motivation to form a relationship with a therapist. The girls preferred to be by themselves, playing with toys and doing crafts. The play therapy group was originated to utilize their motivation for play, to allow them an outlet for nonverbal expression, and to improve the girls' reality-testing abilities and social skills through interpretation of their behaviors and interactions in a group.

TREATMENT: Seven hospitalized girls between sixteen and twenty years of age participated in the group. All of these girls had manifested disorders of psychotic proportions with some schizophrenic features before admission, and six had long histories of difficulties and were considered chronic patients. In addition to the schizophrenic features, several of the girls exhibited disorders such as mental retardation and seizures. Three patients had been assaultive, and three had tried to injure themselves at the time the group was formed.

For the first three months, the group met five times a week for one hour. For the next seven months, hourly meetings were held three times a week. Sessions were held in a special room equipped with toys and games (for example, knittng materials, board games, darts, guns, paints, cards). Because of the destructive potentialities of the members, two therapists were always present. The sessions were run nondirectively, but rules against injury to oneself or others were strictly enforced. One therapist took a passive, observing role; the other took a more active role. Even the active leader avoided initiating activities. Interpretations "were offered as the necessity arose." Following each session, "trend notes" and diagrams of each patient's movements were made.

RESULTS: Analysis of the data collected, including frequency counts, clearly demonstrated that assaultiveness, destructiveness, temper tantrums, and self-injury decreased over the course of therapy. The activities engaged in also changed. Gun play and war games occupied the interest of the group in the first two months. The middle period, the next four months, was filled mostly with arts and crafts activities. In the last four months, the group mainly played board games and card games.

There were also geographical changes over time. The girls scattered through the room for the first six months, engaged in isolated play. By the group's end, after ten months, the girls gathered around one table. Even when engaged in solitary endeavors, the girls no longer isolated themselves physically.

In summary, objective data demonstrated that, as the group progressed, the amount of time spent in talking increased, individual activity was supplanted by group activity, aggression decreased, and the patients tended to congregate together.

These findings seem to have generalized to situations outside the group. The patients, according to staff reports, demonstrated "a marked decrease in stubbornness [and] negativism and were no longer considered disciplinary problems within the hospital." They became more sociable and less seclusive. Although there was a diminution of some of their serious mental symptoms, delinquent acts—such as drinking, promiscuity, and running away—remained unchanged.

After two years, follow-up data indicated that four of the girls had improved significantly over any previous level of adjustment. Their employment records and ability to live away from their families were encouraging, especially since one of the girls had been institutionalized for over two years.

Although length of known psychotic illness was insignificantly related to outcome, length of hospitalization was inversely related. In contrast to the usual pattern of chronic patients, five of the six patients who returned to the community accepted outpatient treatment.

COMMENTARY: Since the girls were receiving medication, individual therapy, and group therapy at the same time, it is impossible to isolate the effects of the group. Being a part of the group seemed important to the girls, however, and on their visits to the hospital, they checked in with each other for chats.

This group method seemed to have a potent socializing effect, which somewhat counteracted the tendency to isolation usually found in seriously disturbed patients. Perhaps the authors found exactly the therapeutic modality (nondirective play therapy) that was suited to the initial developmental level of the girls and then provided the stimulus for further maturation. A good example of this maturational process is to be found in the change from isolated play to the more mature level of parallel and cooperative play.

SOURCE: Rose, D. M., Butler, M. C., and Eaton, F. L. "Play Group Therapy with Psychotic Adolescent Girls." *International Journal of Group Psychotherapy,* 1954, *4,* 303-311.

Short-Term Group for Severely Disturbed Youths

AUTHORS: Jo Rosenberg and Theodore Cherbuliez

PRECIS: Activity group therapy used with hospitalized, severely disturbed children for diagnostic and treatment purposes

INTRODUCTION: The authors conducted an ongoing group therapy program for children in a psychiatric hospital. The group was used for diagnostic purposes but was also intended to have a curative, therapeutic impact on the members. A nondirective psychoanalytic approach proved unsuccessful with the group; instead, the authors believe that a more directive approach and more active involvement by therapists are needed.

TREATMENT: The group was open to children on the unit between eight and twelve years old. There was a high turnover rate on the fifteen-bed unit, so the group composition was constantly changing. The children had been admitted for reasons of suicidal behavior, fire setting, running away from home, homicidal threats, and autistic withdrawal. Their diagnoses included childhood psychosis, behavior disorder, depression, unsocialized aggressive reaction, and borderline personality organization. The group met weekly for one hour and was led by a male child psychoanalyst and a female psychiatric social worker.

During the first year, the leaders attempted a psychoanalytic approach, taking a nondirective stance and emphasizing verbal confrontations and interpretations. They found that this approach did not work, because the children's severe ego disorganization led to chaotic, agitated sessions with no clear motivational themes, and interpretations were not heard or were ignored.

The therapists added more structure to the group, physically restraining members from running in and out of the room and from fighting. However, the children then began fighting in order to derive comfort from being touched and held. The therapists began to participate more in the children's activities and addressed group behavior verbally through interpretations.

RESULTS: The therapists stated that the group became a positive experience for the children, who looked forward to the sessions. Overall, the added structure increased periods of constructive group activity in which the therapists' interpretations were responded to. There was a lower level of anxiety in the group and the therapists. Although the group was not designed as intensive treatment, it was a therapeutic experience that provided a pleasure-laden, warmly anticipated experience, an opportunity to interact with peers, and exposure to interventions aimed at improving self-esteem.

COMMENTARY: Some practitioners have found a psychoanalytic approach effective with severely disturbed patients. However, most practitioners find, as these authors did, that the therapists must take a more active role in the group.

SOURCE: Rosenberg, J., and Cherbuliez, T. "Inpatient Group Therapy for Older Children and Pre-Adolescents." *International Journal of Group Psychotherapy,* 1979, *29,* 393-405.

Seriously Disturbed Boys in Residential Treatment

AUTHOR: Holly Van Scoy

PRECIS: A special activity group for boys ostracized by the other boys in a residential treatment center

INTRODUCTION: Every aspect of a residential center is group oriented, and residents are socialized and treated within the group milieu. Even in this setting, however, some boys are so disturbed or so different that they are ostracized and scapegoated by the other residents. They do not fit into the group network and therefore have little opportunity to benefit from the corrective influences of the group milieu.

The author identified five such boys who needed extra help to gain acceptance by the residents and thus profit from the treatment milieu. To provide these boys with an opportunity to be group members, she developed a group just for them. This activity group was the first positive and consistent group experience that any of the boys had had. The therapist/author believed that the small group would be less threatening for the boys than a larger group and that they could receive more intensive observation and feedback from the therapists, who encouraged socialization and provided positive reinforcement.

TREATMENT: The five boys ranged in age from eleven to fourteen. They came from different cottages, where they were constantly being removed from the larger group because of behavior problems and fighting. Their IQs ranged from 62 to 112. One youngster was diagnosed as a childhood schizophrenic with a history of autistic behavior, paranoid delusions and hallucinations, and aggression toward peers. A second child, diagnosed as a severe personality disorder, had feminine mannerisms and preoccupations and expressed wishes to have a vagina and produce babies. A third youngster, diagnosed as adjustment reaction to childhood, had overt sexual difficulties; he masturbated in public, attacked female staff with his teeth, and attempted to engage other boys in sex play. Another boy, also diagnosed as adjustment reaction, was considered inept by everyone and cried and clung to staff members. The last member, diagnosed as a childhood schizophrenic, had a low IQ (62) and was obese and aggressive toward staff. All these boys had been considered "untouchable" by peers for two months prior to the inception of the group, yet none was aware of this label or his isolation from others.

Two therapists met with the boys weekly for two-hour sessions for seven months. Initially they provided structured arts and crafts activities. The sessions were chaotic, but the boys settled down and worked to receive treats at the end of the sessions. After the fourth session, the boys asked to go off campus, a privilege they were usually denied individually because of their behavior. The boys made their own "rules" to follow on off-campus trips. They were required to behave in public, and serious misbehavior would result in early termination of a session and no refreshments. All sessions culminated with the purchasing and eating of food. The principal rewards, then, were continuing the activity and eating, and the negative responses were ending the activity early or withholding food.

By the ninth session, the group developed some cohesiveness and chose a group name and song. They also began to assume responsibility for each other's behavior. For example, one boy confronted another boy's irrelevant speech and suggested that he talk about people; another boy confronted a peer's whining and told him to make an appropriate decision so that they would not miss treats.

As the group progressed, interventions by the therapists decreased, and the boys became more interested in verbalizing and socializing than in the activity they were doing. Some activities, such as bowling and swimming and visiting public monuments, did not foster group cohesiveness. The boys remained isolated and unsure of themselves on these outings. Activities that involved food, such as trips to the pizza parlor or doughnut shop, were more productive; the boys were more relaxed, and sitting around a table was conducive to conversation as they waited for their reward.

RESULTS: Data from "trend notes," which were made by the therapists after each session, provided estimates of antisocial behavior (physical or verbal attacks on other members or the therapists, destruction of property, self-injury, temper tantrums, bizarre verbalizations, and similar inappropriate behaviors) and estimates of the number of interventions by the therapists. The author reports that each member showed a marked reduction in antisocial behavior over sessions. All were considered by the cottage staffs as more sociable and less withdrawn. The effeminate member behaved in a more masculine way, and all five were accepted by the other residents in their cottages.

COMMENTARY: This small, structured, intensive group experience appears to have prepared these seriously disturbed boys to socialize in the larger groups found in the residential treatment milieu, where they could then be "in touch" with the corrective influences of group living.

SOURCE: Van Scoy, H. "An Activity Group Approach to Seriously Disturbed Latency Boys." *Child Welfare,* 1971, *50,* 413-419.

Additional Readings

Ardmore, J. K. "A Special Kind of Love." *Family Health,* 1977, *9,* 28-31.

Autistic children have great difficulty in interpreting and responding to environmental stimuli and the people around them. A once-a-week program was instituted at a residential center for autistic children to improve their communication and social skills. Special education teachers, psychology students, and interested adults supervised the children in activities, including group games, arts and crafts, physical play, and group projects.

Carlin, A. S., and Armstrong, H. E. "Rewarding Social Responsibility in Disturbed Children: A Group Play Technique." *Psychotherapy: Theory, Research and Practice,* 1968, *5,* 169-174.

Children on an inpatient ward for seriously disturbed children were becoming increasingly aggressive and out of control. A short-term play therapy group was instituted as a crisis intervention measure. The children met four times a week in a playroom. The group received token reinforcement that was contingent on group behavior. The rationale of the system was that patients made responsible for other patients' behavior as well as their own would learn to apply group pressure for cooperation and would grow more circumspect in their social reinforcement of each other's behavior. For cooperative play, the group received tokens that could be used to purchase candy and small toys. If any members were disruptive or aggressive, the group was fined. Efforts by members to help each other or to solve a problem were also rewarded. Aggressive play decreased immediately in the sessions. As the children learned to enjoy the social rewards of cooperative play, aggressive behavior on the ward also diminished. The group was terminated after five weeks.

Herrick, R. H., and Binger, C. M. "Group Psychotherapy for Early Adolescents: An Adjunct to a Comprehensive Treatment Program." *Journal of the Academy of Child Psychiatry,* 1974, *13,* 110-125.

To provide socialization experiences, group psychotherapy was used as a phase-specific, temporary addition in an overall treatment program for severely disturbed adolescents. The disturbed youngsters were also involved in individual therapy. To be eligible for group therapy, the youngsters had to be able to form a relatively conflict-free and trusting relationship with an adult. The youngsters' development in the group was a recapitulation of the normal growth cycle: the individual formed a positive relationship with an adult who taught him self-control, learned to function more independently, and then socialized and worked with others.

Soble, D., and Geller, J. J. "A Type of Group Psychotherapy in the Children's Unit of a Mental Hospital." *Psychiatric Quarterly,* 1964, *38,* 262-270.

Emotionally disturbed children, ages six to twelve, were treated in therapeutic groups. To achieve maximum communication and understanding among group participants, the children were divided homogeneously by developmental level rather than by age. The ninety-minute sessions were divided into three parts. The first thirty to forty minutes were spent on group discussion, in which the general principles of psychodynamic group therapy were applied. A thirty-minute activity period followed the discussion and provided the opportunity to release tensions built up in the earlier phase. The sessions concluded with a relaxation and refreshment period of milk and cookies.

This phase provided closure to the sessions by smoothing over the excitement generated in the discussion and activity.

Trafimow, E., and Pattak, S.I. "Group Psychotherapy and Objectal Development in Children." *International Journal of Group Psychotherapy,* 1981, *31,* 193-204.

The authors discuss the theoretical structure of the object line of development (A. Freud, *Normality and Pathology in Childhood: Assessments of Development,* New York: International Universities Press, 1965) to conceptualize the group dynamics of severely disturbed adolescents. The development of object relations—the ability to relate to others—provides the framework for understanding interactional processes, therapeutic techniques, and the impact of the treatment group on children's psychic growth.

The authors worked with several severely disturbed adolescents who were functioning at the early object stage: their relationships with others were tenuous, and they appeared to still be separating from their mothers. Group therapy helped promote the object development and psychic growth of these adolescents as a result of three general aspects of group process: (1) a treatment group provides several peers who may serve as models to members who need, for example, to see how others cope or assume caretaking roles; (2) therapists may also act as models for appropriate behavior, feelings, or attitudes; (3) the group evolves a group identification, which recreates the symbiotic relationship with the mother; the group as a whole contributes to the gratification and protection necessary for further experimentation by and development of individual members.

Four clinical cases are discussed to illustrate this theoretical framework.

Mental Retardation

Professionals who work with mentally retarded people realize that their emotional problems are often more incapacitating than their intellectual deficits. The label of "retard" and the failure these youngsters experience in trying to fit in with their peers are highly frustrating and demoralizing. They are often rejected or treated differently from their normal siblings, which engenders anxiety and acting-out behavior. In school they are surrounded by more competent peers, which again increases their anxiety and feelings of being different and inferior. A large percentage of retarded clients in state institutions had retarded parents (familial retardation) and came from broken and inadequate homes, and often a number of foster homes, before coming to the institution. Thus, retarded youngsters often exhibit poor frustration tolerance, aggressive acting out, poor peer relations, poor self-image, and poor academic motivation; and they are often neurotic, anxious, withdrawn, and hostile. Depending on the children's developmental level, play group therapy, activity group therapy, and verbal discussion groups are effective in ameliorating these symptoms.

Returning Institutionalized Retardates to the Community

AUTHOR: Rudolph Kaldeck

PRECIS: Conventional group therapy to help institutionalized mentally defective youngsters return successfully to the community

INTRODUCTION: Kaldeck believes that many of the mentally retarded with emotional problems are searching for a substitute family even into adulthood, and this search interferes with their adaptive functioning. In one case, he cites, the patient made an excellent initial adjustment as a helper in a restaurant. The owner was so pleased that he wanted to hire another patient from the institution. However, the first patient was unable to share the attention he had been receiving from the employer, whom he related to as a father substitute. He returned to the institution after having lived successfully in the community for eighteen months.

The author proposes that many retarded persons with IQs above 45 or 50 are able bodied and could function well in the community except for emotional problems. With psychotherapy, he believes, many of the institutionalized retarded could be returned to the community. At the time of this article, however, many psychiatrists who ran state institutions believed that mental retardation was a contraindication for psychotherapy. Furthermore, there were overwhelming numbers of patients and few trained therapists able to do this kind of work. Kaldeck overcame these obstacles by developing a program for a state institution that utilized a small number of therapists to treat a large population. Through the group process, he sought to help the patients learn to interact with others more effectively. Because of their intellectual limitations, he did not expect them to develop insight.

TREATMENT: The author, a therapist, trained professionals in the institution—a physician, two psychologists, and four social workers—to conduct therapy groups, and he closely supervised them throughout the program. The therapists were to be permissive, stay in the background, and make minimal interpretations. The women therapists worked with groups of women, and the male therapists worked with groups of male patients. Criterion for group membership was an IQ near 50 or above. The therapists concentrated on patients under thirty years old; however, older patients were accepted if they offered some prospect for improvement. Each group contained ten to twelve members, and the therapists mixed personalities of members to include overactive and withdrawn, aggressive and submissive patients in the groups. The groups met twice a week for an hour. Ages ranged from seventeen to forty-eight. Initially there were 68 participants in six groups; with turnover, a total of 104 patients were involved. Participation was voluntary.

During the first sessions, the patients griped about the institution and staff. A particularly emotional issue to the members was the selection of patients placed outside the institution, a process the members considered capricious and unfair. The therapists did not intervene but left confrontation up to other group members. In one group a female participant confronted another by spontaneously setting up a role-playing situation. As the groups progressed, patients grew more confident and discussed issues involving parents, siblings, and situations in their past foster homes. Some gained insight into the factors responsible for their emotional problems. The therapists were concerned, however, about the inappropriate behavior and attitudes that were not being confronted; so they shifted tactics from a dynamic, permissive approach to a more active approach, in which they strongly encouraged and supported group members who verbalized socially appropriate attitudes. This approach proved more productive, since the patients were able to express their anxiety and hostility but still behave in socially acceptable ways and establish better attitudes in relating to people.

RESULTS: The author concludes that these continuing groups improved the interpersonal relationships and daily adjustment of the patients, so that many could return successfully to the community. The program also sensitized the staff to the emotional problems and needs of the patients.

COMMENTARY: Although the state institutional system has moved away from large, warehouse types of institutions for the retarded and has developed more community-based projects, programs for our retarded citizens are drastically underfunded and cannot afford the "luxury" of addressing their emotional problems, except in extreme cases. In these extreme cases, authorities all too often solve the problem by sending the psychologically distraught retarded to a mental institution. In fact, the brevity of this section bespeaks the paucity of literature, research, and program development in the area of the mental health of retarded persons. When and if the powers that fund mental health programs recognize this need, this article suggests that conventional group therapy with some modifications can be useful in treating the psychological problems of the mentally retarded and helping them achieve more adequate levels of emotional and interpersonal adjustment.

SOURCE: Kaldeck, R. "Group Psychotherapy with Mentally Defective Adolescents and Adults." *International Journal of Group Psychotherapy,* 1958, *8,* 185-192.

Nondirective Play Therapy

AUTHOR: Benjamin Mehlman

PRECIS: Using nondirective play therapy with retarded children to improve their emotional and behavioral adjustment and self-image

INTRODUCTION: Although many authorities believe that the mentally retarded cannot benefit from psychotherapy, Mehlman proposes that retarded children may benefit from nondirective play therapy, which does not require strong verbal ability and stresses emotional rather than intellectual expression as a means of achieving psychological growth. The child does not concern himself with his problems in therapy. Instead, nondirective play therapy is based on the philosophy that humans possess a drive toward "maintenance and enhancement" of an adequate self. This drive toward psychological health is not free to operate, however, when the individual is under stress and becomes fixated at a primitive, inadequate level of functioning. Nondirective play therapy provides a safe atmosphere with a protective and supportive adult and frees the child to express his feelings and explore his environment. This free experimentation allows the child to achieve a new synthesis of his environment as a source of satisfactions and to develop a positive self-image and more adequate adjustment.

TREATMENT: Eleven youngsters with endogenous mental retardation were seen in two play therapy groups. They ranged in age from seven to twelve and ranged in Binet IQs from 52 to 78. Each group met with the therapist twice a week for fifty-minute sessions. They met twenty-nine times over a sixteen-week period.

RESULTS: According to pre- and posttest measures, the children showed improved personality adjustment on the Rorschach and on the Behavior Rating Scale by Haggerty-Olson-Wickman. There were no such changes in matched control groups. However, there was no improvement in intelligence quotients, as Mehlman had hoped there would be.

According to Mehlman, several factors may have detracted from the effectiveness of the program. First, the groups were too large for the therapist to interact with all the members in as personal a way as he had wanted to. Some of the children were too aggressive and frightened other members. Also, the program did not have the support of the children's teachers or staff, who considered the program too permissive, too noisy, and too disruptive to the routine.

COMMENTARY: Although this group was conducted to assess whether play therapy is effective in improving the emotional and behavioral adjustment of mentally retarded children, the participants were from a "normal" retarded population; that is, they were *not* behavior problems or poorly adjusted to begin with. Thus, these children were not necessarily under threat or stress in developing their "adequate self," and a ceiling effect may have detracted from the more dramatic results that Mehlman had hoped to achieve. Nevertheless, Mehlman's article is important because his approach suggests that nondirective play therapy is effective with retarded children, and even enriched retarded children who were not emotionally disturbed.

SOURCE: Mehlman, B. "Group Play Therapy with Mentally Retarded Children." *Journal of Abnormal and Social Psychology,* 1953, *48,* 53-60.

Activity Therapy for a Dull Boy with Multiple Problems

AUTHORS: Saul Scheidlinger, Morton S. Eisenberg, Charles H. King, and Roland Ostrower

PRECIS: Activity therapy for a boy with severe physical, emotional, and family problems

INTRODUCTION: This article describes a boy of low intelligence (IQ 74) who was enrolled in an activity therapy group after he had not responded in individual treatment in a year and a half. His attendance was poor at individual sessions; he had attended only twenty-five sessions over the eighteen-month period. The therapist believed that the boy might profit from activity therapy, since he had limited ability to develop self-awareness and activity therapy might improve his poor self-image (body image), which caused many of his problems. The therapist also hoped that this approach would be less threatening to him and to his mother, who resisted therapy herself.

CASE EXAMPLE: Carl was a ten-year-old boy when he enrolled in the group. He had a history of physical problems, beginning with his birth, which was two months premature. His mother, who was fifteen at the time, did not know how to parent, and he walked at thirteen months only when a neighbor held him up on his feet and showed her that he was ready to walk. His mother had three other children by different friends, and Carl was pushed into the background and was the least liked of all her children. He apparently received harsh discipline from his mother, who resented having children.

Carl was underweight and had a chronic nasal drip and a scaly skin condition for which his mother would not seek medical treatment because they were "hereditary." He had poor vision and wore huge glasses. He also had a tremor of the hands and poor coordination. A neurological examination was recommended, but his mother resisted. (He did have such an examination years later and was found to have Little's disease, a congenital disorder of the central nervous system characterized by spastic stiffness of the limbs.) Carl had been referred for treatment by the school, after his teacher reported that he had marked learning problems and did not know any letters or numbers, could not get along with peers and was teased by them, and told "imaginary tales."

Carl entered an activity group of five boys and a therapist, who had already met for five sessions. In the first session, he came into the room, where all the boys were quietly working, and called out loudly to the therapist. He began to work on a small crafts project but broke the object's material with his clumsy efforts, and the others laughed at him. He ignored them and talked to the therapist. He later attempted to play follow-the-leader games with the other boys, but he could not keep up with them physically and ended up watching from the sidelines. In later sessions, he tried craft projects but was not too successful. He would call loudly to the therapist if other boys teased him, but he never moved toward the therapist for protection. In the fifteenth session, he worked hard on a project and told the object "I'm going to finish you." The other boys were supportive in the face of his ineptness, but if he bragged and presented himself as competent, they would tease him. His attendance was excellent, and although he occasionally regressed and would cry and complain, he generally developed improved reality perception and frustration tolerance.

At the end of a year of therapy, he still made grandiose statements that angered peers. When anxious, he did not withdraw but depended on the therapist to rescue him. He was quite resilient and would return again and again to a situation he was trying to master.

In the second year, he got along better with peers by reducing some of his annoying behaviors and listening carefully to the boys when they helped him on a project. He was now more secure in the group, since the other boys accepted his limitations and tried to help him. He was making no academic progress at school but had made progress with peers. He had a best friend with whom he shared toys and overnight visits, and he got along with his classmates. He occasionally would fight back when attacked by others, whereas previously he did not know how to defend himself. His mother did seek medical attention, which lessened his skin and nasal drip problems; and his grooming improved, so that he looked more normal.

In the third year, Carl would come late to therapy and would seem to derive pleasure out of the warm welcomes of the others. He would engage in structured roughhousing, which had been too threatening before. He could take temporary rejection or rebuff without a tantrum. The others continued to teach him craft and game skills; and when they told him he was acting "crazy," he would stop. He went to the school counselor to find a job, since his mother did not give him spending money. At camp the staff reported that he was accepted by his age mates for the first time and was socially poised and perceptive. He also became the champion of the weak and would protect younger boys.

In the fourth year, his attendance continued to be perfect.

He discovered a talent for playing bongo drums and was recognized by the other members for this ability. He declined to play organized games such as baseball because he was so unskilled, but he was pleased when the other group members insisted that he should play because he was part of the group. Carl became a leader in getting other boys to control their impulses. He often thought of good projects that he could not do himself but that the group members could do together, such as building a birdhouse. He complimented the work of others.

After treatment Carl moved to a "rough" neighborhood and got into fights, but he also made several friends. He took part in sports at school and joined a neighborhood boys' center. He had a job in a supermarket and was receiving vocational training. Results of a Rorschach showed many improvements over four years of activity therapy. He was less rigid, less concerned with authority, less ritualistic, and more relaxed, and his depression had lifted.

COMMENTARY: The structure of the group provided safe relationships, which were a marked contrast to Carl's earlier relationships. Because the group was able to accept his deformities, Carl was able to accept them himself. The more his peers accepted him, the more Carl was able to relax and identify with the group members in a positive way.

Although many group practitioners and theorists believe that youngsters with physical deformities and mental deficiencies should be excluded from such groups, the authors point out that the group represented Carl's only major source of emotional security and support. Activity group therapy worked when other treatment efforts did not and were not accepted by Carl or his family.

SOURCE: Scheidlinger, S., Eisenberg, M. S., King, C. H., and Ostrower, R. "Activity Group Therapy of a Dull Boy with Severe Body Ego Problems." *International Journal of Group Psychotherapy,* 1962, *12,* 41-55.

Additional Reading

Moore, C. L. "Activity Group Failure: Verbal Group Therapy Success in a Special Education Program." *International Journal of Group Psychotherapy,* 1981, *31,* 223-231.

Activity group therapy was instituted with six educable mentally retarded children, ages eight to twelve. The children exhibited low self-esteem, poor peer relations, withdrawal, and classroom management problems. The goal of the activity group was to enhance problem-solving ability and improve self-esteem through involving members in activities and interpersonal interactions. The group met once a week for ninety-minute sessions over a period of four months.

Although the children manipulated the toys provided, they preferred to sit together on the play mat and talk. They initiated such topics as separation and loss, being different, anger, and sadness. The cotherapists encouraged the children to express their feelings and discuss solutions to the problems as they identified them. The children enjoyed warm physical contact with the therapists and each other, and showed much insight and support with each other's problems. The children's teachers reported that the youngsters showed less withdrawal and aggressiveness, were more assertive, and had improved in overall social functioning in the classroom. Their parents reported similar improvements at home.

Learning Disabilities and Underachievement

Many children with learning problems have been labeled by peers or themselves as "retards" or failures. They lack motivation in academic areas because they feel that they cannot achieve. Group therapy for the learning disabled generally focuses on improving motivation, self-esteem, and peer relations through a verbal discussion format. Though researchers have found self-esteem and motivation to be highly correlated, some of these groups improved self-esteem but not motivation, and some improved motivation but not self-esteem.

Academic Underachievement

AUTHORS: Ben C. Finney and Elizabeth Van Dalsem

PRECIS: Improving underachieving students' attitudes toward school through group counseling

INTRODUCTION: Group counseling was instituted with ninety-two students who were academically able but were underachieving. The goals of the counseling program were to improve the students' attitudes toward school and increase their grade point averages. It was assumed that academic and personal adjustment could be improved if the students' academic (and personal) problems and the motives behind them could be identified and alternative solutions found.

TREATMENT: Sophomore students from six high schools were given the Differential Aptitude Test Battery (DAT). Students with a DAT at or above the 75th percentile were considered academically able. Students whose grades were below the mean for all students at their DAT level were considered underachieving for the purposes of this research study. (Thus, to obtain enough students for experimental and control groups, the authors rated half of the students above the 75th DAT percentile as underachievers.)

There were ninety-two students in the eight treatment groups and eighty-five students in the control groups. The treatment groups ranged in size from five to fifteen members. This wide range occurred because twenty-three treatment students moved away and therefore dropped out of the groups. The groups met weekly during school over a period of two school years. Each group had its own leader—a school counselor who had volunteered to participate. The leaders attended one year of weekly training sessions on group therapy prior to the treatment, and they were supervised weekly during the treatment program.

The students approached the group in the same way that they approached their school experience; that is, they wasted time and tried to blame their lack of progress on others. They spent much of the time criticizing the school, teachers, parents, the social system, and the government; and they avoided introspection regarding their academic difficulties and the feelings behind their actions. The inexperienced therapists were heavily invested in the success of their groups, and were conflicted over when to assume responsibility and guide the group and when to remain passive until the group members took responsibility for themselves. The sessions often consisted of trivial or confused discussions or anxious silences. Gradually, the sessions became more productive, and members expressed personal feelings and fears. The program was supposed to last a year but was continued for another year because modest changes in members were beginning to appear and the leaders believed that the group identity and process had just coalesced. By the end of the second year, the students were discussing meaningful topics, although they never shared "deep" material.

RESULTS: Several measures were used to assess the effects of treatment. Unfortunately, the main treatment goal, academic improvement, did not occur; there was no change in grade point averages. There was significant improvement in the students' attendance records, however, and teachers reported that the students had better attitudes toward the school and learning. The teachers further reported that the students were less rebellious, exhibited less passive resistance, and were more attentive and willing to ask for help. On the California Psychological Inventory, the group participants were more self-confident, outgoing, ambitious, and resourceful after treatment. The students themselves believed that the program was worthwhile, although they tended to see more change in other members than they saw in themselves.

COMMENTARY: The authors conclude that the group therapy program improved the students' attitudes toward school but did not improve their performance. The treatment effects, the authors admit, may have been minimized because the therapists were inexperienced and the students were not motivated to change. In fact, in order to get enough students for the therapy and control groups, the authors had adopted a rather loose criterion for underachievement; and the students in treatment had been rated superior to average in overall adjustment on the California Personality Inventory before treatment even began.

This article exemplifies the difficulties in doing therapy with adolescents who do not want it and do not believe they have problems. The progress was slow and frustrating, and the sessions were characterized by much resistance and avoidance in members. We still believe that group therapy is the treatment of choice with underachieving students, but we recommend that participation be voluntary and for students with serious achievement problems that they themselves wish to modify.

SOURCE: Finney, B. C., and Van Dalsem, E. "Group Counseling for Gifted Underachieving High School Students." *Counseling Psychologist,* 1965, *16,* 27-44.

Affective Needs of the Learning Disabled

AUTHOR: Gary W. Ledebur

PRECIS: Using group therapy to develop self-worth and academic motivation in learning disabled schoolchildren

INTRODUCTION: The author observes that learning disabled elementary students often have more difficulty in mastering developmental tasks than regular students do, especially in social areas and personal self-esteem. The learning disabled student often has had a long history of academic failure, peer ridicule, pressure to work harder, and low self-esteem; and placement in special classes is socially and emotionally traumatic for the child. The LD classroom itself is laden with stress and neglects the emotional needs of the child; the teacher is under pressure to bring the child up to grade level, and a positive relationship rarely develops between the child and the teacher or between classmates.

Ledebur advocates that the school psychologist take an

active role in facilitating the social and emotional development of the LD student, since the psychologist is usually the person who refers the child to the class and is a consultant to the LD class. Ledebur proposes that a therapeutic group can be conducted by the psychologist to deal with the affective and social problems of these youngsters. Such a group can help LD children develop self-understanding and self-acceptance, social understanding and social relatedness, personal values and an understanding of the values of others, and problem-solving and language skills to compensate for their deficiencies.

TREATMENT: The group should include four to seven students, with an ideal size of five. A group with fewer than four students, in Ledebur's opinion, does not permit sufficient group interaction and places too much pressure on individuals to participate. For children under nine years old, sessions should be limited to thirty minutes; for older children, sessions may be extended to forty-five minutes. The groups should meet in a small, quiet room (other than the classroom) where the children can sit on the floor in a circle. Finally, prior to any meeting of the group, the leader should meet individually with each student to explain the purpose of the group, to begin to develop a positive therapeutic relationship, and to invite the child to participate.

In the first session, the leader reviews the purpose of the group and establishes the rules. Ledebur uses two rules in his groups: (1) Everyone must listen without interrupting when others are talking. (2) No hitting, poking, tickling, or fighting. Reminding the children of the rules is usually enough to help them control themselves. If that does not calm them, the session should be terminated and the situation discussed in the next session.

The leader's main role is to establish a group atmosphere of trust and acceptance, so that members feel they can share important concerns. The leader should be empathic and reflective and show positive regard. The children generally introduce topics, and the leader facilitates conversation and the group process. As the children become more comfortable with each other, the leader initiates topics relevant to LD children, such as special class placement, being teased, and feeling dumb. The leader focuses on understanding feelings so that they are less threatening. He also helps the members deal with their problems, emphasizing that problems can be dealt with in adaptive rather than maladaptive ways. Finally, the leader encourages confrontation between members. The confrontation can be negative, as in pointing out a member's disruptive behavior. It can also be positive, as in reassuring a member with a poor self-image that he or she is not stupid and has important ideas.

The author has used the process group approach for three years and finds it valuable in developing self-worth and self-acceptance in LD children. It also provides the psychologist with insights into the children's problem behaviors. For example, one child related in the group that his parents tried to teach him "sounds" at home and scolded him if he did not meet their expectations. This situation caused him much anxiety that interfered with his learning. When the parents were asked to stop tutoring him, he became more relaxed in school and his grades improved.

COMMENTARY: This article considers the need for schools to address the emotional concerns of schoolchildren with learning disabilities. These youngsters have average or near average intelligence yet are unable to learn. They often have a poor understanding of their problem and are poorly motivated in academic areas, since they do not perform well academically and are often labeled slow or retarded by relatives, peers, and themselves. Group therapy can provide an emotional outlet for them to express their feelings and learn more about their learning disability and its effect on them. The group also helps them identify their strengths, improve problem-solving skills, and develop self-worth. Thus, the group can improve the children's attitude and motivation toward academics.

SOURCE: Ledebur, G. W. "The Elementary Learning Disability Process Group and the School Psychologist." *Psychology in the Schools,* 1977, *14,* 62-66.

Group Therapy with Underachievers

AUTHOR: Judith Mishne

PRECIS: Giving children with learning and behavior problems an opportunity to talk about their problems

INTRODUCTION: Children with average and above average IQs were experiencing learning and behavior problems and had difficulty relating with peers. They did not respond to tutoring; in fact, the individual attention increased their anxiety and academic frustration. The teachers were aware that these children had emotional problems that were interfering with school performance. They had referred the children for treatment, but the families did not follow through in contacting outside agencies. Since the teachers had the responsibility for educating these children, they hoped that group therapy might alleviate some of the emotional problems that were interfering with learning.

The children all came from families that were filled with turmoil because of continuing marital and financial problems. All the families had a "family secret," such as a seriously ill parent or sibling, that had been kept from the children. The mothers fostered an overdependent relationship between them and their children. Two of the mothers shared bedrooms with their sons. Each child was the youngest or one of the youngest in the family and had a long-standing physical and verbal conflict with an older sibling.

The goals of therapy were to provide the children with supervised socialization and discussion to help them identify with peers and separate from their families, with the expectation that their school anxiety would then decrease and they would be more open to learning.

TREATMENT: Five boys, ages eight and nine, met with the school social worker twice a week for thirty minutes. The time was extended at the request of the boys. The group met in a small tutoring room around a table to limit mobility and facilitate discussion. The children were told that the group would help them improve their behavior and their schoolwork. Much discussion time was devoted to examining their behavior and attempting to modify it. They talked about problem encounters with their teachers and the principal.

Several techniques were used to stimulate relevant discussion. The children made clay puppets and pretended that they were teachers and their puppets the pupils. The children were also asked to bring in good papers and poor ones, so that they could discuss their work and see what problems they shared. The therapist discovered that the boys had an unrealistic notion of the amount of effort required for the mastery of learning tasks. They all employed magical thinking and day-dreamed in class. Since they found mathematics easier than reading, they were asked to bring in a favorite book and to take turns reading in group. The boys were eager and competitive in reading. By reading to one another, they recognized each other's reading problems and gained insight into their own. One boy went so fast that he changed words. Another never looked carefully at word endings. The boys were noncritical and supportive in talking about each other's reading problems. The worker also required written work in the group, which brought about discussions of sloppy work and "I don't care" attitudes.

The worker pointed out the boys' disruptive behaviors in the group session and discussed how those same behaviors got them into trouble in class. The children spontaneously compared their acting out in class with peers to their behavior at home with siblings.

All the children asked to meet individually with the worker to discuss personal problems and ask for advice, such as parents' pending divorce, a mother's illness, and a boy's embarrassment at sharing his room with his mother. The worker encouraged these meetings to give the boys support and avoid exposing the situations to the whole group.

RESULTS: After four months of treatment, the children were still anxious in taking achievement tests. However, their reading scores improved eight months to their proper third-grade level, and their mathematics scores improved to their proper level. Teachers reported improved social adjustment, increased motivation and interest, better conforming to classroom routines, improved acceptance by peers, and less anxiety in class.

COMMENTARY: The boys in this group seemed to recognize each other's problems and became a cohesive, working group almost immediately. They welcomed the opportunity to meet with boys who had similar problems. As peer relationships and rapport improved, academic material was introduced in a nonthreatening way. The program appears to be useful and effective for a regular school setting where a number of children need help and their parents resist treatment.

SOURCE: Mishne, J. "Group Therapy in an Elementary School." *Social Casework,* 1971, *21,* 18-25.

Additional Readings

Johnson, L. S. "Group Hypnotherapy with Learning Disabled Children." Paper presented at annual convention of the Rocky Mountain Psychological Association, Las Vegas, 1979.

Hypnotic and self-hypnotic training groups were developed for learning disabled children that used hypnotic suggestions related to improvements in academic performance and self-esteem. The children improved in self-esteem but not in academic performance compared to a control group. The learning disabled children were found to be more hypnotically susceptible than a sample of normal children.

Kilman, P. R., Henry, S. E., Scarbro, H., and Laughlin, J. E. "The Impact of Affective Education on Elementary School Underachievers." *Psychology in the Schools,* 1979, *16,* 217-223.

Fourth through sixth graders who were identified as underachievers by their teachers participated in affective education counseling groups. After fifteen weekly sessions, the children showed significant improvements in their reading skills and described themselves as more warm-hearted, emotionally stable, venturesome, and vigorous than their control counterparts described themselves.

McCollum, P. S., and Anderson, R. P. "Group Counseling with Reading Disabled Children." *Journal of Counseling Psychology,* 1974, *21,* 150-155.

Reading disabled children from three schools participated in group counseling. After ten treatment sessions, the children showed improvements in oral and reading vocabulary skills. There was no improvement in sentence comprehension.

School Behavior Problems

One of the problems in developing a group for children with classroom behavior problems is that the published reports on these groups often do not include results and many of the programs lasted only six to fourteen weeks. Since behavior problems often are related to more serious emotional problems, the effects of short-term treatment are often not conclusive or enduring. Many authors in this section relate school problems to the inability to get along with peers, and therapy is aimed at improving peer relationships to improve the children's attitudes toward the school environment.

Affective Education for Severely Disturbed Children

AUTHORS: Nancy Anderson and R. Thomas Marrone

PRECIS: Psychiatric treatment for children in classrooms for the emotionally disturbed

INTRODUCTION: Children attending special classes for the emotionally disturbed in a public school were seen in individual psychoanalysis three to five times a week through a private psychiatrist or a clinic. The following problems developed with this procedure: the parents experienced financial and emotional strain; a large amount of staff time was consumed in attempts to coordinate therapy and educational programming; the teachers complained that the therapists did not understand the children's classroom behavior and made unrealistic recommendations; and the therapists complained that the teachers did not understand the psychodynamics of the children's behavior and mismanaged them in class.

The treatment was moved into the classroom, where a child psychologist and a child psychiatrist led therapeutic discussion groups, and the teachers and teachers' aides were included as cotherapists.

In trying a variety of group approaches, the authors ruled out packaged affective education programs on the market, concluding that these programs promote intellectualization rather than true internalization of the concepts presented. They ruled out behavior modification, believing that this approach is useful in managing some classroom behavior but that these children need to feel loved and cared for without the attention's being contingent on appropriate behavior. They found that the children were interested in discussing problems and feelings with each other in a group where interpretations are made.

TREATMENT: The authors suggest guidelines that they conclude have been most successful in structuring discussion groups for youngsters with diagnoses ranging from schizophrenia to primary behavior disorders.

First, the group is held in a fairly small room, so that the children cannot remove themselves too far from the group. The children sit in a circle in chairs, so that they cannot move around too much and so that overdependent children do not cluster around the adults and ignore their peers.

Second, the teacher is kept in charge, providing control and making the child feel comfortable in talking, without fear of being ridiculed by peers later.

Third, the basic ground rules are that no hitting is permitted and that the sessions are confidential. Initially, the children are required to raise their hands to be recognized. This helps the leaders be more aware of children who dominate the conversation or children who do not participate. As the group progresses, this rule is dropped.

Fourth, the children choose the topics for discussion. The authors state that a hidden agenda or theme will always develop. The therapists keep the discussion focused and facilitate involvement. Occasionally, a child will introduce a topic that is too anxiety producing for the other members. In this instance, the therapist should say that the topic is appropriate for a group discussion but perhaps at a later time. Initially, the children may talk about their favorite activities, television shows, and so forth. Such apparently "idle" talk helps the children become comfortable in the group and provides the therapists with valuable information about individual children's self-esteem, concerns, and conflicts.

Throughout the discussions, the therapists try to promote self-awareness and understanding of self and others by reflecting and interpreting feelings and conflicts and encouraging the children to talk out and solve their problems instead of acting them out.

COMMENTARY: This approach coordinates and maximizes the involvement of the therapists and teachers and gives them an understanding of each other's roles and problems. The therapists are able to see the children's peer interactions and improve them directly, which they cannot do in individual sessions. The teachers are able to understand the children better and learn therapeutic techniques of managing their behavior in the classroom.

SOURCE: Anderson, N., and Marrone, R. T. "Group Therapy for Emotionally Disturbed Children: A Key to Affective Education." *American Journal of Orthopsychiatry,* 1977, *47,* 97-103.

Group for Behavior Problem Children in Inner-City Schools

AUTHORS: Avner Barcai and Esther H. Robinson

PRECIS: Conventional verbal group therapy resulting in marked improvements in classroom behavior problems of fifth and sixth graders

INTRODUCTION: According to the authors, group psychotherapy with preadolescent children (ages ten to twelve) has been limited to activity therapy. They developed a project to evaluate the use of conventional verbal group therapy with preadolescents exhibiting school behavior problems and underachievement. The therapeutic goals were to help the children recognize their own feelings about significant events in their lives, to become aware of the effects of their behavior on others, and to understand how other people's behavior affects them. The authors believed that with these insights the children would begin to show more responsible behavior in the classroom.

TREATMENT: Fifth- and sixth-grade teachers at two inner-city schools were asked to refer for treatment all children who exhibited problems in academic achievement or classroom behavior. The children came from communities characterized by overcrowding, broken families, and poor physical surroundings.

Sixty-one children were referred. After a brief interview, all were treated for six weeks with dextroamphetamine sulphate and for another six weeks with a placebo. Seven children dropped out of treatment, twenty-three responded to medication, sixteen showed minimal improvements with medication, and fifteen showed no change. Group therapy was instituted with the children who did not respond to the drug or who showed minimal response. In each school eight children participated in the therapy group, and the other children participated in an art group to serve as a control comparison group. Half of the members were males, and half were females in each of the groups.

The therapy groups met once a week for fifty minutes during school hours, so that there would not be a problem with attendance. There were two cotherapists. The groups met in conference rooms, where they sat around a long table. The groups met for eleven sessions.

In both groups the children were told that they would be meeting together weekly to talk about problems at school or at home. In Group A one girl immediately began talking about a situation in her home, and others talked about similar situations in their own lives. The therapists interpreted underlying feelings to the group and supported group discussion. At the next session, one child acted withdrawn, and another commented that she was getting too much of the group's attention and should be ignored. She gradually rejoined the group. In the next sessions, the children began testing the limits by teasing and talking in small groups. The therapists focused on the impact of the children's behavior on each other and interpreted their defensive maneuvers. By the fourth session, a few children began trying to exert control over the disruptive behaviors of others, and became more and more successful as the weeks passed. The children were able to understand that their present behavior was influenced by the past. The children's behavior improved in the group, and they were much less impulsive and more attentive.

In Group B, at the other school, the children complained about the school, and two children were constantly fighting and disrupting the group. The children never achieved enough control to be a productive group. In only one meeting, when three of the seven members were absent, was any progress made. Toward the end the children complained about the absence of rigid rules. Two boys who had been more involved expressed anger at the group for blocking progress.

RESULTS: Teacher reports and evaluations of the group members showed that, of fourteen children who completed treatment, eight made marked improvement and six were somewhat improved, the children in Group A showing greater improvement than those in Group B. In the art control group, two of the thirteen children who completed the program showed marked improvement, six were somewhat improved, and five showed no change.

COMMENTARY: The authors conclude that verbal therapy is helpful for preadolescent, lower socioeconomic children, even though many writers in the field believe that these children do not possess sufficient verbal skills to participate meaningfully in verbal therapy. They believe that Group B was less successful than Group A because its members were more aggressive and the school was less supportive. For example, teachers repeatedly interrupted Group B by asking a child to run an errand, and the therapists arrived several times to find that all the children had gone on a field trip. The authors suggest that, with more aggressive children, smaller groups of four or five should be used.

Apparently the children in Group A viewed the sessions as a positive opportunity to discuss their problems, and several children were psychologically ready to begin to share concerns from the start. Perhaps an initial, individual interview with each child would help minimize problems that occurred in Group B by letting the children know ahead of time what is expected of them.

This article shows that often a therapist cannot help individuals unless the school system that maintains their problems is changed. Group B's school system was not amenable to change and simply wanted someone to come in and "cure" the "sick" children. In many ways this partial treatment is worse than no treatment at all, because the children get the message that no one can help them and that they are beyond hope.

SOURCE: Barcai, A., and Robinson, E. H. "Conventional Group Therapy with Preadolescent Children." *International Journal of Group Psychotherapy,* 1969, *19,* 334-345.

Group Counseling with Disruptive Seventh Graders

AUTHOR: Janet C. Goodman

PRECIS: Reducing disruptive classroom behaviors by giving adolescents an opportunity to talk about their problems

INTRODUCTION: Nine seventh-grade children were referred to the school counselor for disruptive classroom behavior and underachievement. The counselor described the children as oversensitive to criticism, moody, impulsive, and anxious. Four came from broken homes. The counselor treated them in group therapy to give the youngsters a chance to release their tensions by talking about their problems and to examine their behavior with the help of their peers.

TREATMENT: The counselor met with each child individually and invited him to join a group to talk about his problems and feelings. The counselor also set forth the ground rules: no racial or religious name calling, complete confidentiality, listening without interrupting, and attending at least three meetings before dropping out.

The children were shy and self-conscious at first, but they were talking freely by the end of the first session. Refreshments were served; but this proved disruptive to the group, and the children chose to discontinue having them. In the next sessions, the children all talked at once and competed for group recognition. The sessions were chaotic and lacked purpose. The counselor decided to divide the group into two groups, to provide more control and give more children a chance to talk.

Both groups quickly became cohesive working groups in which the children discussed their problems with teachers and learning and revealed their fears and feelings of inadequacy. They ventilated their feelings and were supportive of each other.

RESULTS: The results of the group treatment were not formally evaluated; however, teachers reported positive behavioral change in seven of the nine participants. They reported that the children were more aware of their disruptive behavior and were able to exercise more control over it. The children made vast improvements in academic achievement.

COMMENTARY: According to statements by the adolescents, the group provided their first opportunity to talk about themselves and to relate meaningfully with peers. As they began to interact more with peers, the adolescents became more sensitive to the effects of their behavior on others and tried to act in more socially appropriate ways.

SOURCE: Goodman, J. C. "Group Counseling with Seventh Graders." *Personnel and Guidance Journal,* 1976, *25,* 519-520.

Behavioral Group for Disruptive Schoolchildren

AUTHORS: Jim Gumaer and Robert Myrick

PRECIS: Using client-centered and behavior modification techniques to reduce disruptive, acting-out behaviors

INTRODUCTION: Twenty-five children in grades kindergarten through six were referred to a school counselor for treatment because they disrupted classes by talking out in class, leaving the desk at inappropriate times, failing to start their work on time, and hitting classmates. The counselor observed the children in order to confirm the teachers' assessment of the problem, to determine possible classroom reinforcers that maintained the problems, to assess the children's ability to verbalize and profit from a group experience, and to identify possible reinforcers to use in the group. The counselor used this information to develop an eight-week group therapy program that combined behavior modification and client-centered techniques.

TREATMENT: The children were divided into groups of about eight members each. The counselor met once a week for forty-five minutes with each group. He provided a minimum of structure to promote group cohesion and focus attention on the children's behavior.

In the first session, the children sat in a circle and introduced themselves. The counselor explained that he would be talking with the children about their feelings and about problems that were important to them and their teachers. The counselor ignored disruptive children and listened attentively to the children who talked with him. At one point two children began fighting, and he restrained them. He told them that they could not hurt each other and that they had to talk the problem out. He also introduced a group rule, that the children had to take turns talking, and he assured them that everyone would get a turn. The children discussed the problem behaviors that brought them into the group, and they identified three behaviors to work on in the group: talking out, leaving one's chair, and being discourteous to others.

In the second session, the counselor did not initiate conversation but charted the children's behavior by marking down each time a child exhibited one of the three targeted behaviors. The children finally asked him what he was doing, and he told them. They were concerned that he was going to tell on them. He assured them that he would not, and they discussed who had the most marks and who had the least.

In the third session, the counselor gave praise and candy to each child who had less than two disruptive behaviors in the first five-minute period. He explained his procedure at the end of the first reinforcement period. By the end of the third session, disruptive behaviors were reduced, and all the children had earned some candy. The reinforcement procedure was used in all but the final session. The children discussed their own topics in the remaining sessions, including being sent to the principal, getting spanked, losing privileges as a punishment, and completing assignments on time. The counselor focused on the causes and consequences of the problem behaviors under discussion.

In the eighth and final meeting, the candy was discontinued, but the counselor continued to praise appropriate behaviors in the group. He summarized the previous sessions and the children's improvements.

In concurrent weekly meetings with teachers, the counselor encouraged them to ignore less disruptive behaviors (such as whispering and passing notes) and to reinforce with praise the positive contributions of the children (such as raising their hands and starting their work on time).

The children all stated that they got along better with their classmates and that they wanted to continue improving their behavior. The teachers reported that the children were much less disruptive in class. However, the improvements did not endure. According to the teachers' reports, the children regressed to previous behaviors about ten weeks after the groups ended.

COMMENTARY: The rapid reduction in disruptive classroom behaviors suggests that behavioral group counseling can be valuable in managing children's classroom behavior. The authors believe that the systematic reinforcement program should be continued by the classroom teacher following counseling. Another option is to meet longer as a group, since one cannot expect lasting attitudinal and behavioral changes to occur after only eight sessions.

SOURCE: Gumaer, J., and Myrick, R. "Behavioral Group Counseling with Disruptive Children." *School Counselor,* 1974, *21,* 313-317.

Group Treatment of Children Alienated from School

AUTHORS: Louise A. Frey and Ralph L. Kolodny

PRECIS: Alienation from school, a consequence of isolation from peers, treated in group therapy

INTRODUCTION: This article describes a treatment program for children who were seriously alienated from the school. Some were overpassive and uninvolved with peers; others were isolated due to their aggressive behavior toward peers. They came from chaotic family backgrounds characterized by divorce, desertion, physical fights between parents, economic deprivation, and in some instances psychotic parents. One member had satisfactory school performance but was enuretic and clung to her teachers; one was hyperactive and depressed; another was effeminate; and several were aggressive. It was hoped that a group experience would help these children separate from their parents by showing them that school could be a source of emotional gratification rather than a place to be feared or fought. The aims of the group were to provide new opportunities with peers that would result in improved social skills, greater self-sufficiency, and a positive view of peer interaction.

TREATMENT: The fourteen participants (broken into a boys' group and a girls' group) were at the same level of social functioning and could communicate verbally with peers. The members were interviewed individually, and all gave an accurate description of the behavior problems that brought them to the group. However, none of them believed they had problems relating to peers, and they all believed they had many friends.

The treatment method used was "social group work," which provided activities that stimulated discussion, gave opportunities for achievement, and helped the children develop informal relationships. Discussions were structured around the activities.

The therapist was permissive and did not stop the children

from running around the school. She did point out that they might get into trouble and would have to suffer the consequences. The children expressed approach-avoidance conflicts about the group because they liked to come and liked the worker but were afraid that other children in the school would call them "mental" or think they were "bad."

About two thirds of the way through the first year, the children formed a strong identity. They began to use the group to work out problems with peers and teachers in the school. Members supported each other and sympathized with each other. For example, they told one boy who was suffering stress in his family that whatever was happening to him on the outside, they liked him and were glad he was a part of the group. Another boy had to move to another neighborhood, and the children supported him and helped him deal with making new friends.

The general approach was to retard regression and encourage the children to express feelings and solve problems. The program lasted two school years.

COMMENTARY: The authors note that alienation from the school is more often related to fear of peers and the social pressures of school than to academic difficulties. Group therapy is an effective method of reducing children's isolation in the school, improving peer relationships, helping the children separate from home, and freeing tensions so that the children can draw greater emotional and intellectual satisfaction from school.

SOURCE: Frey, L. A., and Kolodny, R. L. "Group Treatment for the Alienated Child in the School." *International Journal of Group Psychotherapy,* 1966, *16,* 321-337.

Parent and Group Counseling to Reduce Behavior Problems

AUTHORS: Edward J. Hayes, George K. Cunningham, and Joseph B. Robinson

PRECIS: Reducing the behavior problems of disruptive schoolchildren through parent counseling and support groups

INTRODUCTION: In developing a counseling program to reduce behavior problems in schoolchildren, the authors discovered that the research was inconsistent on whether the child or the parents should receive treatment. This article describes a study that compared the effectiveness of both methods with a minority student population.

TREATMENT: Ninety-two fifth and sixth graders in four schools were identified by their school counselors as having behavior problems: fighting, failing to complete assignments, getting out of seat without permission, leaving the room without permission, talking back to teachers, disturbing peers, and walking the halls without permission. The children were assigned to one of eight groups. Four groups served as controls and received no treatment. Two groups received group counseling. The parents of the children in the remaining two groups received group counseling, but these children received no direct treatment. All four treatment groups met for twelve weekly sessions.

In the group counseling with students, the counselors used three types of interventions. The first was to role-play situations clearly related to poor school attendance and poor academic motivation and achievement. The role play was followed by a discussion of alternatives to inappropriate behaviors. The second intervention was to encourage involvement in extracurricular activities, with the expectation that the children would develop a positive identification with peers and the school. The counselors found this a very effective technique. Finally, the counselors led occupational and career choice discussions, which were supplemented with guest speakers and field trips.

This exposed the children to a variety of positive role models and vocations.

The parents met in informal discussion groups that focused on their children's behavior and school performance. The counselors spent much of their time helping the parents develop communication and listening skills, so that they could understand their children's point of view and possibly begin to change their own behavior and reactions. A workshop on Parent Effectiveness Training (Thomas Gordon, *Parent Effectiveness Training,* New York: Wyden, 1970) was held as part of the group. Parents were given a small stipend to defray the costs of attending the workshop, and lunch was provided for the three workshop sessions.

RESULTS: The authors report that the parent groups influenced the children's behavior indirectly. The children's academic motivation, overall anxiety, and self-esteem improved significantly; and this treatment was superior to direct counseling with children. However, the authors caution that the effects may reflect differences in the counselors themselves rather than differences in the treatment methods.

COMMENTARY: The results of this study, as well as the inconsistent results reported in earlier studies, may indicate that the expertise of the individual therapist determines the effectiveness of therapy. Also, other research has shown that changes in behavior at home are not necessarily carried over to behavior in the school, and vice versa. The effects of this treatment might have been more significant if the groups had met longer.

SOURCE: Hayes, E. J., Cunningham, G. K., and Robinson, J. B. "Counseling Focus: Are Parents Necessary?" *Elementary School Guidance and Counseling,* 1977, *11,* 8-14.

Group Modification of Discipline Problems

AUTHORS: Eugene W. Kelly and Doris B. Matthews

PRECIS: Using behavior reinforcement and discussion to decrease discipline problems in fifth and sixth graders

INTRODUCTION: Children who are persistent discipline problems in the school impede their own academic progress and interfere with the teacher's ability to instruct other children in the classroom. Whether the child's discipline problems are the result of an inadequate home life, a disruptive or disadvantaged neighborhood, or inadequate adult models, schools must continue to work with the children that come to them. The authors believe that these children have developed inappropriate ways of thinking and behaving, which bring them into constant conflict with teachers and school personnel. To help these children develop more appropriate patterns of thinking and behaving, the authors established a group counseling program where the children openly discussed their problems and where behavioral principles were used to shape behaviors related to classroom functioning.

TREATMENT: Teachers in the fifth and sixth grades of a racially integrated elementary school in a low-income community were asked to refer their most serious discipline problems for treatment. Twelve children were selected from those referred. The group met eight times over a period of ten weeks for hour-long sessions. Two counselors met with the group. Members were required to sit heterogeneously—mixing races and sexes—in a tight circle.

The basic guidelines for the sessions were that all problems and concerns of any member or the group were appropriate for discussion. The discussions were directed toward solving problems realistically and without blaming or judging anyone. Group members chose topics for discussion. The counselors kept the discussion from wandering and guided discussions toward assessment of values, making decisions, and solving problems. The counselors also encouraged quiet members to participate, reinforced socially appropriate behavior, and protected members from harmful self-revelation.

Beginning with the third session, the behavioral aspect of the group was introduced. Members were told that they were expected to participate in an orderly fashion (raising their hands, waiting to be recognized, and talking to the group) and to listen quietly to the person speaking. They were told that they would be directly rewarded for these behaviors. One counselor kept a tally of the appropriate behaviors and rewarded members with a penny Tootsie Roll or a piece of taffy for every three target behaviors performed. At the end of each session, the member with the most points received a candy bar.

RESULTS: Ratings by the teachers indicated that the students who attended regularly made positive improvements in classroom behavior, but the improvement was not statistically significant ($p < .10$). The authors conclude that the combined methods they used were effective in modifying disruptive classroom behaviors but that the groups should have met more frequently and/or over a longer period of time than eight sessions. They believe that the combination of insight methods and behavior modification produces immediate behavior change and can effect deep and long-lasting positive growth.

COMMENTARY: Of the twelve members, only seven attended regularly, and the eight sessions were spread over a ten-week period. The low attendance and the low number of sessions suggest that the members had little opportunity to form a group identity or group cohesion that is the core of the group process. We agree with the authors that more time is needed to effect the significant and long-lasting attitudinal and behavioral changes they believe can be achieved with this combined method. We believe their approach is valuable because it treats both the overt behavioral symptoms and the underlying emotional components of the problem.

SOURCE: Kelly, E. W., and Matthews, D. B. "Group Counseling with Discipline-Problem Children at the Elementary School Level." *School Counselor,* 1971, *18,* 273-278.

Activity Groups for Children with Behavior and Learning Problems

AUTHORS: Robert O. Pasnau, Lois Williams, and Frank F. Tallman

PRECIS: Activity groups, conducted by specially trained teachers, for children with emotionally based learning problems

INTRODUCTION: This article summarizes the results of a twelve-year project in which over 350 children between the ages of six and fifteen were treated in therapeutic activity groups. The program utilized teachers as group leaders. The teachers were released for a half day to prepare for the session, spend an hour with the children, and record detailed observations. The activity groups were designed to bridge the gap between the school and formal psychiatric services; thus, they constituted a preventive mental health program.

TREATMENT: The children targeted for treatment were those who—in the opinion of a psychometrist, the director of guidance for the school, the classroom teachers, and the teacher/leader of the group—had emotionally based learning and behavior problems. Children with severe emotional problems were screened out, as were children who had problems that could be remediated with special help in the classroom.

The teacher/leader met once a week for an hour with a group of five to seven children. Age-appropriate play materials were provided, to encourage the children to explore, interact, and learn about their impact on others. Food was also provided.

The teacher/leader's role was to be available to assist with play and project materials. The teacher/leader did not initiate activities and did not make interpretations but accepted a wide range of verbal and nonverbal behaviors and built a positive, secure atmosphere in the sessions. The leaders found that balanced groups composed of shy and aggressive children needed fewer controls than more aggressive groups did.

RESULTS: The program was rated a success by a variety of sources:

A follow-up study of sixty-nine children one to five years after their participation in the group showed that in social relationships 25 percent were rated quite good, 43 percent fair, 24 percent poor, and 9 percent very poor. Academically, 66 percent were doing average work or above in all academic areas.

The group members reported that they viewed the group as a positive experience in which the adult allowed them much freedom, protected them from the hostility of others, and was someone who "helped." The children reported that they had learned to get along better with others and to control their anger and frustration better.

Independent consultants rated the children initially as anxious and competitive in the group, and they rated the group as disorganized and lacking cohesiveness and cooperation. At the end of four months of activity group meetings, they rated the youngsters as showing no hostility, anxiety, or jealousy and the group as cooperative and organized and providing the members with a sense of security.

Most teachers felt that the groups were useful and should be continued. The program also boosted teacher morale, since the teachers felt that the administration showed interest in them and the children by giving them extra help with these problem children. The teachers who were leaders believed that the groups improved the members' attitudes toward school and peers. They noted that the children became more cooperative and less tense in the group. They also felt that they had become better teachers and more sensitive to the emotional needs of acting-out children.

Finally, the parents reported that the children spoke highly of the group and that the children's attitudes toward school had improved.

COMMENTARY: This group method appears successful in helping emotionally disturbed schoolchildren without having to refer them to formal mental health services outside the school. It overcomes parents' resistance to seeking mental health services and reaches the children before more serious problems develop. The program was relatively inexpensive to the school, since it utilized teachers as group leaders rather than mental health professionals.

SOURCE: Pasnau, R. O., Williams, L., and Tallman, F. F. "Small Activity Groups in the School." *Community Mental Health Journal,* 1971, *7,* 303-311.

Time-Limited Discussion Groups

AUTHOR: Sonya L. Rhodes

PRECIS: Highly structured discussion groups for improving school and social adjustment in problem children

INTRODUCTION: A time-limited group treatment program was utilized at a school with a large number of children needing counseling. The school had asked parents to seek mental health services for their children's multiple problems, but the parents did not follow the recommendations. The children exhibited disturbances in learning, behavior problems, and difficulties relating to peers. This short-term group stressed behavior change. It was offered to modify a specific area of academic functioning (that is, behavior) in the same way that speech and remedial reading are offered to avoid parental resistance.

TREATMENT: Parents were contacted to obtain permission for their child to participate. In individual interviews prior to group treatment, the children were told about the group and its goals. The therapists hoped that these interviews would help to establish rapport and develop motivation for positive behavior changes. The twenty-two participants were from the third through fifth grades. There were four groups; two met for six sessions, and two met for eight sessions.

Since the program was time limited, the therapists were active in providing direction and limits on group behavior and content. Interpretations were made in the group to reflect feelings and conflict areas. The therapists then related the problems in the group to similar behavior problems in the classroom. They stressed behavior change by pointing out alternative coping skills. Throughout the discussions, the therapists implied that the children could make choices for themselves, exert self-control, and find alternatives.

A prevalent theme was the children's aggressive impulses and fantasies. The therapists reflected the feelings and emphasized reality by commenting that the "stories" the youngsters made up told what the children felt like doing to their teachers and other adults but knew they couldn't. This technique allowed for expression of fantasy and strengthened ego functions and social judgment.

Children's fears of failure and feelings of hopelessness in academic areas were expressed and examined in the group. The therapists helped the members differentiate between their strengths and weaknesses, in order to make some academic achievement in their stronger school subjects a possible personal goal for all of them. Other themes included the children's desire for peer acceptance, feelings of being at an "in-between" age, anger at teachers, getting attention, and name calling. The therapists encouraged the children to act out their feelings in situations while they verbalized them, to help them start to talk out their conflicts rather than act them out.

RESULTS: Despite the time limits of the program, behavioral changes did occur. Teachers rated motivation for learning, academic functioning, social adjustment, peer relations, and self-control. Of twenty-two children, nine showed marked improvements, nine showed slight improvements, and four showed no change. These effects endured to the end of the school year (three months). Diagnostic information gathered in the sessions prompted the school to refer six children for further treatment. Two of these children asked for additional treatment after the program ended.

COMMENTARY: This short-term treatment stimulated enough self-understanding and coping skills to motivate many of the participants to control their behavior. It would have been helpful to know whether the number of sessions was related to the behavioral improvements, since we know that some of the children received six hours and some eight hours of treatment. In any event, this article demonstrates that some disruptive children respond to short-term group counseling with specific goals and direction.

SOURCE: Rhodes, S. L. "Short-Term Groups of Latency-Age Children in a School Setting." *International Journal of Group Psychotherapy,* 1973, *23,* 204-216.

Developmental Approach to Reduce Aggression in the Classroom

AUTHORS: Romeria Tidwell and Vickie A. Bachus

PRECIS: Teaching prosocial values to fourth through sixth graders in order to diminish classroom aggression

INTRODUCTION: The authors delineate group treatment methods that have been successful in reducing aggressive behavior in schoolchildren, including behavioral reinforcement, behavior rehearsal, modeling, group activities, and time out. In developing their own group for aggressive boys, Tidwell and Bachus proposed that instilling values of cooperation, empathy, and helping others would reduce fighting and injurious physical contact. They believed that their approach would help the boys think before they act.

TREATMENT: Aggressive boys in the fourth through sixth grades met in groups of six with one therapist. They met for one-hour sessions twice a month. Each of the eight sessions focused on a relevant theme, such as empathy, cooperation, decision making, and finding alternatives. Each session required the boys to use skills learned in previous sessions. Techniques used to make the concepts concrete included the solving of hypothetical problems, to examine the benefits of helping others; a blind "trust" walk, to instill empathy; and planning a group project, to promote cooperation, decision making, and taking responsibility. In final sessions, the boys were encouraged to describe previous aggressive incidents and the feelings involved and to come up with alternatives reflecting the concepts they had learned in the group.

COMMENTARY: The structured group approach described here could easily be adapted to a classroom by teachers or counselors. To extend the effects of the program from the group to the classroom, we suggest that the therapist discuss with the teacher certain cues or phrases used in the group, to remind the boys of the values they learned.

SOURCE: Tidwell, R., and Bachus, V. A. "Group Counseling for Aggressive School Children." *Elementary School Guidance and Counseling,* 1977, *11,* 2-7.

Behavior Problems in Junior High School

AUTHOR: Carole T. Webster

PRECIS: Using group psychotherapy with students and consultation with teachers to modify discipline problems

INTRODUCTION: A junior high school principal asked a local mental health office to assign some staff time to the school, so that the faculty could learn to work more effectively with students who had behavior problems. The school was located in a deprived, rural area that used to be a mining town. The residents were primarily blue-collar workers or living on assistance, and there were no social services of any kind. The agency assigned a staff person to the school one day a week to set up a group treatment program for the students to help them develop more positive behavior patterns.

The social worker assigned to the school found that the faculty were skeptical of the program and considered the students with behavior problems "lost causes." They preferred to spend their energy with students motivated to achieve. Thus, another goal of the worker was to serve as a liaison with the teachers and gain their cooperation. The long-range goal was to make the group program self-perpetuating through the use of faculty members as group leaders.

TREATMENT: The worker emphasized that her role was to support the teachers by working with their problem students. The worker met with teachers informally in meetings and consulted individually with them regarding any concerns in the classroom or with particular students.

The teachers and principal suggested eight students for the first group, and the principal contacted the parents to obtain consent. Four boys and four girls from the seventh and eighth grades participated. They ranged in age from twelve to fourteen. Participation was voluntary, and all eight students agreed to attend for ten sessions. At the end of the ten sessions, they asked for the group to be extended to the end of the school year, approximately twenty weeks.

The worker explained at the first meeting that the purpose of the group was to establish more positive behavior patterns through improved communication among the students, the worker, and the faculty. The rules for the group were the general rules of the school; for example, no smoking was allowed, and the students had to be on time for their next class. The students initially tested the rules—for instance, by passing out cigarettes—but soon stopped when they saw that the worker did not get angry but continued to support members who were more involved in sharing their concerns. The group members began revealing their feelings and conflicts to each other, and a strong group identity was established.

As the group process continued, members began to recognize that their anger toward their parents engendered acting-out behavior in school. The worker and then the group supported members who tried to modify their provocative behavior. The group became a problem-solving resource for the members. For example, one boy was the "class clown" in all his classes and also joked around in the group. The members confronted him with his self-destructive attempts to gain attention and said he did not have to act up or degrade himself for people to like him. Group members who were in his classes agreed to confront his clowning in class and help him stay out of trouble. The boy formed close friendships in the group. His teachers reported marked improvements in his behavior and grades. The boy shared his background in one meeting. He spoke with anger of his father, who had deserted the family; his alcoholic mother; and her alcoholic boyfriend, who beat him and his siblings. The group supported him as he expressed his anger and self-doubts.

The students' major problem areas were with parents, teachers, and peers. The worker stressed that their parents were not likely to change but that they could work out ways in the group to deal more effectively with the problems. The students were able to deal maturely with their situations, such as ignoring messages of rejection and learning to draw emotional support from other resources, including other members in the group. The participants were also able to effect some changes in the school, such as modifying the school dress code and obtaining a suggestion box for the school.

RESULTS: The author reports that the teachers, the principal, and the participants themselves judged the group treatment a success in ameliorating the behavior problems of the participants. The success of the group work and consultation with the teachers produced changes in the disciplinary attitude of the faculty. The teachers were sensitized to the students' problems and began dealing with the students' difficulties directly, rather than referring every infraction to the principal for discipline.

One faculty member expressed an interest in participating in the group treatment program and was trained over the summer to work with groups. Later, two more teachers were trained to lead groups, and the program became self-perpetuating, with minimum involvement from the social worker.

COMMENTARY: The group was viewed as a positive opportunity by the students from the beginning; however, the therapist had to gain the cooperation and support of the faculty. The principal readily acknowledged the problems in discipline and supported the therapist's interventions at every point. The therapist helped the teachers see that these youngsters could change and helped them feel more confident in their ability to work with the students more effectively.

SOURCE: Webster, C. T. "Group Therapy for Behavior Problem Children in a Rural Junior High School." *Child Welfare,* 1974, *53,* 653-657.

Additional Readings

Casella, D. A., and Schrader, D. R. " 'Tripping' with Borderline Dropouts." *School Counselor,* 1975, *23,* 48-50.

This article describes an activity and discussion group for students who wanted to drop out of high school. The activity group consisted of a variety of field trips and "urban encounters" that were followed by discussions of opinions and feelings. The students demonstrated improved self-concepts, academic performance, and productivity as a result of treatment.

DeEsch, J. B. "Group Counseling with Disruptive Students." *Journal for Specialists in Group Work,* 1979, *4,* 117-122.

Students in the seventh through tenth grades who were frequent referrals to the principal's office as discipline problems were invited to participate in a counseling group. In individual sessions prior to the group, students were required to formulate their own goals and committed themselves to working on their own goals and helping others in the group. The program lasted ten weeks. The students helped each other improve study skills, classroom discussion skills, and test-taking skills. Results indicated that the counseling had improved their self-confidence, diminished disruptive classroom behavior, and improved their academic performances and grade point averages.

DuPleiss, J. M., and Lochner, L. M. "The Effects of Group Psychotherapy on the Adjustment of Four Twelve-Year-Old Boys with Learning and Behavior Problems." *Journal of Learning Disabilities,* 1981, *14,* 209-212.

Psychodrama techniques were used with a small group of learning disabled boys who were experiencing problems with peers and school adjustment. The authors emphasize the usefulness of starting with a concrete activity and the value of having cotherapists of the opposite sex. The students showed improvements in communication, attitudes, and general adjustment.

Fournier, M. J. "A Self-Enhancement Activity Group for First Grade Repeaters." *Elementary School Guidance and Counseling,* 1977, *2,* 267-276.

An activity group was provided for first-grade repeaters

to provide an opportunity to share common feelings about repeating, improve social skills, and increase self-confidence. The group met twice a week for five weeks at the beginning of the school year. Specific games and books were used to enhance the children's egos. Teachers reported that the students made outstanding adjustments to their new class.

Kern, R. M., and Hankins, G. "Adlerian Group Counseling with Contracted Homework." *Elementary School Guidance and Counseling,* 1977, *2,* 284-290.

The effects of Adlerian group counseling combined with behavioral contracts were compared to Adlerian group counseling alone and to an untreated control condition in children with poor school adjustment. Adlerian group counseling consisted of (1) establishing a therapeutic rapport, (2) psychological investigation, (3) interpretation, and (4) reorientation. Children in the contract treatment group were also given specific homework contracts, designed to help the students with their problems outside the group setting. Both treatment groups were superior to untreated controls in school adjustment, and the treatment group with the behavioral contracts (homework) was superior to the group without homework.

Krivatsy-O'Hare, A., Reed, P., and Davenport, J. "Group Counseling with Potential High School Dropouts." *Personnel and Guidance Journal,* 1978, *56,* 510-512.

A group counseling program was designed to offer psychological support to girls identified as potential dropouts. The girls were persistently truant, had minimal academic achievement, expressed antischool attitudes, and had family and drug or alcohol problems. A program evaluation indicated that many of the participants benefited from the group counseling.

la Greca, A. M., and Mesibov, G. B. "Facilitating Interpersonal Functioning with Peers in Learning Disabled Children." *Journal of Learning Disabilities,* 1981, *14,* 197-199.

A social skills training group was used with learning disabled boys, ages twelve through sixteen, with poor peer relationships. The modeling, coaching, and behavioral rehearsal strategies were designed to improve their ability to initiate social interactions and carry on appropriate conversations. The training increased frequency of interactions with peers and improved interpersonal skills.

Nagle, J. "Truancy Intervention Among Secondary Special Education Students." *School Psychology Digest,* 1978, *8,* 464-468.

Several group counseling techniques were investigated to reduce habitual truancy in high school special education students. The most effective method in increasing attendance was nondirect counseling combined with contingency contracting.

Impulsive-Aggressive Behavior

Group therapy with impulsive-aggressive children typically requires additional structure and the presence of two cotherapists. The use of multiple therapists allows immediate intervention during a crisis, as well as increased attention for the group members. Many therapists use an activity (such as model making, sports, or games) followed by a discussion period. Additionally, certain target behaviors for each group member may be identified and reinforced. The purpose of group therapy is to develop skills in social interaction and to emphasize self-control.

Directive Verbal Discussion Group for Impulsive Adolescents

AUTHORS: Norman Epstein and Sheldon Altman

PRECIS: Converting a conventional activity group into a verbal interchange group for impulsive boys

INTRODUCTION: A conventional activity group was initially used with a group of impulsive boys, ages nine to eleven. The authors chose this approach because they assumed that the boys could assume responsibility for their behavior, discuss their problems, and work to resolve them. The therapist initially permitted much inappropriate behavior, assumed a passive role, and used only minimal verbal interventions. The primary purpose of the activity group was to provide a springboard for examining feelings and encouraging peer interactions. However, parents and teachers were not satisfied with the behavior of the boys; so the format of the group was changed.

TREATMENT: The first step in converting from an activity group to a verbal discussion group was to introduce more structure. Thus, limits and expectations of behavior were implemented during the serving of refreshments. The rationale for this course of action was twofold. First, the refreshment period was the most difficult period in the group session and was in need of more order. Second, the group members were seated around a table for their refreshments—an arrangement conducive to verbal discussions. If a boy failed to control his behavior (for example, walking about the room), the therapist initiated action to ensure compliance. For example, physical restraint was used on occasions to return disruptive boys to their seats. Also, group censure of behavior was invited by the therapist. The boys willingly joined in the initial requests for censure, suggesting to the therapist that they desired to identify with him and win his approval. The therapist capitalized on this desire and proposed the formation of a new group culture—"The Common Sense Club."

The purpose of "The Common Sense Club" (the evolving activity group) was to help boys develop skills in social interaction. This was done through confrontation and questioning inappropriate styles of behavior. Both the therapist and the group members participated in the process. Alternate methods for dealing with problems were explored by the group, and self-control was emphasized as the highest attribute of masculinity and adulthood.

The group was receptive to the changing format and was able to meet in the therapist's office rather than in the activity room. The smaller office was advantageous for at least two reasons. First, it seemed to encourage more verbal interchange. Second, the therapist was close enough to all the boys to be able to reinforce verbal interchanges by using physical contact. During each meeting, boys were encouraged to report problems encountered that week. The boys were prodded by the therapist to discuss different methods for handling the problems that arose outside the group.

As the group continued, the therapist decided to include parents in at least one group session each month. Some advantages of utilizing the parents were as follows: (1) Parent-child confrontations allowed the therapist to deal with distortions. (2) Parents were provided with the opportunity for discussions with their boys, focusing on mutual problem solving. (3) Praise and recognition from parents were utilized to reinforce acceptable behavior. The authors conclude that verbal discussions are not beyond the scope of the young child and that verbal interchange group therapy is preferable to the loosely structured activity group.

COMMENTARY: This article illustrates the need for structure in group work with impulsive children. It also accentuates the need for openness, flexibility, and creativity on the part of the therapist. Finally, the article illustrates the importance of proper diagnosis and needs assessment of children before inclusion in any type of therapy group.

SOURCE: Epstein, N., and Altman, S. "Experiences in Converting an Activity Group into Verbal Group Therapy with Latency-Age Boys." *International Journal of Group Psychotherapy,* 1972, *22,* 93-100.

Multiple Therapists for Groups of Acting-Out Adolescent Boys

AUTHOR: Arthur I. Kassoff

PRECIS: Using multiple therapists in activity group therapy for acting-out adolescent boys in order to provide support, attention, different adult personalities, and increased structure

INTRODUCTION: The author describes an activity group for acting-out adolescents which required multiple therapists in order to be maximally therapeutic. Initially, additional therapists were utilized because of the level of acting out and the resulting disruption of the clinic routine. However, the presence of more than one therapist was also beneficial for the following reasons: (1) The demands for attention by the emotionally disturbed boys were more easily met. (2) A therapist and a boy could "pair off" at any moment in order to meet the boy's needs for support and attention. (3) Different cotherapists provided a variety of adult reactions to which the group could adjust. (4) Immediate intervention during acting-out episodes was possible.

TREATMENT: The group was an open group (boys could initiate or terminate participation at any time) of eight to twelve boys, ages twelve to sixteen, described as "desperate referrals" because they had repeatedly committed delinquent acts. The group met weekly for one-hour sessions. The boys engaged in the following activities: model making, football, baseball, and bowling. The purpose of the group was to discuss issues arising from the boys' participation in these activities.

Although the advantages of using multiple therapists were numerous, complications arose since the therapists did not always agree on which interventions to make in the group and were unable to work cooperatively. Differences between therapists increased the anxiety level among group members. However, the author concludes that the use of multiple therapists is essential in groups involving acting-out adolescent boys.

COMMENTARY: This article illustrates the need for structure and control in group therapy with acting-out adolescents. Regardless of one's theoretical orientation, the use of multiple therapists provides a solution for lack of self-control among the acting-out adolescents. Additionally, the article emphasizes the need for cooperation and open, honest communication between cotherapists. Also, consultants, observers, and/or video recordings of sessions seem to be viable aids for ensuring cooperation between cotherapists.

SOURCE: Kassoff, A. I. "Advantages of Multiple Therapists in a Group of Severely Acting-Out Adolescent Boys." *International Journal of Group Psychotherapy,* 1958, *8,* 70-75.

Activity Group Therapy Plus Verbal Therapy for Aggressive Children

AUTHORS: Florence Marks and Neal Keller

PRECIS: Combining traditional activity group therapy and verbal therapy within a behavior modification structure to improve behavior and facilitate discussions of problems by aggressive children

INTRODUCTION: The authors designed their therapeutic approach in order to explore dynamic issues and to improve behaviors among the children treated.

TREATMENT: Five boys, ages seven to eight, participated in the twelve weekly, one-hour sessions. The group members were referred by the schools for aggressive behavior, hyperactivity, and learning difficulties. Most of the boys were from single-parent homes. One therapist was a female doctoral-level psychologist, and the other was a male graduate student. The therapists set limits, discussed and demonstrated expectations for behavior, and avoided regressive play materials.

The first session was devoted to introductions, explanations of general expectations, and screening of the boys. All of the boys were judged to be acceptable candidates for treatment. Based on their histories and observations during this initial session, a single specific behavior was selected as a target behavior for each boy (for example, staying with one game, approaching another child, or maintaining eye contact with the therapist during conversations).

During the eleven subsequent group meetings, the one-hour sessions were devoted equally to activities and discussions. Activities included individual games and activities, games for pairs (such as checkers), and group games (such as bingo). During the discussion periods, the boys were encouraged to talk about their school experiences and hobbies. Each boy's target behaviors were reinforced when emitted. Also, certain general behaviors applicable to all members were rewarded. Reinforcers for the eleven sessions following the initial screening session were play dollars, which were redeemable for rewards such as car models, games, candy, pencils, and crayons. Each time a boy's behavior was reinforced, the reason for the reward was explained. The rules for the group were as follows: "Attend regularly. No interrupting. Talk about happenings at home and school. Help one another talk about and solve problems. No hurting one another or stealing." Goals for the boys were explained as follows: "Finish a game. Stay in one's seat. Hold a conversation. Assist in clean-up activities. Do not be a nuisance."

In addition to the work with the boys, three monthly evening sessions were conducted with the parents to discuss the purpose of the group and the ways that parents could assist in generalizing gain made in the group. Discussions focused on behavioral management approaches to improving behavior. Also, parents were asked to observe and record their child's behavior. Similarly, teachers were asked to record behaviors at school.

RESULTS: The boys formed a cohesive group within a few weeks. The reward system increased verbalizations and provided dynamic material for further discussions by the boys and therapists. While positive therapeutic results were attributed to the reward system, the authors also concluded that improvements were related to the degree of parental involvement and to the severity of problems initially exhibited by each boy. Although teachers generally reported improvements in behavior, these gains were not as substantial as those described by parents, and the boys' behavior at school typically deteriorated on termination of the group.

COMMENTARY: This article describes an innovative combination of activity therapy, verbal therapy, and behavior therapy used to improve behavior and explore feelings related to dynamic issues. It highlights the importance of flexibility and openness by therapists working with aggressive, impulsive, and learning disordered children. Furthermore, while minimal work with the parents was effected, no systematic treatment was initiated with teachers. As a consequence, improvements were not adequately maintained outside the group. Thus, the importance of working with the child's total system (family and school) cannot be emphasized enough.

SOURCE: Marks, F., and Keller, N. "A Short-Term Goal-Oriented Latency Boys' Group at a Child Guidance Center." *Group Process,* 1977, 7, 66-75.

Group Work in Residential Treatment

AUTHOR: John Matsushima

PRECIS: Using a group composed of individuals from various cliques to reduce antisocial behavior in an institution

INTRODUCTION: Matsushima describes the evolution of a group program at the Children's Aid Society, a residential treatment setting for children between the ages of six and fourteen who manifest problems with wetting, soiling, running away, fire setting, impulsivity, unmanageability, and destructiveness. Drastic and deleterious changes occurred in the institutional social structure after an administrative reorganization. The confusion among staff members regarding roles and responsibilities resulted in a clear power structure and scale of behavioral standards among the older boys. Several distinct cliques emerged, including the following: a tough, demanding "king," who was idealized and imitated despite his use of physical intimidation; followers, who administered beatings at the "king's" command; manipulators, who organized allowance "payoffs" for protection and coerced others into forbidden activities or submission; those who had little interest in becoming active participants in aggressive relationships; and frightened, passive, smaller boys, who "needed" to be the victims.

TREATMENT: Following the administrative reorganization, a recreation program was initiated in an attempt to influence peer group values and structure. As the children began to develop more self-control and the ability to compromise, small-group treatment was initiated.

A group was formed of five boys, ages twelve through fourteen, each from a different layer of the social hierarchy previously described. The required meetings were held twice each week and included sports, table games, outings, and snacks. In deciding on activities for each session, the group often failed in its initial stages to reach a compromise. Rather, group meetings often developed into fights. When a crisis developed, the activity was temporarily halted so that the group members could discuss the crisis together. Fighting was slowly replaced by arguments and ultimately by attempts at compromise.

At first, pseudodemocratic decisions were made as group members of lower status submitted to those of higher status; however, more passive members gradually began to assert themselves. As changes occurred in similar groups throughout the institution, a more favorable social climate developed.

COMMENTARY: This article illustrates the importance of group composition for therapy groups conducted in a residential treatment setting. Although groups were formed with the specific intent of remediating the difficulties inherent in the setting's social hierarchy, the principle of using a socially stratified group is a useful one. Such a group more closely approximates cottage living in the residential treatment context, as well as life in general in our society.

SOURCE: Matsushima, J. "Group Work with Emotionally Disturbed Children in Residential Treatment." *Social Work*, 1962, 7 (2), 62-70.

Therapy Group as Substitute Family for Aggressive Children

AUTHOR: Ethel Perry

PRECIS: Utilization of a group as a surrogate family for the psychoanalytic treatment of aggressive juvenile delinquents

INTRODUCTION: Perry suggests that small groups be used as symbolic families for aggressive children. In an outpatient setting, the group is particularly suited to providing a bridge between the child's inner and outer worlds. Group members can assume roles as objects of transference, as archetypal familial figures, or as individuals in their own right. The psychoanalytic aspects of this therapy include interpretation, transference, permissiveness, acting out, and regression.

TREATMENT: Groups or "surrogate families" consisted of two to six children meeting for up to twenty-seven months. Some of the families were heterogeneous with regard to sex distribution, while others were homogeneous. The family groups were carefully composed in order to maximize the therapeutic effect derived from the interpersonal contacts. The groups met in two rooms. The "dirty room" was used for the cathartic discharge of aggression and was built of tile walls and a concrete floor. The "clean room" was more conventionally furnished and provided a setting for verbal interactions.

Each group was led by a male and a female therapist, symbolic of the father and mother of the family. The author suggests that children who have experienced inconsistent parents feel secure if authoritarian attitudes adopted by therapists prove unbending. Therapists were prepared in the initial stages to take an emotional buffeting as part of the transference process. The therapists' participation, observation, and interpretation were utilized when the situation warranted.

RESULTS: The author suggests that "family group therapy" resulted in individuals merging with the group and, thus, the strengthening of relationships with peers. Additionally, as fantasy was resolved and aggression cathartically discharged, familial figures were available as objects for the redistribution of freed libido. Through this exploration of the self, children were able to relate their "family group" experiences to situations at home and in school.

COMMENTARY: Although Perry describes treatment within a psychoanalytic framework, there appears to be therapeutic potential in such an arrangement, regardless of one's theoretical orientation. That is, the interactions and relationships arising from the group are rich with opportunities for learning, insight, and growth. The use of male and female therapists appears to be a key component in symbolically approximating the child's family.

SOURCE: Perry, E. "The Treatment of Aggressive Juvenile Delinquents in 'Family Group Therapy.' " *International Journal of Group Psychotherapy,* 1955, *5,* 131-149.

Group Approaches for Socially Deprived Children

AUTHOR: Saul Scheidlinger

PRECIS: Using three different group approaches with deprived latency-age children

INTRODUCTION: The author reviews three different group approaches used effectively with deprived children. Although the three approaches differ in a variety of ways, they all utilize similar motivational forces for change and growth inherent to small-group interactions. The three groups are labeled as follows: experiential treatment groups (a clinical method), para-therapeutic activity groups (emotional support plus academic and vocational enrichment), and para-military cadet corps (a social and recreational program).

EXPERIENTIAL TREATMENT GROUPS: This nondirective approach operates on two levels. On one level, the environment and social interactions provide a here-and-now experience that focuses on the reality of the child's present situation and behaviors. On a deeper level, the group and its leader assume a symbolic meaning wherein the adult leader represents the parent figure and the group members represent other family members. This symbolic level allows the child to regress in order to retrieve and ultimately resolve earlier conflicts.

The three major therapeutic elements of this approach are

guided gratification, guided regression, and guided upbringing and socialization. Guided gratification operates on both the real and the symbolic level. The purpose of guided gratification is restitution for past deprivations and the minimization of current frustrations. In therapy many meaningful interactions between a group member and its leader may revolve around food—its purchasing, cooking, and serving. Guided regression is another therapeutic element wherein participants are led to relive conflicts from earlier times but with different actors and different endings. Guided upbringing and socialization result from the growing attachment between the adult leader and the group. Utilizing this relationship, the adult group leader is able to make gradual demands for control and socialization.

In experiential treatment groups, the optimal group size is seven. The role of the therapist (the group leader) is that of an accepting adult.

PARA-THERAPEUTIC ACTIVITY GROUPS: These groups are used to help socially disadvantaged, intellectually superior children realize their academic and vocational potentials. The major focus is to strengthen ego functions through individual interventions and group discussions.

Meetings are held in rooms where special materials such as science sets, educational games, music instruments, and maps are provided. The elements of gratification, regression, and socialization are underplayed or ignored; instead, there is more focus on reality considerations. The group utilizes invited speakers, indigenous peer leaders, and an adult leader as models for identification. Group members are encouraged to talk about their futures as mitigated by the realities of their present life situations.

The optimal group is from nine to ten members, and the duration of the group is usually about two years. The therapist/leader serves as an accepting adult, an active stimulator, a guide, and a teacher. She offers the group realistic praise and support, plus confrontation regarding undesirable behaviors.

PARA-MILITARY CADET CORPS: This social and recreational form of group organization assumes that a group with an emphasis on action methods, uniforms, discipline, ranks, and ceremonies is more appealing than "traditional" social-recreational programs to disadvantaged youngsters. The ideology of such a group is similar to that of the Boy Scouts; that is, to conduct oneself with honor and courtesy, to wear the uniform proudly, and to develop oneself as a leader. In weekly meetings utilizing free play, military drill, and learning skills (such as knot tying), youngsters gain improved social skills, improved physical skills, enhanced self-esteem, social responsiveness through community tasks, religious education, "character building," and academic motivation and/or remediation (using a cadet manual as a text).

Groups are composed of ten to twenty youths and are led by indigenous, older peer leaders who are supervised by adults.

COMMENTARY: The author's presentation of the three group approaches addresses the emotional, educational, and recreational aspects of treatment. While overlap certainly exists, the use of these methods or adaptations is particularly warranted in such settings as residential treatment centers. The groups as previously outlined might meet a variety of needs and be led by professionals from numerous disciplines (for example, psychologists and social workers, teachers and counselors, and recreational therapists). Although the para-military cadet corps is currently outdated and lacking in popularity, variants such as Boy Scout groups would serve a similar function.

SOURCE: Scheidlinger, S. "Three Group Approaches with Socially Deprived Latency-Age Children." *International Journal of Group Psychotherapy,* 1965, *15* (4), 434-445.

Empathy and Nonpossessive Warmth in Treating Female Delinquents

AUTHORS: Charles B. Truax, Donald G. Wargo, and Leon D. Silber

PRECIS: Time-limited group psychotherapy utilizing relatively high levels of therapist-offered empathy and nonpossessive warmth

INTRODUCTION: The authors reviewed previous studies and concluded that there is empirical support for the use of accurate empathy and nonpossessive warmth in group psychotherapy with hospitalized mental patients, neurotic outpatients, and college underachievers. They sought to apply these therapeutic principles to a group of forty delinquent girls, ages fourteen to eighteen. Subjects were inmates at Kentucky Village and were described as upper-lower-class to lower-middle-class girls from urban and rural areas. A control group of thirty inmates received no group psychotherapy.

TREATMENT: Four therapy groups of ten girls each met twice weekly for a total of twenty-four sessions during a three-month period. The four groups were randomly assigned to two therapists who had participated in a similar research project with hospitalized mental patients. During group sessions, the therapists sought to express accurate empathy through the communication of moment-to-moment understanding of a patient's feelings, experiences, and perceptions from the patient's vantage point. Similarly, the therapists displayed a nonpossessive warmth through their unconditional acceptance and respect for patients' feelings, experiences, and current verbalizations.

RESULTS: Girls receiving accurate empathy and nonpossessive warmth remained out of institutions during a one-year follow-up to a significantly greater extent (54.4 percent of the time) than did controls (40 percent). Also, the score for the group psychotherapy girls on the *C* scale of the Minnesota Counseling

Inventory (MCI) suggested greater understanding of the need for social organization, less rebelliousness toward authority, and more responsible behavior. However, while the results of the MCI were significant from pre- to posttherapy, the scores were still indicative of delinquent-prone behavior. Data obtained from a modified version of the Butler-Haigh Q-Sort for self and for ideal self suggested that effective psychotherapy was mediated through changes in self-concept toward greater self-valuing and a sense of adequacy and by changes in attitude toward parents, seeing them as reasonable and sensible.

COMMENTARY: This study elucidates the importance of the therapist's communicating acceptance of each group member's feelings, experiences, perceptions, and verbalizations. Although the clinical significance of these results was limited, the study provides promising guidelines for the group therapist involved with delinquent adolescent girls.

SOURCE: Truax, C. B., Wargo, D. G., and Silber, L. D. "Effects of Group Psychotherapy with High Accurate Empathy and Nonpossessive Warmth upon Female Institutionalized Delinquents." *Journal of Abnormal Psychology,* 1966, *71,* 267-274.

Short-Term Group Therapy on a Children's Psychiatric Ward

AUTHORS: Jay Williams, Claudeline Lewis, Florence Harris, Landrum Tucker, and Laurie Feagan

PRECIS: Evolution of a group approach incorporating techniques from Slavson, Redl and Wineman, and Vinter

INTRODUCTION: Noting that group therapy has been seen as

a method for treating carefully composed outpatient groups of children over long periods (more than a year), these authors questioned whether the modality might be usefully employed under different circumstances. The special circumstances dictated that the time period would be brief (two to six months), admissions and departures would be staggered, and membership could not be predetermined and ideally balanced. They developed a model group on a nine-bed facility serving children between the ages of three and twelve. The problems of the children that resulted in hospitalization included unsocialized aggressive reactions, psychosomatic disorders, and a wide range of other disorders within the neurotic, borderline psychotic, and behavior disorder spectrums.

TREATMENT: The primary goal of the group was to promote the child's social development, especially as related to impulse control, cooperation, and observing ego development. The nine children on the ward were placed in two groups of four and five. Each group met weekly for forty-five minutes. There were usually a male and a female cotherapist in each group. The group room was sparsely furnished and was outfitted with a one-way observation mirror so that other staff members could observe.

Initially a Slavson-like model was tried (S. R. Slavson, *An Introduction to Group Therapy,* New York: International Universities Press, 1943). Slavson recommends passive-permissive leadership to facilitate regression to levels of developmental fixation, so that a corrective emotional experience can promote growth. This proved to be diametrically opposed to the goals of the childcare staff. Their goal was to provide a structured milieu, so that children with poorly internalized controls could experience some success. In response to the criticisms of the childcare observers, the group therapists modified their approach, borrowing techniques such as "playful ignoring," "antiseptic bouncing," and "tension decontamination through humor" (F. Redl and D. Wineman, *Controls from Within*, New York: Free Press, 1952) and using these techniques to deal with destructive behaviors. Additionally, behavioral techniques were incorporated from Vinter's Rehabilitation Social Groupwork Model

(P. Glasser, R. Sarri, and R. Vinter, *Individual Change Through Small Groups,* New York: Free Press, 1974). These included contracting with individual members to work toward specific behavioral and social changes and contracting with the group to model socially accepted norms and values as well as to induce conformity through group pressure. These changes meant that the leaders took a more active role in limit setting, thereby behaving more in harmony with the total program.

Group members learned to indoctrinate new members by stating the informal contract: "Group is where we talk about feelings and help each other work on problems." In line with Slavson's recommendations, attempts were made to balance the composition of the group as far as possible. For example, an aggressive child would be placed with a withdrawn child, so that the former would be provided with a more controlled model and the latter with a more assertive one.

The techniques used by the leaders to strengthen impulse control included the following: encouraging verbalizations of feelings, interpretations, modeling and stating expectations, specifying goals and contracting to work toward them. An example of encouraging the expression of feelings might be a leader's remark, "Jimmy, tell me how you felt when Bobby grabbed your pencil." An example of interpretation might be: "Charles, you appear angry today. Sometimes it's difficult to accept a new member into the group." An example of modeling and stating expectations would be the therapist demonstrating cooperation by sharing blocks with another child and commenting, "Share those blocks with Randy as you have done before." Techniques providing external control of group members included limit setting, time out, diversions, and physical restraint. Finally, individual and group goals were formulated—the group goals establishing the group as one with common tasks to perform.

Play materials (puppets, paints and inks, clay, drawing materials, mandala designs, lego blocks, drama, and music) helped to provide structure for the sessions as well as a medium for the expression of fantasy. Also, the play materials provided a medium for working on social skills and gave group members the opportunity to produce something.

COMMENTARY: This article illustrates the importance of adapting group approaches to meet the needs of the group members involved in therapy. Furthermore, it elucidates the need to modify one's approach in order to satisfy the goals of other staff members involved in treatment. That is, the therapists apparently considered the political issues involved in contradicting the goals of the inpatient staff. The end result of design and compromise was an eclectic approach that utilized a number of effective but seldom combined techniques.

SOURCE: Williams, J., Lewis, C., Harris, F., Tucker, L., and Feagan, L. "A Model for Short-Term Group Therapy on a Children's Inpatient Unit." *Clinical Social Work Journal,* 1978, *6,* 21-32.

Additional Readings

Bardill, D. R. "Behavior Contracting and Group Therapy with Preadolescent Males in a Residential Treatment Setting." *International Journal of Group Psychotherapy,* 1972, *22* (3), 333-342.

The author discusses insights gained from a behavior-contracting group therapy model for emotionally disturbed young boys over an eight-month period. Since the boys were limited in their ability to verbalize their concerns and feelings, action was used as a primary mode of communication. To offset this, a point system was established wherein boys were awarded for good conduct and therapeutic responses. Points could later be redeemed for rewards (such as special privileges or money). Marked improvement was noted in the ability of all but one boy to verbalize aggressive feelings and to refrain from disruptive behavior.

Epstein, N. "Activity Group Therapy." *International Journal of Group Psychotherapy,* 1960, *10,* 180-194.

The author describes an activity group conducted with seven delinquent boys in residential treatment. There was a balance of acting-out and withdrawn boys in the group. The boys met for thirty-nine sessions and participated in activities focusing on arts and crafts, games, and refreshments. Materials provided to the boys included hammers, saws, screwdrivers, chisels, leather, wood, clay, plastic models, chess, checkers, and ping-pong. The therapist sought to create an atmosphere of acceptance so that the boys could act as they wished without fear of admonishment. Several case presentations are offered as illustrations of the success achieved with this approach.

Herrick, R. H., and Binger, C. M. "Group Psychotherapy for Early Adolescents: An Adjunct to a Comprehensive Treatment Program." *Journal of Child Psychology and Psychiatry and Allied Disciplines,* 1974, *13* (1), 110-125.

The authors describe a two-year experience of group psychotherapy with seven to ten boys, ages eleven to fifteen, referred for specific learning disturbances, behavior disorders, personality disorders, and psychoses. The group experience allowed direct observations and interventions with these outpatients, who were experiencing difficulties in interpersonal relationships. The patients were told that they could say anything they liked; however, they were not allowed to harm themselves, others, or the meeting room. The authors present case illustrations of progress made during the phases of the group. During the first phase, the inactive phase, members were constricted and inhibited. They were preoccupied by inner concerns, fearful, and unable to trust. During the second phase, the partial activity phase, attachments to the therapists were formed, discussions ensued, and conflict areas were identified. During the third phase, the phase of disruption and the beginning of self-control, physical and verbal activity increased, and the adolescents tested the therapists' willingness to offer nonretaliatory external control. Group members gradually mastered their own behavior during this phase, developed self-confidence, and formed new attachments with one another. The fourth phase, the phase of integration, was marked by greater trust for one another and an increase in talking (as opposed to physical activity). From these experiences the authors conclude that work in groups is basically the same as work with individuals; that the young adolescent forms vertical relationships with the therapists before forming horizontal relationships with peers; that two therapists are more effective than one; and that collaboration between individual and group therapists, probation officers, schools, and community agencies is essential.

Maier, H. W., and Loomis, E. A. "Effecting Impulse Control in Children Through Group Therapy." *International Journal of Group Therapy,* 1954, *4,* 312-320.

Six impulsive boys, ages nine to eleven, found a common denominator in similar fantasy material and their readiness to reveal it. Through identification they experimented with new roles when playing with one another. They accepted controls in the group setting and achieved a new orientation to a sibling situation.

Weisselberger, D. "Developmental Phases in Activity-Interview Group Psychotherapy with Children." *Groups,* 1977, *8,* 20-26.

Developmental phases in group psychotherapy with children are discussed, and the practice of group psychotherapy with children is evaluated. Group therapy with children is essentially aimed at providing a corrective emotional experience, so that, on the basis of a trusting relationship with the therapist, the children can learn to accept and gratify some of their dependency needs and give symbolic rather than direct expression to their hostile impulses. As a result of experience, it is considered possible to reduce the impulsive excitability and increase the frustration tolerance and self-esteem of the children. Indications, contraindications, and selection criteria are noted. The group is used as a means of enhancing personal competence in coping with problems of child/parent, child/teacher, and child/peer relationships.

Wineman, D. "Group Therapy and Casework with Ego-Disturbed Children." *Social Casework,* 1949, *30,* 110-113.

The application of casework techniques in group therapy for children with severe ego disturbances is demonstrated. An institution offered a flexible activity climate for boys between the ages of eight and eleven who were strongly fixated on primitive action symptomology. Therapeutic recreational programming was based on the principle of meeting the need of the child. Interview therapy was used when necessary to make the children aware of problems they caused and of ways to resolve those problems.

Delinquent Behavior

One of the striking characteristics of delinquents is their lack of motivation for change. This resistance to change implies rejection of community values as reflected by the adults in the adolescent's environment. In the articles presented in this section, delinquency is viewed as a denial of responsible living following some failure to identify with suitable models of behavior. Goals of therapy are for the therapist(s) to present a firm, competent, limit-setting model whom the adolescents gradually identify with so that they will incorporate the therapist's prosocial values. In therapy the therapist must break through the delinquents' rigid defenses. Several techniques are included to utilize with very resistant groups. The therapist stresses realistic thinking, problem solving, and awareness of cause-effect relationships. She also helps the delinquents develop social skills.

Group Therapy Application of Behavioral Principles

AUTHORS: Nuha Abudabbeh, Jogues R. Prandoni, and Diane E. Jensen

PRECIS: Using token reinforcement to increase verbalizations in a therapy group of delinquent boys

INTRODUCTION: Behavior modification techniques that reinforce appropriate behaviors in a group setting have been successful with juvenile delinquents. Reinforcement techniques were used to increase desirable behaviors of these youngsters in both the classroom and the institution; as a result, their behavior on the street also changed. Assuming that delinquents act out their feelings rather than verbalize them, the authors used token reinforcement to attempt to increase productive verbalizations in a therapeutic group of juvenile delinquents at a mental health clinic.

TREATMENT: The participants were five adolescent boys, ages thirteen and fourteen, who were committed to a juvenile facility and transported by bus twenty miles to a clinic once a week for group therapy. All the boys were inner-city youths with a history of parental neglect, rejection, and a chaotic family situation. Their IQs ranged from 77 to 91, and they all were committed for various forms of robbery; one was also committed for assault with a deadly weapon. This was the only treatment they received.

There was one therapist for the group and one observer who recorded the frequency of behaviors. The first five weeks were used to collect baseline data. Therapy was nondirective during this time; and a variety of activities, such as table tennis, puzzles, and drawing materials, was available for participants.

In the first phase, participants were given one poker chip for each unit of speech produced. They were not told the basis for reinforcement or the purpose of the study. At the end of each session, chips could be exchanged for candy, money, or a phone call. Verbalizations did increase, and after seven weeks the second phase was instituted. In this phase, the criterion for reinforcement was changed so that only personally relevant statements were reinforced; thus, only a discussion of the participant's own behavior at the facility was reinforced. This phase lasted for five weeks, when again the criterion for reinforcement was changed. In the third and final phase, only verbalizations of feelings, personal problems, and statements relating to the group itself were reinforced. This phase lasted for five weeks.

The reinforcement was conducted within a therapeutic group context in which the therapist and the observer conveyed their interest in and concern for the participants and gave them verbal reinforcement. The token reinforcement procedure did increase the number and quality of verbalizations, with members progressing from merely being involved in game activities, to talking about impersonal topics such as sports and school, to discussing their feelings about the therapist and their personal and sexual concerns. Although this progression occurs in any successful group, the authors believe that the reinforcement produced the change more rapidly.

COMMENTARY: In addition to the reward aspect of the poker chips, the tokens also served to structure the group goals for members, making clear what was expected in the group. The chips also reduced anxiety about talking in a group, since members could claim, if teased by peers, that they were talking only to earn chips. Most important, the members became competitive in acquiring chips and would lie about how many chips they had and attempt to steal chips—thus providing an immediate opportunity for the therapist to deal with these delinquent behaviors, which simulated the boys' behavior on the street. In other words, the chips elicited behaviors that otherwise were denied by members or would not have been discussed and interpreted as meaningfully without this stimulus.

SOURCE: Abudabbeh, N., Prandoni, J. R., and Jensen, D. E. "Application of Behavior Principles to Group Therapy Techniques with Juvenile Delinquents." *Psychological Reports,* 1972, *31,* 375-380.

Observer-Cotherapist in Group Therapy

AUTHOR: James E. Allen

PRECIS. A "silent observer" included in group therapy with delinquent boys to act as a catalyst in accelerating group action

INTRODUCTION: Training schools are handling more and more young offenders each year and must prepare them for reentry into society as quickly as possible. Many of these youths need intensive therapy, yet the institutions do not have the resources or staff time to provide individual therapy. This particular training school, like many institutions, utilized group therapy. However, conventional group therapy did not work with its population, since the group members were extremely passive and reluctant to discuss personal problems in front of peers. As a result, the therapist spent a great deal of group time trying to establish a therapeutic relationship.

A catalyst was needed to accelerate the formation of a therapeutic relationship within the group; therefore, a second therapist was added as a silent observer. The author states that the group members may relate to the silent observer in any number of ways theoretically—as a warm and understanding person providing nonverbal support, as an object to direct nonverbal hostility toward, as an anxiety-provoking figure, as an animal or pet, or as an integral part of the group.

TREATMENT: The therapist and the silent observer met with six boys for one hour twice a week. They ran two consecutive groups, one for eighteen sessions and one for nineteen sessions. The group members were homogeneous in age, intelligence, and length of time spent at the training school. The groups focused on dealing with authority and authority figures through use of role playing, group discussion, and interaction; also, a blackboard was used for illustration and interpretation. The leader fluctuated from a directive to a nondirective role as the situation demanded.

The role of the silent observer was explained to the groups at the beginning. He would attend all meetings but would remain silent throughout the sessions, would not answer questions or take notes, and would not show any reaction to discussions. The therapist and the silent observer met briefly before each session and up to an hour after each session to discuss individual and group reactions and ramifications. They also met periodically with the boys' caseworker and were totally involved in the boys' overall treatment.

RESULTS: This technique stimulated the group by decreasing resistance to group discussions. The groups were cooperative, spontaneous, and characterized by productive interactions, even in early sessions. The author believes that the silent observer, a second adult to whom the participants could relate, decreased some of the immature reactions found in previous groups. In fact, in two sessions where the therapist was absent, the silent observer maintained his own role and the group was able to continue productively, with a group member assuming leadership. Also, when a different silent observer appeared for several sessions, the group process was not affected in any way.

COMMENTARY: Since the silent observer was less involved than the leader, he could provide objective observations about the group and pick up on individual reactions that the leader missed. Thus, he provided a second clinically oriented analysis of group and individual dynamics. As a second therapist, he also suggested methods and treatments for particular problems. Having two therapists added to the intensity of movement in the group and achieved the short-term therapeutic goals of self-understanding, support, and insight.

A further advantage to the institution is that this method

provides an excellent training opportunity for staff members not experienced in conducting group therapy. Participation as observers exposes staff members to the group process and a variety of techniques, diminishes their anxiety about running a group, and answers many questions they have about group therapy. The silent observer is also able to stimulate experienced therapists through his observations.

SOURCE: Allen, J. E. "The Silent Observer: A New Approach to Group Therapy for Delinquents." *Crime and Delinquency,* 1970, *15,* 324-328.

Analytic Group Treatment of Delinquents

AUTHORS: Norman Epstein and S. R. Slavson

PRECIS: Modified analytic group therapy used with hardened, institutionalized delinquent boys

INTRODUCTION: The authors describe an analytic group for delinquent boys at a residential treatment center. They felt that the group would provide a change from the normally highly structured routine and that the change would promote discussion.

TREATMENT: The group consisted of eight boys, ages fourteen to sixteen, and two therapists. The boys had been in individual casework for over one year but displayed marked resistance to forming an individual relationship and had not responded to treatment. Seven of the eight boys had severe character disorders, and the eighth was a psychoneurotic boy with schizoid features. The group met for fifty-two weekly sessions.

In the first fifteen meetings, the boys resisted talking about anything personal and interrupted any boy who attempted to discuss significant material. They complained about the institution and bragged about their aggressive and delinquent acts and about their sex lives. The therapists had difficulty distinguishing reality from fantasy. They made few comments and waited for an opportunity to introduce a subject for discussion that would break through the boys' acting out and did not involve emotionally laden material. This opportunity arose in the sixteenth session, when the boys brought paper noisemakers into the room. One of the therapists commented that it sounded like an airplane breaking the sound barrier. A boy asked how planes break the sound barrier. The therapist answered, and the boys began firing questions about various natural phenomena at the therapists. The boys wanted to know what causes dreams and what they mean. They shared some of their dreams and asked for interpretations. This discussion marked a breakthrough; the boys talked about their dreams and freely discussed the feelings and conflicts in the dreams. In subsequent sessions, the boys asked the therapists other questions that concerned them. These topics included their parents, sex, incest, guilt about sex and masturbation, homosexual fears, fears of loss of control, how to save face when challenged by peers, and problems they would encounter when released. The boys spontaneously spoke of the relationship between their mothers' criticism of them and their feelings of inadequacy. The boys then progressed to being able to discuss concerns freely and offer suggestions to one another. Their swearing and bragging dropped out completely and were replaced by more responsible and reality-oriented attitudes.

The authors also describe the progress of a boy in a similar group. This boy acted out more than other members, who wanted to kick him out because of his constant disruptions. They gradually accepted him and let him use the group to release tensions related to his chaotic family situation. They also provided support and confronted his unrealistic ideas. His concerns provoked discussions of similar concerns in other members. The group helped him express his anger at his parents and promoted ego strength and self-esteem. He became less agitated and formed some friendships. However, he formed a neurotic transference with the therapist, whom he related to as his older brother. The authors state that this type of transference cannot be resolved in the group but needs individual therapy. The teenager left the institution and did not receive treatment. He regressed to delinquent behaviors and was incarcerated within a year.

COMMENTARY: Many theorists would not attempt this type of therapy with boys as disturbed as these. Once the initial resistance was overcome, however, these delinquents were able to develop insight into their behavior and to identify with the therapists. They made significant behavioral and attitudinal changes in one year of analytic group therapy.

SOURCE: Epstein, N., and Slavson, S. R. "Further Observations on Group Psychotherapy with Adolescent Delinquent Boys in Residential Treatment." *International Journal of Group Psychotherapy,* 1962, *12,* 199-224.

Promoting Understanding of Cause-Effect Relationships

AUTHOR: Girard H. Franklin

PRECIS: Using group treatment to decrease negativism and aggressive behavior in boys committed to a state training school

INTRODUCTION: Group therapy was an integral part of the total treatment program at a boys' training school. The therapy group was used to help the boys adjust to the institution, to promote an understanding of the causes and effects of their behavior, and to improve their interpersonal relationships and attitudes toward themselves.

TREATMENT: Each group consisted of five adolescent boys

and a therapist. They met twice a week for hour-long sessions in the therapist's office. The groups lasted for six months. The therapist explained that the purpose of the group was to help the members understand themselves and their problems better by examining problems and interactions that occurred in the group. After the first session, attendance at the remaining meetings was voluntary but strongly encouraged by the staff. The group followed a discussion format.

The therapist's primary role was to foster insight into the behavior of the group members. The boys were free to introduce their own topics for discussion. However, the therapist attempted to focus the discussions, as much as possible, on interactions occurring during the sessions. He challenged members to examine the ways in which their feelings and needs motivated their behavior and to keep those needs and feelings in mind when they considered alternative solutions. He also provided emotional support and praised the boys for positive contributions in the group and for positive behaviors they exhibited outside the group.

RESULTS: A number of changes took place in the boys' behavior as a result of treatment. The boys progressed from being hostile and alienated to developing group cohesiveness and interest in each other's ideas. They did not trust the therapist at first, but later understood that their mistrust was a defense against confiding personal information and fears of becoming too close to people. They were able to understand that the negative reactions and rejections they received from people were caused by their own threatening and hostile behavior. The boys initially insisted that their aggressive behavior was a defense against the attacks of others, but they were able to understand that their own hostile attitudes provoked the aggression. The author concluded that—although the group experience helped the boys understand that their poor relationships with people were related to their own rejecting, hostile attitudes—six months was not really long enough to develop positive self-other attitudes. However, since the boys were able to perceive interpersonal relationships more realistically, he hoped that they would feel less threatened and more capable of dealing effectively with their difficulties and, therefore, less destructive and antisocial in the community.

COMMENTARY: The adolescents in this group, like most delinquents, were narcissistic and indifferent to people around them. They had poor comprehension of why people reacted to them negatively and no understanding of cause-effect relationships. By focusing on the boys' behaviors and interactions in the group, the therapist sensitized them to others, and they were just beginning to be able to see another person's point of view. They were able to understand causes and effects of their behavior and learned how to achieve the interpersonal effects they desired in socially appropriate ways. They began blaming others less and took more responsibility for their behavior.

SOURCE: Franklin, G. H. "Group Psychotherapy with Delinquent Boys in a Training School Setting." *International Journal of Group Psychotherapy,* 1959, *9,* 213-218.

Summer Work Group

AUTHORS: Harry E. Grob and Eric E. VanDoren

PRECIS: A therapeutic summer experience for delinquent boys under the guidance of counselors

INTRODUCTION: At a private institution for teenage delinquent boys, the planned summer program had to be scrapped because of a shortage of cottage parents. The director and a social worker devised a substitute work program to provide relief for cottage parents, demonstrate to the staff principles involved in working with delinquent boys, help the community by cleaning up an eyesore, and provide the boys with a therapeutic group experience. The idea was to clear and beautify a swampy, overgrown area of the campus. The therapists would work side by side with the boys to provide role models and guide group interactions.

TREATMENT: Three mornings a week for three months, the two therapists took two groups of boys to the area to be cleared. Each group consisted of all the boys in one cottage, about ten boys. There were six cottages, which meant that each boy worked one morning a week on the project. Each work session lasted four to five hours. Boys were given the choice of working or sitting close by and watching the others work. Usually all the boys ended up working.

The therapists encouraged the boys to make their own goals and work plans for the day. They taught the boys how to use each tool properly and safely, and they encouraged the boys to learn how to use their favorite tool on a variety of tasks. The therapists also taught the boys to replenish their body with salt in the heat, to pace themselves in the heat, to bathe after strenuous work, and similar health-related procedures. They used the opportunities that arose in the daily work to encourage cooperation, decision making, and creative thinking. The therapists also answered questions that the boys asked about plants and wildlife they encountered.

The boys were quick to recognize a member who was not working, and reminded him that he didn't have to work if he didn't want to. In the work group, the boys came to respect each other more. For example, several unpopular boys came up with creative engineering ideas to solve problems about removing trees and developing drainage. This increased their status and acceptance in the work group and in the cottage.

The therapists found that, in rotating the cottages across the workweek, they had to keep in close contact with each cottage to maintain morale and interest. The boys were informed of progress and problems that were encountered each workday.

The therapists met weekly with cottage staff to keep them informed of the progress and point out important contributions and creative ideas made by each boy. The therapists hoped to impress on the staff the boys' productive response to democratic processes. In one cottage, the staff complained that this process made the boys think they were the boss. They cited two instances of boys getting out of control. In examining the issue closer, the therapists discovered that the staff had left the boys unsupervised "to see what they would do." In general, the cottage staffs supported the projects and listened enthusiastically to the boys' stories of their work. Sometimes the staff suggested that ideas the boys used in the work group should be adopted in the cottage.

The community support was favorable. Members of the police force dropped by on off hours to see how the project was going and encourage the boys. The boys were surprised that the police showed positive interest in them.

The project was terminated with a community-wide dedication ceremony in which the boys made speeches about what the project meant to them and received awards.

RESULTS: The project gave the boys a sense of accomplishment and taught them problem-solving skills, social skills, and responsible behavior that was carried over into their behavior in the cottages.

COMMENTARY: This therapeutic work program for older adolescent boys offered the group interactions and experiences that activity group therapy offers young children, at a more age-appropriate level. The project provided the boys with success experiences, fostered creative and independent thinking, improved their self-esteem, and provided them with positive skills and attitudes that might carry over into their future employment. The therapists' involvement was somewhat unconventional and more physical than perhaps some of us might want to attempt, but their work worked.

SOURCE: Grob, H. E., and VanDoren, E. E. "Aggressive Group Work with Teenage Delinquent Boys." *Children,* 1969, *16,* 103-108.

Structuring and Limit Setting with Delinquents

AUTHORS: Martin A. Jacobs and Jacob Christ

PRECIS: Modifications necessary for conducting discussion group therapy with disturbed, delinquent boys

INTRODUCTION: In developing a therapy group for delinquent teenagers, the authors modified standard group therapy techniques to take into account their age and their pathology. The following deviations were anticipated:

1. Outputs must be provided for tension reduction. Adolescents have a greater propensity for action than adults; and delinquents, in particular, act out stress rather than think about it. The authors expected these teenagers to defend against anxiety in the sessions by flight-or-fight reactions. The fight reactions may include throwing objects, doing damage to the room or each other, yelling, pounding on furniture, and running around the room. The flight reactions may include leaving the room or the building. The boys sometimes hid in the building, implying a need to be found or rescued. A third anticipated defense was regression to seeking oral gratification; thus, time for refreshments was provided at the end of the session. Activities were provided to release tensions.

2. A formal structure must be provided to control the anticipated action. For example, if refreshments were to be served, appropriate arrangements would have to be made in the group in an orderly fashion. Since delinquents have difficulty with impulse control and distinguishing fact from fantasy, structuring makes the situation as concrete and unambiguous as possible. The main method of structuring is setting limits or rules. The authors state that rules are defensive and progressive functions. Rules that indicate what the group is, when it will meet, and where it will meet are progressive because they build group cohesiveness and continuity. Letting the boys make the rules is also progressive, since they conform better to the rules and this democratic process fosters cohesiveness. Rules against destruc-

tive acting out are defensive in their control function. However, they are also progressive in providing an atmosphere of safety and control of dangerous impulses.

3. The therapists must be flexible in enforcing the rules. Since therapy is anxiety producing, explosions will occur if pressure is applied. The authors believe that a certain amount of release of tension must be allowed if full expression within the group is to occur. If the boys are not allowed some acting out, they will withdraw in the group and act out in the community. In addition, by allowing some acting out, the therapists can make interpretations about the behavior and thereby promote self-understanding and modifications of such actions.

TREATMENT: The group included six boys, ranging in age from fourteen through seventeen, who were seen on an outpatient basis. Their police records included kidnapping a policeman's son, stealing, and assaulting young girls. All the boys showed psychotic processes, and several had passive, feminine identities. The group met once a week for an hour. This article covers the first twenty weeks of treatment.

The boys in the group were markedly cohesive from the beginning. The least bit of change in the group, such as changing the meeting time, was perceived as rejection by the members, and they reacted angrily. In this instance, they broke pencils and threw objects, talked disruptively, and ran wildly around the room. When the leader called a halt to this, they cleaned up the room and raided the refrigerator. Two boys hid in an upstairs closet to prolong the session.

The therapist had to establish his authority and let the boys know he would not let them hurt themselves or each other. He earned their respect and established his authority by dealing with crises in the group rather than by calling the police when the boys acted out. The therapist also became one of the group by sharing refreshments, paying dues, voting on issues, and having a stake in the continuity of the group. He asserted his authority when necessary; but by becoming a group member, he sided with their egos instead of their superegos, which fostered identification with him.

The sessions were marked by swift and dramatic mood changes. Typically, several productive sessions would be followed by sessions of wild rebellion. This "breaking away" from the rules represented the boys' need for independence. When the leader restored control and order, the boys experienced guilt over the destructive aspects of their aggression. They then determined to work together, to start with a clean slate. Several productive sessions then followed, in which members enjoyed the support and warmth of this substitute family. If the sessions led to too much closeness and too much submission, the boys again rebelled with defiant behavior. Through group therapy, the goal was to limit the range of these mood swings, so that the boys could integrate affection and compliance with independence and aggression for a more balanced personality. Identification with the leader was the primary mechanism for resolving this ambivalence.

COMMENTARY: This article does not discuss results, since the group was ongoing; in any event, theoretical aspects of therapy with delinquents are stressed. The formation of a strong group identity suggests that the boys remained committed to the treatment group. Treatment is a long and arduous process with youngsters as disturbed as these. The article presents excellent descriptions of defenses and processes in treating delinquents.

SOURCE: Jacobs, M. A., and Christ, J. "Structuring and Limit Setting as Techniques in the Group Treatment of Adolescent Delinquents." *Community Mental Health Journal,* 1967, *3,* 237-244.

Task-Oriented Group Therapy

AUTHORS: Jo Ann Larsen and Craig T. Mitchell

PRECIS: A task-centered approach for mobilizing the group to identify and work on self-defeating behaviors

INTRODUCTION: Delinquents in a treatment group create confusion and disorder to avoid self-disclosure and taking responsibility for themselves. They tell self-serving stories, enter power struggles, recite endless grievances, and direct vicious put-downs at other group members. The authors state that a well-structured format, in which the worker elicits adherence to the structure and provides positive feedback, can make the group more productive. They describe a task-centered approach, in which the individual enters the group with behaviors he wants to change, and the group helps each member formulate and review relevant tasks to help him attain his goals.

TREATMENT: The worker makes an initial contact with the individual and explores the problems that led to the youth's incarceration. The worker explains that she is assigned to work with the youth and that they will meet weekly. The worker then encourages the youth to come up with some problems he needs to resolve, rather than attempting to force unwanted changes and social values on him. If the worker thinks that the youth can attain his goals through the group, the worker suggests that he participate. The worker explains that the group members assist each other in identifying and working on goals and tasks relevant to the behaviors they want to change. It is stressed that group participation is voluntary, and if he joins the group, he must work on his problems in it. The worker and youth then sign a contract.

In the first meeting of the group, the worker helps the group develop a decision-making process that stresses group consensus. The worker also identifies the steps of a decision-making process as follows: (1) defining the problem, (2) brainstorming alternate solutions (members are not to criticize suggestions), and (3) choosing a solution that meets the needs of all the members. To help them learn to use this method, the worker identifies issues that need to be resolved, such as how to select topics for discussion, how much time to allot to different problems, and how to deal with disruptive behaviors.

The worker gives positive feedback on the group's progress and on individual progress, such as task-oriented statements, proposing solutions, and problem resolution. The worker also encourages the group members to give positive feedback to each other. The authors state that positive feedback is an important element of treatment, since research has shown a causal relationship between low self-esteem and delinquency. In their own experience, youths who showed positive changes in self-concept had lower recidivism rates than youths with no change or negative change in self-concept.

In weekly individual sessions, which last fifteen to twenty minutes, the worker praises the youth's progress, however small, and mentions specific examples of progress. These experiences gradually enhance self-esteem and help him perceive himself as an effective, competent person. The worker also focuses on disruptive behaviors the youth displayed in the group and may make mini-contracts to resolve the dysfunctional behavior. For example, instead of belittling other members, the youth will make three positive statements about others in the group meetings.

The group described in the article was composed of five boys who had committed serious criminal offenses such as assault, armed robbery, murder, and rape. The group met for one-and-a-half-hour sessions once a week for eight weeks, and individuals met with the worker once a week. There was one therapist, who was the boys' social worker.

The initial sessions were chaotic and difficult to control as members manifested many negative behaviors. With the influence of the individual sessions, which focused on these negative behaviors and worked to resolve them, the group became more productive. By the fourth and fifth sessions, the members would not allow disruptions and took full responsibility for working on problems and assigning tasks to members.

When helping a member with a problem he had contracted to change, the group presented specific examples of how the behavior had occurred. For example, if someone had an explosive temper, the group would tell the circumstances under which it occurred, the frequency of loss of temper, significant others who were involved, and the physiological signals of the impending loss of temper (such as tensing of muscles). They then suggested replacement behaviors, to be tried during the week, that might avert the negative chain of events. For example, a youth with a temper problem might agree to put his hands in his pockets, count to ten, and walk away from "trigger" situations when he experiences physiological signs of anger.

RESULTS: In contrast to a control group, the youths in this group had significantly improved self-concepts and were rated by the staff as more responsive to supervision, improved in personal hygiene, and more appropriate socially after only eight weeks in treatment.

COMMENTARY: The authors' approach fosters adolescent autonomy by making membership in the group voluntary and by allowing members to choose which behaviors they want to change. Thus, the adolescents are responsible for their own behavior; youngsters who may sabotage treatment are not included in such a group. The worker can use any small problem a member may wish to solve to motivate him to participate in the group. The worker also creates a positive atmosphere in the group sessions, which provides the youngsters with positive messages they may not have encountered before; for example, the fact that an individual can change—and that the group can effectively help him to do so.

This type of group treatment demonstrates that teaching delinquents positive methods for solving their problems and giving them a sense of self-worth is really the only treatment that will have enduring results. We suggest that such groups meet on a long-term basis since the members are so disturbed. Once they have had a positive group experience, disturbed adolescents may be more willing to work on other problems. Behavioral contracts could be renegotiated every eight weeks, or members of the short-term task-oriented group could be given the option of joining an ongoing group.

SOURCE: Larsen, J. A., and Mitchell, C. T. "Task-Centered, Strength-Oriented Group Work with Delinquents." *Social Casework,* 1980, *61,* 154-163.

Discussion Group Therapy at a Boys' Industrial School

AUTHOR: Jaime Lievano

PRECIS: Conventional discussion group therapy used with delinquent boys aged fifteen to seventeen

INTRODUCTION: Group therapy aimed at helping boys communicate effectively with adults was conducted. Many of the boys had not had any positive relationships with adults and were mistrustful and uncommunicative in individual sessions. The therapist was not attempting deep personality reorganization but anticipated that a voluntary group with ego-supportive qualities would foster identification with the therapist and improve self-control, self-understanding, and ability to relate with adults.

TREATMENT: Seven boys met with the therapist for forty-two hourly sessions. The therapist was permissive and encouraged the boys to talk about whatever was important to them. Although the boys had had to write letters stating their motivation to attend group therapy, they had difficulty discussing relevant material and forming any group cohesion. They acted out in the sessions and told the therapist that he was wasting his time with them because they were hopeless causes. Common themes included their feelings of hopelessness, anger at their parents, asking the therapist to tell them what to do, complaints that adults always tell them what to do, and blaming others. The therapist focused on the present and pointed out their self-defeating and impulsive behaviors.

The author discusses resistances encountered in working with these delinquent boys. For instance, there were prolonged silences, absences, and disruptions of the group. Moreover, the boys would leave the room, exclude the therapist from the discussion, and tell the therapist that they knew he didn't like them but was paid to work with them. They were also preoccupied with sexuality to the exclusion of other topics.

In the twenty-fifth session, new boys were added to the group. This aroused unresolved sibling rivalry conflicts in the old members, who acted out and threatened the new members. The therapist reflected their resentment of the new members and anger at himself. By the thirty-second session, the boys formed a group identity and enough trust to share significant material and feelings. Some of the boys began to identify with the therapist and sought his approval. The therapist concluded that the group was a success because the boys were able to form a meaningful relationship with him, opening the way for them to trust other adults and work more productively in their individual sessions with their caseworkers.

COMMENTARY: While some therapists prefer to use a highly structured and behavioral approach and confront resistances head on, a more permissive approach such as this one is also productive. It provides opportunities for delinquent youngsters to develop self-direction and new ways of relating to an adult who reacts to them as no adult before has.

SOURCE: Lievano, J. "Group Psychotherapy with Adolescents in an Industrial School for Delinquent Boys." *Adolescence,* 1970, *5,* 231-252.

Video Playback in Groups of Delinquents

AUTHORS: Robert C. Marvit, Judy Lind, and Dennis G. McLaughlin

PRECIS: Group sessions of antisocial adolescents recorded on videotape and played back to improve reality testing and reduce denial

INTRODUCTION: Delinquent youths are a particularly difficult population to treat. They often do not agree with society that they have a problem and thus are not motivated to change. They are frequently nonverbal and uncooperative with treatment and deny experiencing any anxiety over the consequences of their antisocial behaviors.

Research has shown that group therapy techniques are helpful with delinquents, particularly when modified to produce changes in antisocial attitudes rather than attempting to achieve psychological insight. According to the authors, the most important component in changing delinquents' attitudes is to confront them with reality and force them to see the world as it really is. They postulated that videotaping the group process and then playing the tape back to the group would force the adolescent to face how he and his behavior appear to others. They also felt that the videotape could act as a positive reinforcer for desirable behaviors.

TREATMENT: Four agencies that deal with delinquent adolescents participated and included youngsters from all socioeconomic levels. The first agency had a guided group interaction program for boys referred by the court, many of whom had been committed to youth correctional facilities. The second agency was a runaway shelter for girls and provided crisis intervention and referral to other sources of help. The third agency was for girls involved with the family court and having histories of law violations. It used a behavior modification approach with a token economy and goal setting for treatment. The fourth agency was a residential treatment center for boys and girls with intolerable home situations and for those who could not return home following court proceedings. The sample from the four agencies included youngsters with long histories of law violations as well as youths who had never been involved with the law.

At each agency a control group and an experimental group were chosen. There were twenty-three participants in the experimental groups to be videotaped, and all gave their consent to be involved. Each group was videotaped for four psychotherapy sessions. The authors used the already established group meeting time at the agencies, which meant that two agencies had four consecutive daily sessions, one agency met once a week for four weeks, and one had two meetings a week for two weeks. Each group viewed the tapes following each session and discussed the content, the group dynamics, and the participants' feelings about seeing themselves.

RESULTS: No one refused to participate in the study, and attendance at all meetings were quite high, suggesting that the videotape increased interest in the groups. Members indicated that they were disappointed in how they looked, and many improved their dress and hygiene during the course of the taping. They also reported that they had a clearer understanding of how they appeared to others. Though the evidence the authors cite is somewhat unclear, they believe that the videotape made members more sensitive to feedback from others and more fearful of criticism and rejection by others. They believe that the group members became more reflective and denied less; thus, they were more aware of their shortcomings and felt less confident. Members also became aware that many of their behaviors would be viewed by others as not worthy of respect or serious consideration. The group supported the members and worked through some of these negative feelings and helped provide members with a more realistic appraisal of themselves.

COMMENTARY: The videotape experience itself is a novel situation for adolescents and can spark interest in the therapy sessions. As a therapy technique, videotape can help adolescents understand and confront self-defeating behaviors. The videotape offers a quick confrontation with reality that the adolescent cannot deny. The recognition of negative behaviors comes from within the individual—instead of being forced on him by the therapist or group members—and the impact of seeing how he really looks to others often catalyzes immediate changes in his behavior and physical appearance. Adolescents also may become more sensitive to feedback from others and practice denial less in subsequent sessions after viewing themselves on videotape. Thus, one may want to employ this technique early in a group therapy program to reduce resistance in the group members.

SOURCE: Marvit, R. C., Lind, J., and McLaughlin, D. G. "Use of Videotape to Induce Attitude Change in Delinquent Adolescents." *American Journal of Psychiatry,* 1974, *131,* 996-999.

Discussion and Psychodrama Groups of Delinquent Girls

AUTHOR: Ralph M. Patterson

PRECIS: Discussion group therapy, psychodrama, and individual therapy compared

INTRODUCTION: To determine an effective and economical method of psychiatric treatment for institutionalized delinquent girls, the therapist compared the effects of discussion group therapy, psychodrama, and individual therapy.

TREATMENT: The girls were fourteen- and fifteen-year-olds from families with several generations of maladjusted individuals. Their homes were substandard: mere tents or shacks with dirt floors. Their families moved frequently; and the parent constellation changed continuously, with parents, foster parents, relatives, and paramours acting as parents. The girls had histories of truancy, stealing, and sexual acting out and had had a number of placements before being committed to the institution. The only criterion for group selection was that verbal girls be placed in the group discussion, nonverbal girls in psychodrama, and neurotic girls in individual treatment.

The candidates for the discussion group were gathered together and the purpose of the group explained. All fifteen girls volunteered to participate. The meetings were held in the library during school hours. The girls sat in a circle in chairs. The therapist placed himself by girls who tended to be disruptive or girls whose egos would be inflated by sitting next to the leader.

In the first session, the leader suggested that they talk about stepparents. The girls readily shared their feelings and experiences and formed a positive group identity by the end of the session. At the beginning of subsequent sessions, the leader would pick an item of interest left unfinished from the previous hour. He then took a "background" role, keeping the discussion focused but not answering questions or making interpretations. As the sessions progressed, the girls became less belligerent, listened to each other reflectively, and competed less to talk in the sessions. They reported improved social relations and self-understanding.

The drama group had ten members. The leader suggested a relevant theme, and the girls volunteered to act out specific parts. The situation was reenacted several times by different members. The leader took an active role in "directing" and frequently played male authority figures, such as a kind or cruel father or a judge. After the role play, the girls discussed the scene. The girls developed a female character, Genevieve, who was a delinquent girl they followed through a variety of problem situations. The girls identified with Genevieve and by projecting themselves onto the character were much freer in discussing their own problems. Most of the girls were able to drop this projection technique and share their feelings directly by the end of four months of treatment. The girls reported a drastic improvement in their ability to express themselves verbally.

They also reported improved interpersonal relationships and improved understanding of parent-child relationships.

Both groups met three times a week for four months. The girls in individual therapy met less frequently, each for ten to fifteen sessions.

The goal of individual therapy was to develop the girls' understanding of repressed hostility; to channel the hostility toward its true target; and to dissipate it if possible, to permit adjustment to substitute parents in the community.

RESULTS: The author realized once the study started that he could not separate the effects of group treatment from the other therapeutic influences of the milieu. He felt that both groups improved the girls' interpersonal relationships and general adjustment and helped them establish a positive relationship with the staff, so that they would seek advice for personal problems—something that would not have happened before. He believes that group treatment cannot replace or substitute for individual therapy.

COMMENTARY: Research has shown that adolescent girls are intensely concerned with interpersonal relationships and peer acceptance; thus, group therapy is an excellent treatment mode for them. The group improves the girls' social adjustment and reduces their feelings of isolation and inadequacy.

SOURCE: Patterson, R. M. "Psychiatric Treatment of Institutionalized Delinquent Adolescent Girls." *Diseases of the Nervous System,* 1950, *11,* 227-232.

Use of Fantasy with Delinquents

AUTHOR: William R. Perl

PRECIS: Discussing fantasied occupational goals with delinquents to break down their resistance to sharing personal concerns in a group

INTRODUCTION: Delinquent adolescents are a difficult population to treat, since they are resistant to talking about themselves and are oppositional with authority figures, including therapists. The author believes that what the delinquent sees as the reality of life has not worked for him—he has failed to learn to deal with reality and feels hopeless about ever being able to succeed in the real world. Thus, he joins the delinquent subculture, an alternate reality. Any attempt to get him to face reality, such as therapy, re-creates the feelings of inadequacy; and he pulls out all his defenses, both conscious and unconscious, to resist. Perl proposes that a more successful therapeutic approach might be to gain entry to his fantasy life, a world that is not as bleak to the delinquent as "hard-hitting reality."

There were two problems with this idea that had to be overcome. First, delinquents have active fantasy lives that contain grandiose and illegal elements, such as pulling off the ultimate crime; and the author did not want the group to be an audience for tales of that nature. Second, because of their weak ego formation, delinquents are defensive about letting anyone enter their all-important, need-fulfilling fantasy lives, for fear of rejection and ridicule. The fantasy of choice for the author was the desire for occupational success, which contains an element of hero fantasy but is not a taboo subject of discussion to delinquents.

TREATMENT: The group consisted of seven boys, ages fifteen to seventeen, who were committed to a children's detention center. They were extremely hostile, aggressive, and unmanageable, with intelligence ranging from upper dull normal to upper average. Participation in the group was voluntary; however, if someone wanted to leave the group, he had to give his reasons and come once more to give the group a chance to change his mind. There was one therapist.

During the first session, there was almost complete silence. In the next five sessions, the boys vented complaints about the institution. By the seventh meeting, they were bored with what they had been doing but did not know what to do next. The therapist thought that one boy appeared ready to go into more meaningful material, but he was sitting between two unresponsive members. (Seating in such groups is important, since the technique is to go around the group circle and ask each member to share. Preferably, then, the first boy chosen to share should be sitting next to someone who is likely to be responsive.) An opportunity arose when another boy, who held high status in the group and was seated next to more responsive members, announced a quite unrealistic expectation of early release. The therapist asked him what he would do after being released:

Patient: Join the Air Force.
Therapist: Want to make it a career?
Patient: No, just for three or four years.
Therapist: Any idea of the occupation you want to follow?
Patient: Mechanic, I guess.
Therapist: Certainly the group would be interested to hear whether this is what you always wanted to be, or did you at some time have other wishes too?
Patient: Other wishes too.
Therapist: But these wishes seem beyond your reach now.
Patient: Yes.
Therapist: Any reasons why you feel they are probably beyond your reach?
Patient: Well, education, I guess, and money.

The therapist commented that the other members of the group, including himself, probably had similar thoughts about what they would like to do. He then asked each member to tell what he would like to be doing in ten years.

Once fantasy is involved, it is easy to move into other areas with questions such as "How would you spend your spare time if you had all that money?" and "Would you like to be married?" The gamelike atmosphere allows group members to share important concerns but not have to accept full responsibility for their statements because it was "just a game."

COMMENTARY: The use of this technique can successfully allow hard-to-reach adolescents to share concerns in a safe way. Their mutual experience of sharing something real with others binds them together and helps them feel less isolated. The author states that the fantasy technique achieves cathartic effect, movement toward interpretation of symbolic fantasy content, and the beginning of a group superego. The group is then able to move on to other concerns and content areas in future sessions.

SOURCE: Perl, W. R. "Use of Fantasy for a Breakthrough in Psychotherapy Groups of Hard-to-Reach Delinquent Boys." *International Journal of Group Psychotherapy,* 1963, *13,* 27-33.

Adolescent Caring Community

AUTHORS: Richard Raubolt, Marcia Strauss, and Thomas E. Bratter

PRECIS: Delinquent adolescents treated in group therapy that evolved into a twenty-four-hour-a-day caring community

INTRODUCTION: Two of the authors formed a treatment group composed of clients from their private practice who had prominent behavior problems, such as drug abuse, promiscuity, truancy, and shoplifting. The goals of the group were to reduce feelings of isolation, provide support and confrontation from peers, provide a miniature social situation to uncover relationship problems not manifested in individual therapy, stimulate new ways of dealing with situations and interpersonal relationships, and provide a sense of protection by an adult who encourages undergoing these changes.

TREATMENT: The two counselors met with eight boys and girls, ages twelve to sixteen. The group met weekly after school for two and a half hours. Refreshments were served to minimize anxiety and foster the counselor-client rapport.

The first six weeks of therapy were described by the authors as a "rap group." The counselors encouraged open discussion, and the members used the time to get to know each other and develop group cohesion and trust by discussing shared interests, such as books, films, and rock groups. The members tested the counselors by cursing, coming late, and jostling each other. The counselors did not interpret behavior but remained informal, interested, and reflective. The counselors used the discussions to reveal members' values. For example, they would ask who the member's favorite book or movie character was and why. When the members introduced more personal issues, such as family problems, the counselors pointed out similarities in group members' behavior, encouraged reality testing by providing different perspectives, and emphasized that there are reasons why people including their parents, engage in certain behaviors. The counselors also revealed some of their own painful memories as they related to the problems under discussion.

In the sixth week, the counselors changed the direction of the group by noting that many personal problems and fears had been raised and that they would use the group to begin working toward solutions. The counselor then turned to the most popular group member and asked him what he would like to change. The leaders particularly focused on self-destructive behaviors and would not accept excuses. Members tried to blame their parents for their difficulties. The leaders repeatedly explained that members could not change their situation but could change their responses to it, and that their parents were not going to change but the members could change. They believed this self-disclosure brought about significant breakthroughs for several participants.

The members recognized the need for change and attempted to make changes in their lives; however, they were unable to maintain their resolutions and unable to follow through. The counselors believed that the youngsters needed more support than the group sessions were providing; so they developed the next phase of their treatment—a caring community.

The caring community concept is based on the peer self-help programs in Alcoholics Anonymous and Daytop Village, where members are encouraged to support one another outside the group. Peers exchange phone numbers and are encouraged to call each other when they are experiencing a crisis or are lonely and want someone to talk to. The twenty-four-hour-a-day support system enables peers to be involved with each other's problems and help each other function more effectively in their daily lives.

The counselors believed that a support system for these youngsters with shattered, uninvolved families would encourage a positive separation from parents by creating healthy peer relationships. They introduced the idea to the group by asking what commitments they were willing to make to help their friends. The members' responses were creative, responsible, and significant. They seemed to know how they could provide assistance to others and who could provide assistance to them. For example, Philip, the most popular member, was failing four of five classes and cutting an average of three classes a day. Each member made a commitment to help Philip in a different way: one member agreed to tutor him; two others agreed to call him in the morning and walk to school with him; and one girl, who was also having problems academically, agreed to go to their teachers with Philip and ask for help.

Philip responded to the assistance of the group by passing all his courses and helping other members become more self-confident. As other members saw the improvements in Philip, they became more determined and hopeful that they, too, had the power to change. The caring community concept developed a positive growth cycle in the youngsters; the more they progressed, the more confidence they had in their own power and creativity.

COMMENTARY: The concept of the caring community can be considered an extension of group therapy. It takes all the advantages of group therapy—such as peer support and confrontation, harnessing social desires in a positive direction, and experimenting with new problem-solving skills—and extends them from two hours a week to twenty-four hours a day. Although these youngsters made progress in the group sessions, their communities were so lacking in emotional resources and support that they were unable to maintain their improvements outside the group. The caring community extended the group into their daily lives. Besides providing direct support to persons calling for help, the caring community concept develops in the "helpers" a self-image of a competent, resourceful, and needed human being.

SOURCE: Raubolt, R., Strauss, M., and Bratter, T. E. "Evolution of an Adolescent Caring Community." *Together: Journal of the Association for Specialists in Group Work,* 1976, *1,* 32-39.

Fostering an Authority-Dependency Relationship with Delinquents

AUTHOR: Irving Schulman

PRECIS: Reducing anxiety in delinquents to promote reflective behavior

INTRODUCTION: Schulman describes characteristics of delinquent adolescents that one must keep in mind when developing a treatment approach. They are impulsive and deal with anxiety by externalizing it and acting it out. They have a fragile ego and a malformed superego. They are concrete and interested only in the present, not the past or future. Their impulsivity limits higher thought activity, including reflection, self-awareness, and empathy for others. They are indifferent or antagonistic toward authority. They have come from homes where parents were rejecting and amoral or dissocial and stimulated aggressive, impulsive behavior in their children. They project their anger on the environment and perceive it as hostile and threatening.

Schulman believes that the etiology of the delinquent's behavior lies in dependency relationships (parent-child) that resulted in emotional harm, confusion, and threat. In his view, the most effective technique in treating these antisocial adolescents is to establish a benign authority-dependency relationship with the adolescent that leads to a different outcome from what he has previously experienced. The expectation is that the delinquent will then incorporate the values of the therapist. Schulman states that, for effective treatment, delinquents must be treated on an inpatient basis. Since these youngsters are poorly motivated to change, outpatient treatment will not work. He believes that the best treatment program incorporates milieu therapy with individual and group therapy. Before the adolescent is institutionalized, the therapist meets with the youngster and informs him that the length of commitment is determined by the therapist and that release is dependent on the adolescent's gaining understanding of what causes him to act in an antisocial way. The therapist then becomes the "meaningful" person—the focus of all the adolescent's manipulations. Both group and individual treatment are aimed at intensifying this authority-dependency transference.

TREATMENT: The therapist takes an active role in treatment. The goal in therapy is to reduce impulsiveness by reducing anxiety and controlling impulsiveness before it escalates. The therapist helps suppress aggressive impulses by structuring the sessions so they do not build up to an aggressive pitch.

The therapist begins the group by stating the purpose,

which is to help group members learn about themselves and their behavior, so that they can be released from the institution. He then allows the group members to structure the interaction until the group inevitably becomes preoccupied with sexual or aggressive matters, or until prolonged silences occur. The therapist then breaks in, informs the group of what he has observed, and wonders verbally how this discussion will help them get out of the Home. The therapist then introduces a topic for conversation, usually an aspect of interpersonal relationships mentioned in passing in the earlier conversation. The therapist does not interpret resistance, since that would increase anxiety and acting out. Instead, insight is paired with release. Most important, the therapist does not get angry with the delinquents, since they will use the anger as a license to retaliate.

The therapist focuses on behavior in the group, so that the group members become more aware of the inappropriate behavior. The therapist also introduces prosocial values and promotes realistic thinking. For example, in a discussion about stealing, the therapist asked a group of delinquent girls how they would feel if someone stole something important from them. Some said they would retaliate; others said that if the girl was smart enough to steal something from them, she should have it. The therapist pointed out that their reactions were not normal and that most girls would react differently. He related an incident where his own watch was stolen. The girls thought this was a terrible thing to happen to him. He used their identification with him to point out how their victims must have felt.

Schulman points out that, even with intensive therapy in a milieu setting, the best prognosis one can hope for is limited control of impulses and a marginal social adjustment.

COMMENTARY: According to Schulman, it is not necessary—as some suggest—that the delinquent be transformed into a neurotic adolescent and engaged in introspective therapy. He states that neurotic manifestations may occur when the youngster has shown some impulse control, but the youngster is unwilling to probe more deeply into the motivation and painful experiences behind his behavior. The approach he proposes is to establish a benign authority-dependency relationship with the youngster and work toward impulse control. Although he believes that effective treatment can occur only on an inpatient basis, this approach could be useful for social workers and probation officers working with delinquents and could be combined with behavior modification techniques.

SOURCE: Schulman, I. "Modifications in Group Psychotherapy with Antisocial Adolescents." *International Journal of Group Psychotherapy,* 1957, *7,* 310-317.

Group Hypnosis with Institutionalized Girls

AUTHOR: Edward M. Scott

PRECIS: Intensive techniques, such as group hypnosis, used to facilitate discussion with delinquent girls

INTRODUCTION: The author observes that most institutionalized delinquent girls have suffered chaotic, physically abusive, rejecting backgrounds. He uses the term *branding* to describe the deep, pervasive influence this rejection has on the girls' self-esteem and self-identity. Therapy, if it "takes," is a long and difficult process with this population.

TREATMENT: Groups of eight to ten girls met weekly with the therapist for one-and-a-half-hour sessions. During the first few sessions, as in other groups in institutions, the girls complained about the staff. After a couple of sessions, the therapist introduced hypnosis to the group. Members were not required to participate, but hesitant members usually became involved by the second or third group hypnosis. In the first hypnosis, the therapist suggested that the girls remember a happy event in their lives. After a short time, they were brought out of the trance and shared their experiences. One of the girls related a traumatic experience she had recalled. The group was very supportive as she tried to sort out her confused and painful memories. In general, the girls recalled significant early events that they were confused about, and the confusion was quickly "cleared up" with the hypnosis and discussion. Traditional talk therapies would take much longer to uncover and resolve these problems, if ever. The "leads" provided by the group hypnosis were used for discussion in the same and future sessions.

The therapist also may introduce existential topics for discussion, including death, suicide, and being a willing victim. Significant areas of treatment are uncovered in these areas, since many of the adolescent girls have become deeply involved in reincarnation and witchcraft. Scott has used hypnosis to "exorcise" members who were obsessed with witchcraft and wanted to stop their involvement but could not. Suicidal gestures and the violence the girls have undergone are also important topics for the group to deal with. A frequent topic of conversation is interpersonal relationships, especially with boyfriends. These girls use sexual intimacy to feel that someone cares about them and to gain self-esteem. However, they generally pick boys with their own pathological problems—boys who use them and reject them. The girls now face double defeat: they have been rejected both inside and outside the home.

Because of their interpersonal concerns and pathological relationships, Scott believes that delinquent adolescent girls have identity disorders, as opposed to the more commonly diagnosed conduct disorders. The goals of therapy are to develop common sense, reality judgment, and self-control and to improve their identity by helping them separate themselves from their traumatic past.

COMMENTARY: The author notes that delinquent girls are interested in gaining self-understanding through discussing "deep levels" of traumatic events. In treating identity disorder rather than conduct disorder, Scott as the therapist stresses insight and self-understanding, to free the girls from the need to act out and to improve their self-esteem, rather than providing structure and limits to decrease symptomatic behavior.

SOURCE: Scott, E. M. "Delinquent Females: In-Depth Therapy and Some Theoretical Opinions." *International Journal of Offender Therapy and Comparative Criminology,* 1982, in press.

Group Treatment of Potential Delinquents

AUTHORS: Marion Stranahan, Cecile Schwartzman, and Edith Atkin

PRECIS: Emotional reeducation in group psychotherapy to produce behavior changes in character disturbed children with neurotic and borderline features

INTRODUCTION: The authors describe techniques and philosophy underlying treatment of potentially delinquent adolescents. The group was designed to be the substitute of a "good family," with the therapist as the "good parent" to provide emotional reeducation and rebuild deficient ego and character functions. The procedures were planned to reduce anxiety and hostility as much as possible. The children could not profit from therapy, the authors believed, until their experiences convinced them that adults could be devoted and responsive to their needs for safety, protection, caring, and fun.

TREATMENT: The youngsters ranged in age from thirteen to fifteen and exhibited serious learning and behavior problems in school, including truancy, stealing, and insubordination. All came from impoverished families in New York City. Most came from broken homes and were sent to relatives and back home again. They had every reason to expect capricious, neglectful, and selfish behavior by adults, since that is all they had known. They were suspicious and nonverbal.

The therapist communicated respect and caring through actions: arranging to have them excused an hour early from school for group, sending them letters reminding them of each meeting, providing carfare to sessions if necessary, meeting in a convenient location, following up on absences, and becoming involved in the children's lives outside the group by making home visits, seeking remedial classes, and accompanying them to doctors' appointments they were fearful of. The therapist sanctioned pleasure by providing play equipment and food at every session (this also reduced anxiety) and by taking them on a trip of their choice every six weeks.

In three years of group treatment, the boys in a boys' group progressed through three stages. Initially they were like two-year-olds who did not relate to each other but desired the attention and favors of the therapist—the female social worker who had done the initial interviews. (The boys were afraid to have a male therapist.) They had difficulty taking turns and sharing food. In the second phase, the boys showed positive feelings toward the group and openly acknowledged their dependency on the therapist. They called her "mother" and sought individual interviews for special problems. They acknowledged needs and requests for help. In the third phase, they readily accepted the involvement of the male cotherapist. They were genuinely concerned about each other and enjoyed working and playing together. They were able to take turns and conversed spontaneously with each other about their activities and expressed their feelings, attitudes, wishes, and concerns. Their delinquency decreased, and their behavior improved. Most joined neighborhood recreational centers, and some began individual therapy when the group ended.

A girls' group followed the same general process as the boys' group did. Identification with the therapist developed slowly, and members began to incorporate her standards. They gradually interacted more with peers. The food and activities took a less important role in the girls' group than it did in the boys' group. The girls talked more spontaneously without the need for activities to facilitate discussion. The girls were more difficult to treat, however, because they were superficially more conforming and veiled their hostility in subtle jokes and facial grimaces. They denied underlying conflicts and feelings. The girls also sought individual sessions with the therapist more than the boys, but did not vie for her attention in the group as the boys did. An important factor that emerged was the girls' ambivalence toward the therapist, which represented their ambivalent relationship with their mothers. Although rebellious against their parents, the girls identified with their mothers, who were overburdened and mistreated by their husbands. The girls believed that they, too, would be mistreated in relationships with men. This attitude was encouraged by the fact that many of them already had to care for their younger siblings and had extensive household responsibilities. The therapist tried to modify their view of femininity and hoped that their identification with her as a person with self-esteem and status would modify their self-identity.

RESULTS: All the children improved their attitudes toward school, and their truancy and delinquency decreased considerably. They showed better social and school adjustment overall. However, they still were referred for individual treatment.

COMMENTARY: The authors view delinquents as emotionally malnourished youngsters who experience the world and adults around them as hostile and threatening, because that is all they have known. The goal of treatment was to provide emotional reeducation so that the adolescents could resolve their most basic needs of trust versus mistrust and security versus insecurity. The use of activity therapy with these delinquents demonstrates the primitive level of their emotional functioning, which results in long and difficult treatment.

SOURCE: Stranahan, M., Schwartzman, C., and Atkin, E. "Group Treatment for Emotionally Disturbed and Potentially Delinquent Boys and Girls." *American Journal of Orthopsychiatry,* 1957, *27,* 518-527.

Group Therapy with Probationers

AUTHORS: Lewis Weber and Trafford Hill

PRECIS: Recommendations for the development of therapy groups for adolescents on probation

INTRODUCTION: The authors conducted eight months of group therapy with boys on probation. The group was mandatory, and the boys resisted participating meaningfully in group interaction because they associated the group with court and probation. They insisted that their only problem was "getting caught." The probation department did not work closely with the therapists, which resulted in continuously changing group membership. Also, the department did not provide them with information about group members, which made it impossible to formulate relevant treatment goals or decide on an appropriate therapeutic model. The article delineates their recommendations for developing a therapy group for older adolescents.

RECOMMENDATIONS: The authors observe that a close relationship with the probation department is essential. The department must understand the goals of therapy and be committed to the success of the program.

In the therapy group itself, resistance of members to treatment can be diminished if (1) the group is run independently of the probation department, except for referrals and problems with nonattendance; (2) attendance is mandatory; (3) members are prescreened, so that very resistant persons are kept out; (4) a heterogeneous group of offenders is used, since homogeneity increases resistance; (5) the group consists of five to seven members, since with too few participants pressure on all the members to talk is increased; and (6) the therapist plans carefully to develop goals and orientation of the therapy before the group is started.

COMMENTARY: The authors point out a variety of problem areas in developing group treatment for adolescents on probation. Their suggestion that the group function independently of the probation department to reduce resistance is overoptimistic. Since members are referred because of their probationary status, it is doubtful that the two authorities would be separated. If the group is mandatory, the therapists must be prepared to deal with heavy resistance and break through it. Alternatives are to have the probation officer as a cotherapist or to have a voluntary group. Though the voluntary group would have fewer members, it would be more productive; and its success, spread by word of mouth, might motivate others to become involved.

SOURCE: Weber, L., and Hill, T. "A Therapy Group of Juvenile Delinquent Boys." *Psychiatric Forum,* 1973, *32,* 25-33.

Behavioral Principles in Groups for Psychopathic Adolescents

AUTHOR: Anne Weinstock

PRECIS: Group therapy for antisocial, developmentally disabled, institutionalized adolescents

INTRODUCTION: Follow-up studies cited by the author reveal that, compared to neurotic children treated in the same conventional child guidance clinics, adolescents with severe character pathology fare less well in later life. Symptoms that are found include a range of antisocial behaviors (for example, child abuse, delinquency, and alcoholism) and forms of acting out that result in arrests. More promising results are reported from institutional programs that employ therapeutic community and group approaches. Additionally, the author notes that behavior modification programs have been frequently used with the retarded and that conventional group therapy and activity group therapy have been prominent modalities of treatment for disturbed youngsters. Her approach combines elements from group therapy, activity group therapy, and behavior modification models of treatment.

TREATMENT: The program treated twenty-seven to thirty-five adolescents, ages twelve to eighteen, at any one time. These patients had behavioral problems of long duration, and most were institutionalized at the insistence of some authority because of unsocialized aggressive delinquency. Eighty-seven percent had been institutionalized previously, and most remained in this institution and the program for over a year. Most of the youngsters had psychopathic personality disturbances characterized by antisocial behaviors, aggressiveness, impulsivity, and an almost total lack of guilt about their many transgressions against their fellow man. All carried one or more secondary diagnoses as well (for example, mental retardation, learning disability, and language deficit). Only 3 to 5 percent were psychotic. The range of IQs was 40 to 92, with a median of 72. The early experiences of these children had been damaging. Discipline and supervision in early years was inadequate, inconsistent, or missing altogether. Parental rejection or absence was frequent.

A token economy was at the heart of the residential treatment milieu. Tokens were earned for appropriate, on-task behavior during program activities and could be exchanged for recreational activities. The day was highly structured, discipline was benign but consistent, and the children were always held accountable for their behavior. The formal program included group therapy twice a day for half-hour sessions, special education classes five hours a day during the week, and individual counseling one or more times a week. Medication was prescribed as necessary by a consulting psychiatrist. Family therapy was available. Routine care, group therapy, and individual counseling were provided by childcare workers and nurses, most of whom had bachelor degrees and "worked under the direct clinical supervision of a small professional staff."

A modified time-out procedure was used when children got out of control during discussions of anxiety-provoking material. These children were asked to sit quietly in a chair outside the group for a period of five minutes. Only after four or five repeated disruptions of the group was a child removed from the room. This had the advantage of allowing the child to listen to the affect-laden discussion from a safe distance. Over time, the need for time out decreased.

Another distancing technique was role playing—the acting out of an actual disturbing situation. A discussion of appropriate alternative responses was followed by replays of the scene, incorporating the new alternatives. At other times a "fictional" situation was played out—a situation sufficiently removed from the actual conflict area to make observation, discussion, and resolution possible.

After a year the patients attained a level of maturity that accommodated the discussion of upsetting material, and the group moved to a new stage. Explicit behavioral goals were formulated for each child. For example, the group helped one girl to stop scapegoating another by encouraging her to substitute nice statements for her negative ones. The members of the group took an active role in providing constructive feedback to her. The behavior changed significantly, and the girl reported liking her one-time victim.

The group leaders had to teach the children how to use this goal-oriented approach. At the start the leader initiated the formulation of goals and gave the child a goal card specifying the target behaviors. Staff members checked these cards when the appropriate behavior was demonstrated. A parallel reward system was added to the token system. After about three months, the card system was no longer needed to keep the goal-oriented approach going.

A specialized program was instituted for four moderately retarded boys (IQs from below 46 to 55), ages fourteen to sixteen, who were very disruptive in the discussion groups. A "new style" of meeting was devised around activities (such as checkers, cards, and crafts) rather than discussion. Teasing continued to be a problem. Systematic reinforcement was introduced in the form of compliments by the group leader for positive social interactions (for example, saying "I like you). Teasing and fighting decreased, and the group became more cohesive.

RESULTS: The author concludes that the groups were helpful in socializing these adolescents. The leaders had to modify the format of the groups and to use varied techniques to maintain control over behavior.

COMMENTARY: In this intensive group program, although the leaders had to be very active and directive, they showed that developmentally delayed youngsters could achieve both self-control and empathy for others through a group discussion format. Even the lowest functioning children were able to incorporate behavioral goals from goal cards into their day-to-day thinking and to generalize the social and support skills they learned in the group to situations they encountered in daily living.

SOURCE: Weinstock, A. "Group Treatment of Characterologically Damaged, Developmentally Disabled Adolescents in a Residential Treatment Center." *International Journal of Group Psychotherapy,* 1979, *29,* 369-381.

Long-Term Therapy with Hospitalized Delinquents

AUTHOR: Jack C. Westman

PRECIS: Analytic group psychotherapeutic procedures adapted for managing severe character disorders in hospitalized delinquent adolescents

INTRODUCTION: The author discusses therapeutic methods of dealing with five categories of treatment needs of delinquents.

The first area of concern in therapy is synthesizing the group. These disturbed adolescents are narcissistic in their object relationships and have difficulty entering and sustaining group membership. To encourage identification within one group, for instance, meetings were scheduled so that the boys missed gym, an activity they all disliked. Refreshments were also served, to make the group seem more attractive. New admissions to the hospital had a waiting period before they could join the group, adding prestige to group membership. Also, boys in the group got "inside" information about new admissions and ward activities. Finally, the roles of the therapist and co-therapist as adults and leaders were strictly maintained, to assist the boys in identifying with each other, albeit against the staff.

A second area of treatment focuses on getting the boys to identify with the therapists; that is, to build a positive transference. To accomplish this, the therapist must gain the respect and admiration of the boys by withstanding their attacks and "testing" behaviors in a firm and decisive manner. The therapist shows that he can "take it" and "dish it out."

The third aspect of therapy is to strengthen reality testing. The therapists attempt to correct the boys' stereotyped fantasies about authority figures by discussion and modeling adult behavior; for example, behavioral controls are introduced as necessary aids to maturation rather than as capricious, punitive actions by adults. Since these boys do not know how to have fun in conventional ways, therapy must educate them in conventional forms of behavior. The group also helps the boys learn that their personal fears and anxieties are not unique but are shared by others.

Strengthening impulse control is another focus of treatment for delinquent youths, who are used to seeking immediate discharge of their impulses. Therapy helps them restrain their acting out, mainly by providing and enforcing structure. Rules are the primary method of structuring the group. In this group the boys must remain in their seats around the table, attendance is mandatory, and the only uncontrolled aspect is the freedom to talk about anything of interest to everyone in the room. Environment also provides structure; this group is held in a classroom, and the boys are seated around a table to create an atmosphere of discipline. The therapist rewards goal-oriented and productive discussion through interest and support and ignores or expresses disapproval of control inappropriate or off-task behaviors. All these are examples of structuring.

The final focus of treatment is stimulating self-awareness. Delinquents are resistant to changing themselves, using denial and projection to avoid introspection. Westman believes that the boys are, in fact, incapable of introspection and use words to conceal rather than express their true feelings; thus, what sounds like a remarkable insight is actually an intellectualization and does not carry over into observable behavior. More reliable cues to delinquents' feelings and attitudes are nonverbal behaviors. Effective interpretation involves observable behavior and is concerned with behavior in the group, which provides an immediate and concrete example that the boys cannot deny or distort.

TREATMENT: The group consisted of eleven boys, ages thirteen to seventeen, with IQs ranging from 93 to 127. Seven were delinquents, two were schizoid personalities, and two exhibited passive-aggressive character traits. The group met twice a week for fifty minutes over the course of one year. The boys were required to attend as a part of hospital treatment. The therapist was a male psychiatrist, and the cotherapist was a female nurse.

In the first month of therapy, the boys resisted the structure by feigning sleep to avoid talking, whispering to each other, and telling exaggerated tales of their delinquencies. An antistaff group and leader emerged. A prostaff group then emerged, mainly to dislodge the leader of the other subgroup; and the boys shifted back and forth between groups. By the third month, the boys began taking more responsibility, such as controlling unacceptable behavior themselves, telling offenders to "get with it," and discouraging running away from the hospital, an act that formerly won respect.

By the fifth month, the boys formed an identity as a group and were meeting on their own prior to the sessions to suggest topics for the group. The boys were also experiencing ambivalent feelings toward the therapist; they verbally attacked his personal mannerisms and appearance, yet the informal leader obtained a crewcut similar to the therapist's. In the seventh month, the group identification was so strong that the boys began calling it a fraternity and hazed new members. When this evidence of cohesiveness and identification with the therapist was interpreted to the boys, they showed overt hostility by drowning out the therapist when he talked. This behavior subsided when the boys hid the therapist's chair, laughed at his embarrassment, and then drew up the chair and invited the "doc" to "come on in" and join the group.

By the ninth month, the boys were concerned with how to get out of the hospital and what to tell people about their hospitalization. They solicited the doctor's comments, instead of rejecting them as they had in the past. By the twelfth month, the boys were interpreting each other's behavior—an important step, since the boys accepted interpretations by other members more readily than they accepted the therapist's interpretations.

COMMENTARY: This article describes a year-long therapy group with two therapists, an arrangement many institutions do not have the time or resources to duplicate. However, it delineates important areas of treatment needs for this type of youngster and reportedly was successful for the boys involved.

Also of interest was the role of the nurse to the boys. Initially she was an observer; then she was drawn into the group during the boys' hostile phase as they attempted to pit her against the doctor, simulating earlier experiences with their parents. Her presence also was a learning experience for the boys, who stated that they had never before seen a situation where the woman did not dominate the man; and they asked her to discuss women's attitudes on issues.

SOURCE: Westman, J. C. "Group Psychotherapy with Hospitalized Delinquent Adolescents." *International Journal of Group Psychotherapy,* 1961, *11,* 410-418.

Additional Readings

Borriello, J. F. "Patients with Acting-Out Character Disorders." *American Journal of Psychotherapy,* 1973, *27,* 4-14.

Acting-out delinquents who expressed even a minimal desire to change were seen in group psychotherapy. All were psychopathic, character disordered individuals committed to a mental hospital after being adjudicated not guilty by reason of insanity for offenses such as rape, murder, arson, assault, and robbery. The therapy method was basically analytic, dealing with transference and resistance in individual members and the group as a whole. The group was used by the therapist as the restructured family, which provided an opportunity for the resocialization of each member. Members were encouraged to confront each other's defenses and narcissism and accompanying affect. This long-term treatment program was considered a success, since twenty-six of thirty-one participants showed positive community adjustment. They were gainfully employed and staying out of trouble with the law, and some had enrolled in school or vocational training.

Bratter, T. E. "Educating the Uneducable: The Little 'Ole' Red Schoolhouse with Bars in a Concrete Jungle." *Journal of Offender Counseling, Services and Rehabilitation,* 1979, *4,* 95-108.

The author describes an educational program that was an alternative to incarceration for twenty-four juvenile offenders, ranging in age from fourteen to sixteen. All had been charged with violent acts, such as assault, armed robbery, and rape. All were members of rival gangs from some of the toughest sections of New York City. Some were on high doses of medication, some were drug abusers, and some were unwed mothers and fathers. All were diagnosed as psychotic and were angry, antiauthoritarian, and aggressive.

The author believed that the only way to reach these youngsters was to get personally involved with them and teach them from a humanistic approach. A central event in establishing rapport was the teachers' challenging the students to a basketball game. In this approach the teachers did not focus on traditional academics but on making the youngsters think for themselves in a productive manner. The teachers devised activities that helped the adolescents discover and use some of their talents. Students were responsible for deciding what they should learn. The staff also told the students when they were behaving irresponsibly and what was expected from them. At the same time, the staff treated them with respect and modeled images of nurturant, wise parents who could help the students discover themselves and the world.

Gersten, C. "Group Therapy with Institutionalized Juvenile Delinquents." *Journal of Genetic Psychology,* 1952, *80,* 35-64.

This was one of the first controlled studies that utilized group therapy with juvenile delinquents and provides valuable insights into the development and process of group treatment with delinquents. The first step was to establish a warm therapeutic relationship with these boys, who had lacked positive relationships with adults. Initially the group followed a discussion format. The therapist encouraged members to introduce topics for discussion and also introduced clippings from magazines and books to stimulate discussion. When handicrafts were introduced, the boys interacted more and were more open in conversation. The therapist felt that the activities reduced the boys' self-consciousness and gave them a sense of achievement; therefore, the activities were continued as a part of the sessions. The boys also responded enthusiastically to stories of famous persons, such as Babe Ruth and Joe Louis, who also had come from underprivileged backgrounds. This study highlighted the need to prevent further delinquency by providing alternatives—such as recreation—to street and gang behavior.

Harari, H. "Cognitive Manipulations with Delinquent Adolescents in Group Therapy." *Psychotherapy: Theory, Research and Practice,* 1972, *9,* 303-307.

In this article delinquents' cognitions and attitudes were assessed to determine their attitudes toward therapy and the therapist and their primary method of coping with interpersonal conflict. This information was used in group therapy to make therapeutic interventions that would be accepted by the individual delinquent rather than defended against and to foster a positive identification with the therapist. For example, it was found that the delinquents do not respond to a nondirective approach in which the therapist presents himself as someone who will help the patient pull himself up by his own bootstraps. These youngsters respond to a therapist who is directive and structured and is perceived by them as powerful and effective.

Head, W. A. "Sociodrama and Group Discussion with Institutionalized Delinquent Adolescents." *Mental Hygiene,* 1962, *46,* 127-135.

Sociodrama, or role playing, has important diagnostic and therapeutic implications with delinquent adolescents. The adolescents reveal their perceptions and conflicts through their choice of roles, identifications, projections, and the content of their portrayals of the enacted situation. It is a projective technique to use with adolescents in much the same way as play therapy is used with young children. In this article sociodrama was followed by group discussion to analyze and interpret significant ideas revealed in the dramatic portrayals. In the discussions the delinquents could talk about the "roles" they played, instead of directly revealing personal material. The sociodrama/group discussions modified antisocial attitudes and behavior problems of members, greatly improved their reality testing and social skills, and was resisted less than traditional therapies in the institution.

Mueller, E. E. "Psychodrama with Delinquent Siblings." *Social Work,* 1971, *11,* 18-28.

Psychodrama was used to treat delinquent boys, ages nine through sixteen, committed to a state facility. These boys had never received consistent discipline and had never learned to associate consequences to their behavior. They perceived the world as a hostile place in which they never knew when something painful—that is, punishment—would occur. The goal of treatment was to teach the boys to understand cause-effect relationships and develop problem-solving and social skills. It was hoped that the new skills would help them perceive their environment more realistically and help them feel capable of solving their problems effectively in socially acceptable ways. The therapy group was an arena for resocialization. The youngsters acted out family dynamics with peers. The therapist helped them relate feelings to their behaviors and resolve conflicts in ways that satisfied their needs without blocking the needs of others. The author lists eighteen psychodrama techniques used in treatment.

Phelan, J. F., Slavson, S. R., Epstein, N., and Schwartz, M. "Studies in Group Psychotherapy in Residential Treatment of 'Delinquent' Boys." *International Journal of Group Psychotherapy,* 1960, *10,* 174-212.

Two methods of group psychotherapy were utilized at a residential treatment center for adolescent delinquent boys. The boys came from impoverished, multiproblem families and suffered a history of rejection and sometimes abuse by their parents. Each group was balanced to include boys who were neurotic, schizophrenic, and behavior problems. The first group described, for boys between eleven and a half and thirteen years old, utilized activities to promote interaction and discussion. The second group, for boys between fourteen and sixteen years old, utilized classical analytic group psychotherapy. In both groups the boys built a strong, positive transference with the therapist, whom they saw as different from other adults they had known, and incorporated his values. The boys in both groups responded enthusiastically to belonging to the group and attained a high level of productivity and insight in the sessions. The boys were less anxious, more assertive and socially appropriate, and able to perceive themselves and others more realistically after treatment.

Redfering, D. L. "Group Counseling with Institutionalized Delinquent Females." *American Corrective Therapy,* 1972, *26,* 160-163.

Research on female juvenile delinquency is sparse, in part because male delinquency is more frequent and in part because male delinquency has more serious social implications. Male delinquents tend to destroy property and harm other people, whereas female delinquents tend to be more self-destructive—

running away, taking drugs, and acting out sexually. Furthermore, females' offenses diminish as they leave school and their parents' authority, whereas many male offenders continue their misbehavior and become adult criminals. Short-term, client-centered group therapy was conducted with institutionalized female delinquents. The girls in therapy showed improvements in attitudes toward themselves and others, attitudes which penal authorities believe impede treatment and rehabilitation if not modified. In contrast, untreated girls showed more negative attitudes—suggesting that incarceration has negative effects on delinquent girls' attitudes toward themselves, their families, and other people.

Redfering, D. L. "Durability of Effects of Group Counseling with Institutionalized Delinquent Females." *Journal of Abnormal Psychology,* 1973, *78,* 85-86.

A one-year follow-up on the effects of short-term therapy with incarcerated girls showed that the positive effects of treatment were enduring. Treated girls were released earlier than nontreated girls and had a lower rate of recidivism. The improved attitudes toward self and others reported after treatment were somewhat diminished a year later, perhaps because the relationships that the girls had idealized while incarcerated proved disappointing within the realities of daily living.

Sarason, I. G., and Ganzer, V. J. "Modeling and Group Discussion in the Rehabilitation of Juvenile Delinquents." *Journal of Counseling Psychology,* 1973, *20,* 442-449.

The authors compared two methods of group treatment that provided juvenile delinquent boys with the training and information necessary for social, vocational, and educational adjustment in the community. The boys themselves suggested situations that were problematic for them—for instance, how to apply for a job, how to resist temptation by peers to commit antisocial acts, how to discuss problems with authority figures, and how to set realistic goals and stick to them. In one method the two cotherapists acted out a situation that involved the theme for the day. They modeled both appropriate and inappropriate responses and then had the boys role-play the same situation. In the other method, the cotherapists discussed the theme for the day in detail with the boys, using a counseling format. Boys in both treatments showed more positive attitudes and behavior changes in the institution and had less recidivism than control subjects. All the boys said that they were impressed with the no-nonsense, well-organized informational approach of both treatments.

Substance Abuse

Effective therapy with substance abusers must be intensive therapy. Alcohol and drug abusers like their drugs and the sensations the drugs produce, and they have built strong defense systems around preserving their addictions. Substance abusers usually seek treatment at the insistence of an external force, such as a spouse or parent, and are not motivated to change. The articles in this section suggest techniques to break through the defenses quickly, in order to engage the person in meaningful treatment. Because of the poor ego functions and strong dependency needs of these individuals, effective treatment requires peer support and confrontation in either a residential community treatment group or a caring community where support is available twenty-four hours a day.

Community Groups

AUTHOR: Thomas E. Bratter

PRECIS: A community-sponsored discussion group as therapy for drug abusers

INTRODUCTION: An upper-middle-class community sponsored a group therapy program for their adolescent drug users to meet with a therapist in a casual atmosphere in the community. The participants attended the same high school, and their parents were well educated, cultured, affluent, successful in their professions, and in some instances socially prominent. The adolescents collectively expressed feelings of neglect and rejection from their parents, whom the youngsters perceived as too busy pursuing affluence and social prominence to show them love and concern. Their parents pressured them to do well, and the adolescents rejected and rebelled against their parents' values. The authors believed that the drug abuse relieved their feelings of rejection and failure and provided a rationale for their lack of success. The adolescents still believed that they could succeed if they wanted to.

TREATMENT: The group met in different locations in the community four times a week. Group participation was voluntary and changed from session to session. The drug abuse ranged from occasional marijuana use to heroin addiction. Most of the participants ranged in age from fourteen to eighteen, but adults were welcomed, and the adolescents seemed to appreciate their company. Average attendance was sixteen, with a range of six to seventy-one. More than 325 students attended at least five sessions over the two and a half years of the program. The participants arrived and left when they wished, and sessions generally lasted about three hours. The length of the session pressured individuals to make commitments to change.

The therapist assumed a charismatic role by proving that he was concerned about the members, committed to helping them, and maintained high expectations that they could function responsibly and happily. He presented a model of a competent, satisfied person with a drug-free life-style. The therapist confronted the members with their unacceptable, self-defeating behavior and continually pressured them to choose a more productive life-style. Finally, the therapist acted as an advocate for the youngsters by intervening with courts, schools, or agencies to help the members return to school, secure a job, or receive probation from court. As an advocate the therapist presented a positive role model and showed members that they could assert themselves in productive and gratifying ways. However, the group itself determined whether the member had earned the therapist's support as an advocate.

The primary short-term goal was to diminish drug abuse by encouraging abstinence. For example, individuals who came to the meeting intoxicated were confronted and criticized. Usually the sessions focused on one person. The group examined and demonstrated to the participant the self-defeating aspects of his behavior. The group stressed the individual's ability to control his own behavior and pressured the individual to accept total responsibility for his behavior. The group insisted that the person could change and asked him whether he would change and act responsibly or whether he would continue to engage in immature, irresponsible, stupid self-destructive behavior. (Such a confrontation is uncomfortable and humiliating and prompts motivation to change.) When the individual admitted a desire to change, the group demanded a commitment and gave specific recommendations on how the person could improve his behavior. Two or three group members were then assigned to that individual as quasi-counselors to make sure that the commitment was fulfilled. The group members expressed their concern for the person by not accepting excuses but insisting that the person could carry out the assignment, such as securing a job. When the individual fulfilled several commitments, he dropped his failure identity and felt better about himself. The person saw himself as more competent and began more positive, responsible behavior with the continued support of the group.

CASE EXAMPLE: Craig was an eighteen-year-old drug abuser

who prided himself on his extensive knowledge of drugs. His father was a businessman who spent little time at home and was punitive with Craig and his two brothers. His mother devoted her life to dieting and pampering herself. She didn't like boys and spent little time with her sons. Both parents spent evenings dining out or at the country club. All three boys referred to their parents as "emotionally dead." When Craig was expelled from high school for truancy and because school officials suspected that he was selling drugs, his parents sent him to a psychiatrist. The parents used his diagnosis of mental illness to avoid responsibility for his problems and to avoid further involvement themselves. The psychiatrist prescribed Librium for Craig, which Craig sold.

Craig attended the drug abuse group with friends and directed hostile comments at the therapist. The second time he came, he was put on the "hot seat." Craig believed that the adolescent group would protect him, and he repeatedly went into elaborate autobiographical explanations to justify his self-defeating behavior. He also used his diagnosis to prove that he could not control his own behavior. However, the group did not accept his excuses but confronted him with questions such as "What kind of person drives a car while tripping?" and "What kind of person deliberately gets himself expelled and then provokes the police?" Under the pressure Craig admitted that he was acting stupid instead of sick and that he had failed in school to avoid the pressure of success.

In searching for more positive behavior, Craig said he would like to try academics again. The therapist convinced his high school to give Craig credit for a psychology course the therapist was teaching. Craig had to promise to abstain from drugs, attend every class, and complete assignments on time. Toward the end of the quarter, Craig smoked marijuana. The whole graduate psychology class focused on his self-defeating behavior. To be able to continue the course, Craig had to petition his high school on his own to be allowed to continue, had to improve his behavior at home, and had to do an extra assignment. He completed the course and eventually returned to high school and was admitted to college. He occasionally violated his commitment and used drugs, but his usage was vastly reduced from previous levels. His prognosis remains guardedly optimistic.

RESULTS: The author reports that there has been no formal evaluation of the group, but thirty members who had been expelled from school returned, six more earned the equivalency of a high school diploma, and nine were employed in meaningful full-time jobs.

COMMENTARY: Bratter finds that firm confrontation and an unwillingness to accept excuses can break through addicts' defenses and mobilize superego functions. The therapy group acts as an auxiliary ego, supporting constructive behaviors, suggesting alternative behaviors, and teaching the individual how to behave to maximize success.

SOURCE: Bratter, T. E. "Group Therapy with Affluent, Alienated Adolescent Drug Abusers: A Reality Therapy and Confrontation Approach." *Psychotherapy: Theory, Research and Practice,* 1972, *9,* 308-313.

Teenage Alcoholics

AUTHOR: Thomas E. Bratter

PRECIS: Confrontation-reality therapy with adolescent alcoholics

INTRODUCTION: Bratter uses the same confrontation approach with alcoholics in this article that he used with drug abusers in the previous article in this section. He explains that adolescent alcoholics are difficult to treat successfully because physicians and professionals are pessimistic about the possibility of improvement with this population, and, as a result, the adolescent also views himself as hopeless. To counteract this view, Bratter builds optimism and high expectations for change into his approach. Although many sources, including the American Medical Association, define alcoholism as an illness and something the individual cannot control, Bratter views alcoholism as a behavior of choice, a self-defeating and antisocial choice. To treat alcoholism, Bratter does not recommend interpretation or insight to effect behavior change. He demands behavior change from the alcoholic, assuming that the person will feel better about himself when he is functioning more appropriately. Bratter recommends that alcoholics be treated in therapy groups, because the peer group can examine the individual's behavior and pressure him to change more effectively than a therapist alone can, and because adolescents desire peer acceptance. Peers can become quasi-therapists and enforce the norms of the group, and a competitive spirit develops between peers as they make progress.

TREATMENT: Briefly, the therapist fosters a strong positive relationship with the adolescent, to demonstrate that he is committed to helping the youngster. Bratter suggests that the therapist disclose relevant parts of his life in the sessions, including his fears, frustrations, and failures, so that the young alcoholic recognizes that other people have problems but have overcome them. Thus, the therapist becomes a human and responsible role model. The therapist and the other group members then point out the alcoholic's self-destructive behavior as well as his strengths and help him devise a realistic plan for change; for example, he may resolve to have one less drink a day instead of trying to quit all at once.

Bratter recommends that the plan be put into written contract form. Each goal in the contract is broken down into small steps, to enable the patient to experience success. To help the patient overcome his failure identity, the group maintains high expectations and treats him as a responsible adult. If a goal is not met appropriately, the group does not accept excuses for failure but requires the patient to fulfill the goal. The contract may be renegotiated. Bratter often makes the new contract even more difficult, to show the patient that the group has faith in his ability. Possible goals for the contract include completion of schooling, attending college or vocational school, or obtaining full-time employment.

Bratter also recommends that the group be turned into a caring community, in which members support each other outside the sessions twenty-four hours a day. The caring community becomes an extension of the therapist but encourages dependence on peers rather than on the therapist. By helping one another, the members themselves learn that they are competent and that others value their ideas and abilities. The more responsible and productive members are sought for advice, and this "earned" status further reinforces a positive identity.

Bratter encourages members to join Alcoholics Anonymous, which further reinforces the goals of the therapy group and provides additional support and comradarie.

At times the therapist becomes an advocate for the patient, helping him cope with bureaucracies that he must face when he tries to get a job or return to school. As an advocate the therapist models for the patient ways to assert himself in a productive and responsible manner.

COMMENTARY: Bratter insists that the therapist must get personally involved in therapy with substance abusers to show them that someone cares about them. When an important person like the therapist values the patient and believes he can make positive behavioral changes, the patient becomes motivated to try to change. As he makes slow but gradual progress in therapy, the experience of success improves his self-esteem and the patient begins to discard his failure identity. Bratter believes in the concept of "self-fulfilling prophecy"; that is, he believes that the therapist helps the patient change by maintaining high expectations.

SOURCE: Bratter, T. E. "Reality Therapy: A Group Psychotherapeutic Approach with Adolescent Alcoholics." *Annals of the New York Academy of Sciences,* 1974, *233,* 104-114.

Marathon Therapy

AUTHORS: Elliot S. Cohen and Kenneth Rietma

PRECIS: Using marathon groups to intensify group processes in conjunction with ongoing group therapy

INTRODUCTION: Many therapeutic communities, including Synanon in Santa Monica and Habilitat in Hawaii, utilize marathon therapy as a part of their ongoing therapy program. Similarly, Cohen and Rietma used a marathon as part of a drug rehabilitation program for enlisted men. Their purpose was to hasten group processes, such as building group cohesion and trust and penetrating individuals' defenses.

TREATMENT: The basic program is a month-long rehabilitation project for drug and alcohol abusers from several area military bases. The patients are enlisted men, ages eighteen to twenty-four. Ten to fourteen patients are admitted into the program on a Friday and remain in the closed program for four weeks. The program is based on group treatment, and the patients participate as a group in physical training, occupational therapy, intensive group psychotherapy, and didactic groups that heavily emphasize transactional analysis and deal with themes such as social training and values clarification.

The marathon itself begins at 3 P.M. on the first Monday after admission and lasts twenty-four to twenty-six hours. Three pairs of staff members rotate as leaders over the three eight-hour shifts. Two of the therapists have primary responsibility for the core therapy for the four-week period, and they are assigned to the final eight- to ten-hour shift. It is always arranged that the cotherapists are of the opposite sex. During the marathon the therapists take process notes of the group unconscious and content notes on each individual's behavior during the experience. At the change of shifts, the therapists overlap for half an hour, and the outgoing therapists summarize the group content and process to the incoming therapists in front of the group.

All meals are brought into the room, and patients are allowed to leave the room only to go to the bathroom. A chair is placed in the corner by a window, and members can go there to smoke at any time unless a therapist has established a no-smoking period for some therapeutic reason. Also, group smoking breaks are taken every few hours at the request of the staff or a patient. Throughout the marathon, coffee and Kool-Aid are available in the room.

The nursing shifts parallel the therapists' shifts, and the nursing personnel are invited to participate by observing group interactions or facilitating group interaction, depending on their ability and level of experience.

The morning following the marathon, the therapists meet with the staff psychiatrist and social worker for three hours to discuss the group process and content. They "track" each patient through the three shifts to clarify his personal themes, concerns, and defenses. The information is used by the team to decide which of the four universal conflicts the person is experiencing, as described by J. Mann in his book *Time Limited Psychotherapy* (Cambridge, Mass.: Harvard University Press, 1973). The conflicts are independence versus dependence, activity versus passivity, adequate self-esteem versus poor self-esteem, and unresolved grief. Once the team decides which of these conflicts is the individual's personal theme, the two primary therapists use this information as the basis of their interventions for the remainder of the program.

The authors report that the marathon is quite successful in achieving the goal of forming strong group cohesion. The patients often feel that they have had a peak experience in self-awareness, and the excitement and motivation to be more productive are carried over into the remaining weeks of the program. The defenses of denial, isolation, and intellectualization cannot withstand the extended group and are broken down. The marathon gives the therapists an opportunity to introduce their expectations and guidelines to the group. It also provides an opportunity for the participants to work through their irrational fears of the therapists (the fear, for example, that the therapist will retaliate against the patient or reject or abandon the patient) and establish a positive therapeutic relationship.

Administratively, the marathon helps the therapists quickly recognize patients who are not appropriate for the program, a process that used to take two weeks. Considered inappropriate are prepsychotic and borderline patients, who are referred out for individual treatment, and malingerers, who are asked to participate meaningfully or return to active duty. The authors emphasize that inappropriate members must be removed early, before they form a bond with the main group and form a countertherapeutic subgroup.

COMMENTARY: The marathon's success in hastening the group process is especially helpful in a time-limited program such as this one. Such a device could be used with adolescents, since the "peak" experience in self-awareness brought about in marathon groups would hook them into treatment when used in conjunction with a longer, rehabilitation program.

SOURCE: Cohen, E. S., and Rietma, K. "Utilizing Marathon Therapy in a Drug and Alcohol Rehabilitation Program." *International Journal of Group Psychotherapy,* 1981, *31,* 117-123.

Confrontation-Reality Therapy

AUTHORS: Richard R. Raubolt and Thomas E. Bratter

PRECIS: Therapy to help addicts terminate their manipulative and self-defeating behaviors and adopt more responsible, productive life-styles

INTRODUCTION: Drug addicts are a particularly difficult population to work with, because they avoid dealing with their problems and reality by escaping to an alternate reality; they are not motivated to begin a therapeutic alliance or to give up their self-destructive behavior; they approach life as if it were a game in which the ability to manipulate others is highly rewarded; they use their history of failure to avoid responsible behavior; and, finally, they are alienated from society and follow a hedonistic pattern of instant gratification without regard for future consequences.

In confrontation-reality therapy, the therapists require addicts to assume responsibility and to act in a self-respecting manner. The approach draws heavily from William Glasser's *Reality Therapy: A New Approach to Psychiatry* (New York: Harper & Row, 1965) and uses confrontation to force addicts to be aware of their behavior and its consequences. This confrontation expedites behavior change by forcing addicts to mobilize their resources into positive action, instead of rationalizing their inaction. Confrontation-reality therapy assumes that people cannot always control their situation in life but they can control their responses. Continually the addicts are asked: "What are you doing?" "Is it helping you?" "Do you choose to continue it?" The progressive treatment goals are to eliminate overt self-destructive behavior; encourage (provoke) expression of feelings; operationalize those feelings into constructive behavior; establish a caring community, in which group members confront and support each other; and support independent, creative thinking and action.

TREATMENT: Confrontation-reality group therapy consists of three stages. The first stage is establishing a positive therapeutic relationship. The therapist must prove in a forceful way that he cares about the members and is capable of helping them. That is, he must show "responsible concern." The authors recommend that at the outset the therapist state clearly to the addicts that he can help them become more happy, productive people but only if they choose to do better and stop their drug usage. At this stage there is no group identity, but members unite against the therapist to try to sabotage him. They play "games" such as "I can't," "Don't blame me," "How would you know, you never took drugs," and "If you straightened out society, we would change." The therapist emphasizes that their problems are not unique and that they have *people* problems, not drug problems. He continually focuses on alternatives to drug abuse and insists that members have the power to change and succeed in life.

This first stage overlaps with the second stage, in which the therapist tries to induce a therapeutic crisis to get the group members to recognize and give up their negative behaviors and self-images. He confronts their "tough" images and games as unrealistic, immature, and stupid. He finishes their statements and phrases to expose their stereotyped thinking. He also confronts their countergroup alliances by asking members to examine questions such as "Is deceit a basis of friendship? Is a friend someone who will lend you ten dollars 'to cop' or someone who refuses to give you the money so you can poison yourself?" As members share important concerns and "excuses," the other members give up their negative alliances and play a new game, "Cure him because he's sicker than me." Here they are able to see problems in others that they cannot yet admit to in themselves. The therapist encourages this display of "concern for others" and suggests that members establish a caring community, in which members are available to confront and support each other twenty-four hours a day. The caring community becomes an extension of the therapist and helps members help each other. In helping each other, members discover more of their abilities and resources and begin to identify themselves as helpful, competent persons. The most responsible members become role models for the others, and this earned "status" further improves and reinforces a positive self-image.

By now the members are aware of their behavior and its consequences and begin to identify with the therapist. They give up their drug dependence but are still dependent on each other for support and assistance. They are also aware, however, that they can exert control over their behavior and future. The therapist's role changes to being a teacher, supporter, and advocate. The group progresses to the third stage, restructuring.

In this third stage, members accept the need for change but are unsure of what or how to change, and they fear the future. The therapist helps the members develop a plan for sequential, progressive action toward a more responsible life-style, such as going to school or getting a job. He insists that they make a written commitment to action. The contract includes long- and short-term goals—for example, "(1) establishing drug-free friendships, (2) securing and maintaining full-time employment, (3) attending school part time, and (4) moving out of parents' living quarters." Excuses for failure are never accepted, and members are held accountable to the contract. As an advocate the therapist uses his profession and position to provide references and pressure agencies on behalf of the members.

COMMENTARY: By understanding the games drug abusers play, the therapist can make interpretations that expose these manipulations. Only when the games and defenses are destroyed can the abuser be motivated into accepting responsibility for his self-destructive behavior and choose a more productive life-style. Drug abusers generally have severe ego deficits, are quite dependent, and have few friends. Therefore, the therapy group must become a caring community that provides support, meaning, and direction to the individual. Dependency on the drug is changed to dependency on peers, who can strengthen the ego functions in therapy.

SOURCE: Raubolt, R. R., and Bratter, T. E. "Games Addicts Play: Implications for Group Treatment." *Corrective and Social Psychiatry,* 1974, *20,* 3-10.

Additional Readings

Bratter, T. E. "The Psychotherapist as a Twelfth Step Worker in the Treatment of Alcoholism." *Alcoholism and Health,* 1979, *2,* 31-58.

The author stresses that the primary goal of alcoholism counseling is abstinence. Therapists who hold out the hope that the alcoholic can drink occasionally do not understand the dynamics of alcoholism and sabotage treatment. Treatment toward reduction rather than elimination almost always ends in relapse. Bratter describes the use of his confrontation-reality therapy approach (which is detailed in previous digests in this section) with alcoholics. An important aspect of this approach is that the therapist must become a friend of the alcoholic, who has no friends, trusts no one, and feels unworthy and unlovable. The alcoholic needs someone who will respect and become involved with him, who will expect and demand his best, and who will struggle with him and not give up. A therapeutic group using the confrontation-reality therapy approach supplies that need.

Bratter, T. E. "Some Pre-Treatment Group Psychotherapy Considerations with Alcoholically and Drug Addicted Individuals." In T. E. Bratter, *Alcoholism and Drug Abuse: A Humanistic Approach.* New York: Free Press, 1982.

Bratter discusses the difficulties encountered in working with substance abusers, including the lack of relevant training for therapists, the lack of theory and practical research related to treatment of this population, and the lack of motivation in the abusers themselves. He describes the confrontation approach, which many practitioners believe is the "most effective therapeutic tool for managing and resolving [the] potentially life-endangering behavior" (p. 72) of substance abusers.

Bratter, T. E. "Treating Alienated, Unmotivated, Drug Abusing Adolescents." *American Journal of Psychotherapy,* 1973, *27,* 585-598.

Bratter discusses the development of his confrontation-reality therapy approach. He emphasizes the importance of the personal involvement of the therapist in treating drug-abusing adolescents. These youngsters, who feel rejected by their parents, equate caring with the amount of energy expended. The louder the therapist yells and reprimands and maintains high expectations, the more the youngster feels assured. Bratter differentiates between the expectations of the therapist, who is not psychologically invested in the success of the youngster, with the expectations of parents. One type of therapist involvement, he suggests, is sending letters of confrontation. He describes letters he has sent to youngsters, challenging them to change; to parents, challenging them to become involved with their children; and to agencies, challenging them to give the youngster a chance. He cautions that parents are fearful of their adolescent's independence and may sabotage treatment by early termination, refusing to pay the bill, or scheduling conflicting appointments.

Author Index

Y

Z

Subject Index

D

E

F

R

S